Savoring Southeast Asia

WILLIAMS-SONOMA

Savoring Southeast Asia

Recipes and Reflections on Southeast Asian Cooking

Recipes and Text
JOYCE JUE

General Editor
CHUCK WILLIAMS

Recipe Photography
NOEL BARNHURST

Illustrations
MARLENE McLOUGHLIN

Oxmoor
House®

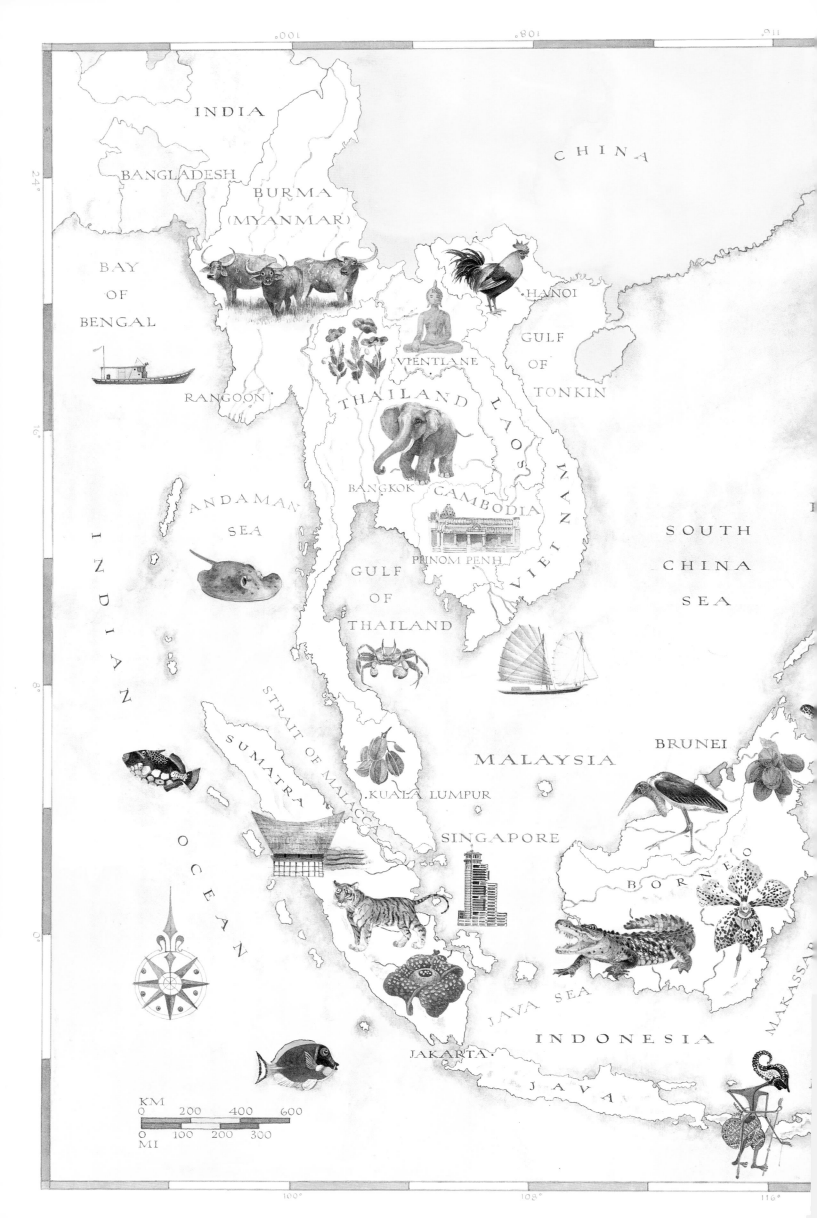

INDIA

BANGLADESH

BURMA
(MYANMAR)

CHINA

BAY
OF
BENGAL

HANOI

GULF
OF
TONKIN

RANGOON

VIENTIANE

THAILAND LAOS

ANDAMAN
SEA

BANGKOK

CAMBODIA

PHNOM PENH

VIET NAM

SOUTH
CHINA
SEA

GULF
OF
THAILAND

INDIAN

OCEAN

STRAIT OF MALACCA

SUMATRA

MALAYSIA

BRUNEI

KUALA LUMPUR

SINGAPORE

BORNEO

INDONESIA

JAVA SEA

MAKASSAR

JAKARTA

JAVA

KM
0   200   400   600

0   100   200   300
MI

Contents

INTRODUCTION

The Southeast Asian Table

MY FIRST VISIT to Southeast Asia was auspicious. I arrived in Bangkok unaware that the city would be caught up in the colorful swirl of Loy Krathong, the most popular festival of the year. Held at the end of the monsoon season, the festival is celebrated throughout the country with street fairs, music, food, and much merriment. The members of the typical extended Thai family work together to weave small boats from banana leaves and flowers, load them with lighted candles, incense, and coins, and launch them onto the river under a starry sky. If the vessels stay afloat, the sins of the builders are carried away downstream, while the coins bring the promise of prosperity for the coming year. The boats double as offerings to Mae Pra Kongka, the Mother of the Waters, the goddess who watches over the rice harvest.

The Thais are not alone in making such offerings. Indeed, rice paddies exist throughout Southeast Asia, and locals everywhere fashion offerings to the spirits who protect this single most important food in the region. Literally hundreds of rice varieties are grown, and the people in each country fancy specific types and ways of cooking them. Thais, Malaysians, Singaporeans, Indonesians,

Above top: On a typical spring morning, bicycles and cyclos for hire fill a tree-lined street in central Hanoi. **Above bottom:** Noodles—flat, round, thin, thick, long, short, made from rice flour or wheat flour—are consumed throughout town and village in Southeast Asia. **Right:** This woman's distinctive clothing identifies her as a member of the Yao, a hill tribe deep in the mountains of the Golden Triangle.

Vietnamese, and Cambodians prefer long-grain rice cooked by the absorption method without salt. The Burmese favor long-grain rice boiled with salt, while Filipinos like slightly stickier medium-grain rice. In Laos and northeastern Thailand, cooks steam short-grain glutinous rice in a conical bamboo basket. In every case, however, rice is a symbol of prosperity and well-being, as evidenced in the phrase with which Asians universally greet one another: "Have you eaten your rice today?"

Water means prosperity as well. Long seacoasts, meandering rivers, and spreading deltas are vital to the overall health of the region. They are the primary source of protein in the form of fish and shellfish, provide much of the water for what are for the most part agricultural economies, and form the infrastructure for transportation and commerce. These waterways have also played a critical role in the centuries of colonialism and of the migration of peoples that have shaped the region's history and defined its table.

In the early sixteenth century, the Portuguese arrived in Indonesia and Malaysia, where they set up a chain of prosperous trading posts. The Dutch followed them one hundred years later, and then the English, who left their mark not only on Indonesia and Malaysia, but on Myanmar (then Burma) and Singapore (then Temesek) as well. The Spanish left a lasting imprint on the Philippines, which they ruled for about 350 years, while the French brought their food—baguettes, beef bourguignon, crème caramel, pâté, even sandwiches—language, and culture to Indochina, now Vietnam, Laos, and Cambodia. Although Thailand was never subject to European domination, it was nonetheless subject to outside influences. Indeed, for centuries before the arrival of the Europeans, the region saw the rise and fall of great kingdoms and the establishment of many trade routes, and both neighbors and more distant peoples—Chinese, Arabs, Indians—regularly crossed over many borders. All of these elements left a lasting impression on the local cuisines.

Europeans introduced an array of New World vegetables to Southeast Asia, as well as the fork and spoon, utensils that replaced

eating with one's fingers in all but the most remote or traditional communities of nearly every country. Arguably the most significant of the vegetables was the chile, which eclipsed black peppercorns, until then the principal source of spicy heat. Malaysians created a table condiment of pounded fresh chiles mixed with the local *blacan* (dried shrimp paste) and lime juice, Thais added chiles to their curry pastes, and the Burmese dried and ground the peppers and added the powder to everything from soups to noodles. The Dutch planted coffee in Indonesia, the French did the same in Indochina, and the British introduced it just about everywhere in between.

Chinese, primarily from southwestern and southern China, migrated to the region in great numbers, bringing soy sauce, fermented bean sauce, bean curd, wheat and rice noodles, and, perhaps most importantly, the wok, now found in kitchens from Myanmar to Malaysia to the Philippines. They also brought chopsticks, which were adopted by the Thais

Left: The British colonial architecture of the Sultan Abdul Samad Building coexists with sleek modern skyscrapers in Kuala Lumpur's urban landscape. Such contrast is common in this city, Malaysia's capital, where elements of the nation's modern life mix with its colonial past and the old traditions and new lifestyles of its mostly Malay, Chinese, and Indian residents. **Above top:** At the famous Shwedagon Pagoda in Yangon (Rangoon), which welcomes tens of thousands of pilgrims each year, a young girl kneels to pray before a saffron-robed monk. **Above bottom:** On its upper three terraces, the Borobudor temple complex in Java houses seventy-two "invisible Buddhas," each hidden inside a bell-shaped, latticed stone *stupa*.

for noodle dishes and by the Vietnamese for eating everything.

Dishes have migrated as well, such as *satay,* the skewered grilled meats that most scholars credit early Arab traders with bringing to Indonesia. A typical Indonesian version uses *kecap manis,* the local sweetened soy, in the marinade for lamb or beef and serves the grilled meat with a relatively simple dipping sauce of peanuts, *kecap manis,* chiles, onions, and lime juice. In Malaysia, where cooks have been heavily influenced by the Indonesian kitchen, the *satay* is eaten with a spicy peanut sauce rich with coconut milk and with cubes of cucumber and *lontong* (compressed rice). Thais, the true spice alchemists of the region, spike the peanut sauce for their pork *satay* with red curry paste and then smooth out the heat with coconut milk and palm sugar. The meat marinade includes coconut cream, and a sweet-sour cucumber relish goes on the table with the *satay* and sauce.

Because Laos is landlocked, ideas and ingredients from elsewhere, such as Indian spices, have been slow to find a place in its kitchens. Yet this geographical isolation has not fully halted culinary exchanges. Cooks in neighboring Cambodia, Vietnam, and Thailand have imitated the traditional Laotian *tom som,* shredded green papaya salad spiked with chiles. Likewise, *larb,* a signature salad of water buffalo meat tossed with fish sauce, lime juice, chiles, and mint, has crossed the southeast border of Laos into Thailand, where it is usually made with pork or beef and local Thai seasonings.

The Filipinos, in contrast, are arguably the region's greatest borrowers. A full menu of Spanish dishes, such as seviche, paella, *pochero* (mixed-meat stew), and *leche flan* (caramel custard), are part of the repertoire of most Filipino cooks, although such preparations always include an island accent. The Chinese influence is pronounced here as well. For example, *pancit bijon guisado, pancit molo,* and *lumpia* are simply Philippine versions of three familiar Middle Kingdom plates, chow mein, wonton soup, and spring rolls, respectively.

But the region's most interesting example of a blended kitchen began in the early 1500s, when Chinese traders living in Malacca, then

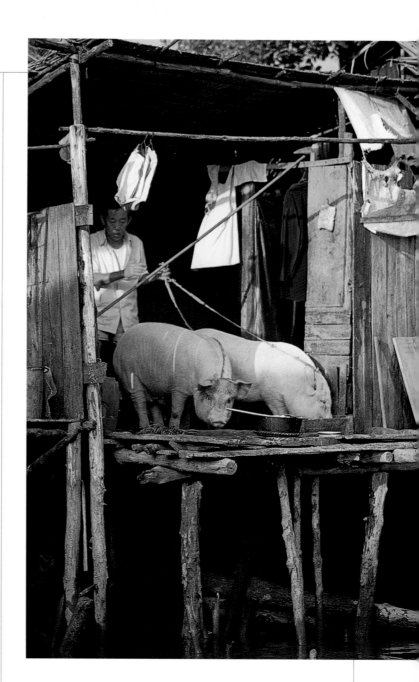

Left: The gold-plated glasses of this bespectacled Buddha require the labor of nine Burmese monks to complete their biweekly cleaning. The Buddha is known for his power to cure various afflictions, especially those related to eyesight. **Above top:** In Vietnam, seasonal flooding along the lacy canals that wind away from the Mekong Delta has made houses on stilts a necessity for residents—and their livestock. **Above bottom:** Burmese shadow puppets, used in traditional storytelling, are poised in patient display outside a temple in the old capital of Bagan (Pagan).

a Portuguese port on the Strait of Malacca, married local Malaysian women. The children from these marriages were called Straits Chinese or *Peranakan,* the latter meaning "born here" in Malay, with the girls called *nonyas* and the boys *babas.* Within a few generations, Nonya cooking, a fusion of Chinese and Malay ingredients and techniques, emerged, putting down permanent roots in Singapore and Malaysia. The melding is complex, with such ingredients as pork, soy sauce, dried mushrooms, and lily buds from the Chinese pantry and *blacan,* lemongrass, coconut milk, and tamarind from Malaysian shelves. Many dishes begin with a Malaysian technique, the making of a *rempah,* or spice paste, which is then combined with meat and vegetables and stir-fried in the Chinese manner.

Clearly, Southeast Asia is home to a rich cross-cultural table, with every country boasting a distinctive cuisine that nonetheless shares similarities with its neighbors. A look at a trio of ingredients highlights these culinary links. The first is fish sauce, a thin amber liquid also used as a condiment. Extracted from salted anchovies packed into barrels and left to ferment, fish sauce is an indispensable item in the kitchens of Thailand, Vietnam, Laos, and Cambodia, and shares cupboard space with soy sauce in Malaysia, Singapore, Indonesia, Myanmar, and the Philippines.

The second ingredient, what some observers call the "heart and soul of Southeast Asian cooking," is dried shrimp paste, a seasoning that adds unique character and an indescribable luster to the regional table. It comes in two basic forms, a hard, sliceable cake and a very thick, spoonable mass sold in a plastic tub. Although the types are different, they both deliver the sharp, pungent flavor that many Southeast Asians have grown to expect on the dinner table. The last ingredient is the ubiquitous coconut, the cream and milk of which are widely used in soups, curries, desserts, and other dishes everywhere in the region.

Of course, these three ingredients are only the starting point for putting together a Southeast Asian meal. Many dishes alone call for more than a score of herbs and spices.

Time-strapped cooks new to the Southeast Asian table may want to prepare a meal composed of only a dish or two and rice, until they are more comfortable with this exotic pantry and can enlist some kitchen help. In Asia, where the tradition of the extended family remains strong, kitchens are often filled with mothers and daughters, aunts and grandmothers, all folding dumplings, filling spring rolls, and chopping vegetables together—just as every extended Thai family looks forward to gathering on the riverbank and launching their handmade boats for Loy Krathong.

Above left: Here, the fresh berries of the pepper plant hang in jewel-like strands, before being dried into peppercorns and then ground for adding to myriad soups, salads, relishes, and other dishes. **Above:** Floating markets are common in central Thailand, and Damnoen Saduak, about sixty miles (100 km) west of Bangkok, is the largest one in the region. Every morning at sunrise, women in narrow boats loaded with fresh fruits and vegetables or outfitted with makeshift kitchens crowd the market's maze of canals to sell their wares to tourists and neighbors alike.

SMALL PLATES AND SOUPS

Myriad snacks sold from roadside stands are the fuel of the Southeast Asian worker.

Preceding spread: Small silver fish dry on a simple rack in the steady heat of a Manila afternoon. **Above top:** In the heart of Kuala Lumpur's thriving downtown, the image of the Jame Masjid mosque, built in traditional Arabian style, is reflected in the mirrored panes of a modern office building. **Above bottom:** Duck is popular in Thailand, where the birds are roasted whole to a rich chestnut brown, Chinese style, or used in a thoroughly Thai red curry, such as *gaeng ped supparot.* **Right:** Vendors in the southern Vietnamese town of Soc Trang look forward to the arrival of the ferry, hoping to sell their fruits and homemade snacks to the disembarking passengers.

WITH THE EXCEPTION OF A BANQUET, serving an appetizer at the beginning of a meal is an imported custom for Southeast Asians. Foods that would be considered appetizers in Western cuisines are more likely classified as snacks in this part of the world, where stopping for a quick bite at nearly any time of the day or evening is commonplace. Indeed, snacks, that is, foods eaten between meals, are ubiquitous and varied. Some are as substantial as a plate of *kway teow,* Singapore wok-fried rice noodles, while others are as simple as a *perkedel,* Indonesian corn fritters.

In a Southeast Asian home, all the dishes for a meal are brought to the table at once, rather than in courses. Cooks rely on simple preparations, too, with most dishes steamed, braised, or poached, and only one or two stir-fried, so that everything is ready to be eaten at the same time. *Tok panjang,* or "long table of food," is an old Straits Chinese dining custom in which a long table is topped with a near overflow of curries, soups, *sambals,* and other dishes. Unlike Western buffets, where guests tend to pile everything onto one plate and

then find a spot away from the food to sit and eat, the *tok panjang* has as many guests as will fit take a seat and eat, picking and choosing from the bounty of choices. As each diner is finished, he or she gets up and the empty place is taken by the next hungry guest.

Southeast Asian cooks are adaptable, however, and over time many of them have altered their age-old dishes to accommodate the Western style of menu planning and dining. Preparations such as *satay*, *cha gio* (Vietnamese spring rolls), *sakoo sai kai* (Thai dumplings), *be ya kyaw* (Burmese split-pea fritters), and others were once only celebratory foods, street-hawker specialties, or sometimes main dishes. But with the French in Cambodia, Vietnam, and Laos, the British in Myanmar (Burma),

Above top: Street-side snack vendors are a typical sight in Malaysia, where midafternoon hunger pangs are readily satisfied by a few skewers of charcoal-grilled *satay*.
Above bottom: The sixteenth-century arrival of the chile in Southeast Asia revolutionized local tables. Varying in shape, color, and degree of heat they deliver, these flavor-packed peppers are sliced and used as a garnish or set afloat in a dipping sauce, pounded into curry pastes, and added to stir-fries or soups whole or chopped. **Right:** On the outskirts of Hanoi, cycling shoppers zip past an outdoor market in a blur of rain-resistant color.

Malaysia, and Singapore, the Dutch in Indonesia, and the Spanish in the Philippines, restaurateurs and home cooks were introduced to the Western notion of the appetizer, and they soon began making concessions to it.

The spring roll, which is time-consuming to prepare and requires practice to shape with skill, is an excellent example of a dish that made the move from festive food to everyday appetizer. Traditionally, spring rolls were made for Chinese New Year, the first day of spring according to the lunar calendar, and every Southeast Asian country has its own version. Eventually, a year-round demand for them developed, however, and they began being served regularly as an appetizer, thus losing their original celebratory significance.

Thai *miang kum* is yet another example. Basically it is a relish tray containing such items as dried shrimp, roasted peanuts, and toasted coconut; a stack of green herb leaves; and a syrupy sauce. An assortment of the "relishes" is tucked into a leaf, a dab of sauce is added, and the resulting packet is popped into the mouth in a single bite. Thais always ate *miang kum* as a snack, until Western influences gave it a second role, as the perfect light opener to a meal.

How these shifts happened is easy to understand. Snack foods are irresistible, whether it is *ukoy,* shrimp and sweet potato fritters, in Manila, or *poat dot,* grilled corn brushed with a sweet oil-seared onion "butter," in Phnom Penh. Because local cooks

understood the pull of these foods, such quick bites easily found a place on the dinner table.

The role of soup in a Southeast Asian meal differs from that of its Western counterpart as well. Some soups, usually broths with a few ingredients floating in them, are served as part of a meal. But rather than being offered before the other dishes, the soup is brought to the table at the same time. Each diner helps him- or herself to spoonfuls from this central bowl throughout the meal. It is enjoyed for itself and also acts as a way to temper hot, spicy flavors, thus readying the diner for the next bouquet of tastes.

Noodle soups served as a main dish for breakfast or lunch or for a snack make up a second category. Vietnamese *pho,* rice noodles in beef broth, is a standard morning eye-opener. In Hanoi, I watched as vendors on their way to the market stopped at a street hawker to buy *pho*-to-go in Styrofoam cartons. With chopsticks in hand and an eye on their merchandise, they slurped their steaming noodles and broth as they awaited their first customers of the day. Anyone who had failed

Left: A young vendor of lotus seeds manages a smile as she makes her way along a street in Phnom Penh. **Below top:** According to legend, the sprawling, gold-spired Shwedagon Pagoda, the most sacred temple in Yangon (Rangoon), was built to enshrine eight hairs of the last Buddha. **Below bottom:** Near Chiang Mai, the largest town in northern Thailand and a popular base for touring the Golden Triangle, a trio of workers take a lunch break from rice harvesting.

Above top: The slopes that rise from southern Vietnam's beautiful Cam Ranh Bay, with its clear, sky blue waters, are a primary salt production site. In the 1960s, this same area, surrounded by groves of coconut palms and banana plantations, was home to a huge U.S. naval installation. **Above bottom:** Emerald green banana leaves are versatile culinary tools, used as plates for richly spiced curries; as sturdy, fragrant wrappers for cooking sticky rice or whole fish; and as a steaming basket for sweet potatoes and other vegetables, as shown here. **Right:** A succession of stone doorways frames a statue of a seated Buddha at Banteay Kdei, a temple in the Angkor complex near Siem Reap, in Cambodia.

to buy *pho* en route to work did not have to worry, however. Women walked the aisles offering bowls of the hot soup for sale.

Soups eaten with rice are yet another category. On my last visit to Singapore, I regularly trekked down to one of the few remaining open-air shophouses specializing in *bak kuh teh,* or pork rib tea soup, a specialty of the Chao Zhou people of southeastern China. The soup is made by simmering small pork spareribs in a broth seasoned with star anise, cinnamon, garlic, and green onions. The tender ribs are plucked out with chopsticks, dipped into a soy-chile sauce, and eaten with rice. Part of the dining ritual includes spooning some of the broth over the rice before eating it and then drinking the remaining broth.

But just as with appetizers, the traditionally defined roles played by soup have been modified. In other words, today travelers dining in the better restaurants of Southeast Asia will likely be served their soup Western style, at the beginning of a meal. Fortunately, such concessions to modern expectations have not brought on compromises in the quality of these classic preparations.

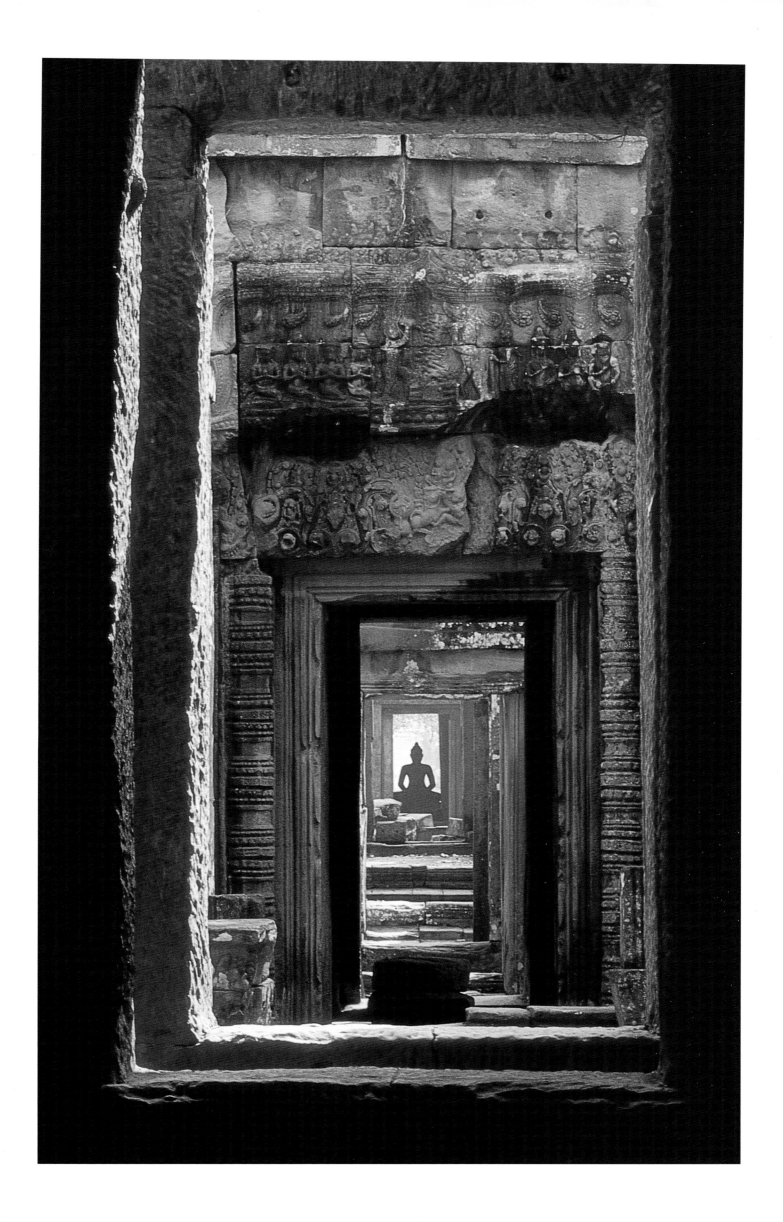

Vietnam

Goi Cuon

fresh spring rolls with hoisin-peanut dip

When making these marvelous spring rolls, don't skimp on the aromatic herbs. In Ho Chi Minh City, I tasted rather plain spring rolls with very little meat, but the abundant fresh herbs made up for the simplicity. The sauce, called nuoc leo, *uses hoisin sauce, a popular Chinese condiment.*

DIPPING SAUCE

1 tablespoon vegetable oil

4 cloves garlic, minced

⅓ cup (3 fl oz/80 ml) hoisin sauce

1 tablepoon fish sauce

1 tablespoon sugar

1 teaspoon chile paste or hot bean paste

½ cup (4 fl oz/125 ml) chicken stock

¼ cup (1 oz/30 g) chopped unsalted dry-roasted peanuts

FILLING

¼ lb (125 g) dried rice vermicelli, soaked in warm water for 15 minutes

2 cups (16 fl oz/500 ml) chicken stock

2 teaspoons fish sauce

¼ teaspoon sugar

pinch of ground pepper

¾ lb (375 g) boneless pork loin, in one piece

12 large shrimp (prawns)

12 dried round rice papers, 8 inches (20 cm) in diameter

12 large, soft red-leaf lettuce leaves, stiff ribs removed

1 carrot, peeled, finely julienned, and tossed with 1 teaspoon sugar

1 cup (4 oz/125 g) finely julienned jicama

leaves from 1 small bunch fresh mint

12 fresh dill sprigs

12 fresh coriander (cilantro) sprigs

❦ To make the dipping sauce, in a small saucepan over medium heat, warm the oil. When it is hot, add the garlic and cook, stirring, until lightly browned, about 30 seconds. Add the hoisin sauce, fish sauce,

sugar, and chile paste or hot bean paste, stir well, and simmer for 15 seconds. Stir in the chicken stock; the mixture should have a thick, creamy consistency. Add the peanuts and let cool. Divide among small saucers.

❦ To make the filling, bring a large saucepan three-fourths full of water to a boil. Drain the rice noodles and add to the boiling water. Boil until just tender, about 2 minutes. Pour the noodles into a colander and rinse thoroughly with cold water. Drain well and set aside. Toss the noodles occasionally to keep them from sticking together.

❦ In a saucepan, bring the chicken stock to a boil over high heat. Add the fish sauce, sugar, pepper, and pork and return to a boil. Reduce the heat to medium and boil gently until the pork is firm and no longer pink, about 20 minutes. Remove the pork from the stock and let cool. Cut into thin strips ¾ inch (2 cm) wide by 2 inches (5 cm) long.

❦ Bring a saucepan three-fourths full of water to a boil. Add the shrimp and boil until they turn bright orange-pink, 1–2 minutes. Drain, let cool, then peel, devein, and cut in half lengthwise. Set aside.

❦ To make the spring rolls, lay 1 rice paper round on a flat surface. Lay another paper next to but not touching it. If space permits, lay out as many as 4 papers without touching. Using a pastry brush, generously brush the papers with warm water and leave them for 30 seconds or longer until they are softened and feel like wet tissue. While working on one, cover the others with a damp kitchen towel. Arrange 1 lettuce leaf on the lower third of the round. Put about 2 tablespoons of the rice vermicelli, a few strips of pork, carrot, jicama, a few mint leaves, and 1 dill sprig on the lettuce. Fold the lower edge over the filling, half covering it and forming a log. Fold in the sides to enclose the ends. Put 2 pieces of shrimp with 1 coriander sprig across the log. Continue rolling the paper over the shrimp to seal the roll. Moisten the ends with water to seal the seam. Set the roll on a tray lined with plastic wrap. Cover with a damp kitchen towel. Repeat until all the rolls are done.

❦ Arrange the rolls, whole or cut into thirds, on a serving tray. Distribute the dipping saucers among the diners. To eat, dip the rolls into the sauce and eat out of hand.

makes 12 rolls; serves 6

Singapore

Kueh Pai Tee

"top hat" filled with crab and vegetables

A great party dish, these dainty, fluted shells, named because they look like upside-down top hats, are filled with a braised mixture of seafood and vegetables. Each shell is made with a steel mold that is dipped into batter and plunged into hot oil. When crisp and brown, the shell slips off the mold. I found molds while rooting around in the night markets in Singapore, and they are also sold there in department stores. Some of the better Southeast Asian markets in the West carry them as well. If you cannot find the mold, you can substitute wonton skins: press a 1½-inch (4-cm) wide, stainless-steel ladle into the middle of a skin and hold it down in the hot oil. Failing that option, use small premade Western pastry shells.

PASTRY SHELLS

¾ cup (4 oz/125 g) all-purpose (plain) flour

¼ cup (1 oz/30 g) rice flour

¼ teaspoon salt

1 egg, lightly beaten

¾ cup (6 fl oz/180 ml) water

vegetable oil for deep-frying

FILLING

¼ lb (125 g) shrimp (prawns)

2 tablespoons vegetable oil

3 cloves garlic, minced

2 teaspoons dried shrimp, minced

1 cup (4 oz/125 g) julienned bamboo shoot

1 large carrot, peeled and finely shredded

½ lb (250 g) daikon, peeled and finely shredded

1 cup (8 fl oz/250 ml) water

1 tablespoon sugar

1 teaspoon salt

¼ lb (125 g) fresh-cooked crabmeat, picked over for shell fragments and flaked

¼ cup (⅓ oz/10 g) chopped fresh coriander (cilantro), plus about 36 whole leaves for garnish

Sriracha sauce (page 251)

To make the pastry shells, in a bowl, stir together the all-purpose and rice flours and the salt. Add the egg, then slowly add the water, stirring until the mixture is the consistency of a thin batter.

To fry the shells, pour the vegetable oil to a depth of 3 inches (7.5 cm) in a wok or deep saucepan and heat to 365°F (185°C) on a deep-frying thermometer. When the oil is hot, season the pastry mold (see note) by holding its handle and dipping it into the hot oil for 1 minute. Remove the mold from the oil, shaking to remove any excess oil, then dip it into the batter up to, but not over, the top edge. Lift the mold out of the batter and let the excess batter drip back into the bowl. Lower the coated mold into the hot oil and deep-fry until the pastry can retain its shape, about 1 minute. With chopsticks or tongs, nudge the top edge of the mold to help release the shell into the oil. Fry the shell until it is golden brown, about 1 minute longer. Remove and drain on paper towels. Repeat until all the batter is used. Let the shells cool completely. (The shells can be stored in an airtight container at room temperature for up to 3 days.)

To make the filling, bring a saucepan three-fourths full of water to a boil. Add the shrimp and boil until they turn bright orange-pink, 1–2 minutes. Drain, let cool, then peel, devein, and cut into ¼-inch (6-mm) dice.

Place a wok over medium-high heat and add the oil. When it is hot, add the garlic and dried shrimp and sauté until the garlic is golden, about 30 seconds. Raise the heat to high and add the bamboo shoot, carrot, daikon, and diced shrimp, and stir and toss in the hot oil for a few seconds. Add the water, sugar, and salt and continue cooking, stirring gently, until the vegetables are tender and all the liquid has evaporated, 8–10 minutes. Remove from the heat and let cool.

Add the crabmeat and chopped coriander to the cooled filling and mix well. Using chopsticks, put about 2 teaspoons of the filling into each pastry shell. Garnish each filled shell with a whole coriander leaf, top with a drop of Sriracha sauce, and serve.

makes about 3 dozen pastries; serves 12

Thailand

Gaeng Liang Fak Tong

pumpkin and coconut milk soup

A soup of pumpkin and coconut milk is one of the many dishes that cross the culinary borders of Southeast Asia. My favorite version comes from Thailand, where the luxury of adding extra spices and ingredients helps develop a more complex flavor.

2 tablespoons dried shrimp, rinsed

1 lemongrass stalk, tender midsection only, chopped

4 shallots, quartered

3 red Fresno or serrano chiles, seeded

1 teaspoon dried shrimp paste

½ cup (4 fl oz/125 ml) coconut cream (page 245)

3 cups (24 fl oz/750 ml) coconut milk (page 245)

2 cups (16 fl oz/500 ml) chicken stock

1½ teaspoons roasted chile paste (page 245)

8 kaffir lime leaves, spines removed

1-lb (500-g) piece pumpkin, peeled, seeded, and cut into 1-inch (2.5-cm) cubes

1 tablespoon fish sauce, or to taste

½ teaspoon sugar

½ cup (3½ oz/105 g) drained canned straw mushrooms

1 tablespoon fresh lime juice, or to taste

½ cup (½ oz/15 g) Thai basil leaves

❧ In a blender, combine the dried shrimp, lemongrass, shallots, chiles, and dried shrimp paste. Process to form a smooth paste.

❧ Put the coconut cream into a saucepan over medium-high heat. Add the spice paste and cook, stirring frequently, until fragrant, 3–5 minutes. Add the coconut milk, stock, chile paste, lime leaves, and pumpkin and bring to a boil. Reduce the heat to medium-low and simmer, uncovered, until the pumpkin is tender, about 20 minutes. Add the fish sauce, sugar, mushrooms, lime juice, and basil and heat through. Ladle into warmed bowls and serve.

serves 6–8

Thailand

Miang Kum

herb leaf–wrapped bundles

My first introduction to this "salad" was a learning experience, for eating it properly is no easy feat. When it was served, it looked like a relish tray, but my host soon showed me that its enjoyment was dependent on a skillful combining of the ingredients. She took a small fresh herb leaf and put one or two bits of each item onto it, spooned a dab of sauce on the mixture, and folded it up into a bundle. Although it sounds simple, my first attempts left a trail of ingredients across the table leading to my plate. Several torn leaves later, I succeeded in wrapping one and consuming the whole small bite at once. It was a memorable mouthful, bursting with textures and flavors.

In Thailand, cha plu *leaves, relatives of betel leaves and sometimes referred to as wild betel leaves, are traditionally used, but spinach or* shiso *leaves may be substituted. It is important to cut each ingredient into the size indicated.*

½ cup (2 oz/60 g) unsweetened grated dried coconut, toasted

½ cup (2½ oz/75 g) unsalted roasted peanuts

¼ cup (1½ oz/45 g) dried shrimp, each about ½ inch (12 mm) long

¼ cup (2 oz/60 g) peeled and diced fresh ginger (¼-inch/6-mm dice)

1 thin-skinned lime, unpeeled, cut into ¼-inch (6-mm) dice

⅓ cup (1½ oz/45 g) diced shallot (¼-inch/6-mm dice)

2 tablespoons chopped green serrano or Thai chile

½ cup (½ oz/15 g) fresh coriander (cilantro) leaves

18 cha plu *(see note),* spinach, or shiso *leaves*

SAUCE

¼ cup (1 oz/30 g) unsweetened grated dried coconut, toasted

2 tablespoons dried shrimp powder

3 tablespoons ground unsalted roasted peanuts

1 slice fresh galangal, ½ inch (12 mm) thick, peeled and chopped

½ teaspoon dried shrimp paste

⅓ cup (3 oz/90 g) firmly packed palm sugar or brown sugar

¼ cup (2 fl oz/60 ml) tamarind water (see sidebar, page 114)

1 tablespoon fish sauce, or to taste

1 teaspoon dark soy sauce

½ teaspoon salt

½ cup (4 fl oz/125 ml) water

☙ Prepare an attractive platter with individual piles of the coconut, peanuts, dried shrimp, ginger, lime, shallot, chile, and coriander leaves. Arrange the *cha plu* or other leaves on a serving plate.

☙ To make the sauce, in a mini food processor or a blender, combine the toasted coconut, dried shrimp powder, ground peanuts, and galangal. Process as finely as possible. Transfer the mixture to a small saucepan and add the dried shrimp paste, palm or brown sugar, tamarind water, fish sauce, soy sauce, salt, and water. Bring to a boil over high heat, reduce the heat to medium, and boil gently, stirring occasionally, until the mixture is syrupy and a dark caramel color, about 3 minutes. Pour into a dipping saucer and let cool.

☙ Each diner takes a leaf and puts a bit of each ingredient onto it. The total of all the ingredients should amount to no more than a small mouthful. Then he or she spoons a dab of the sauce on top, folds up the leaf, and pops it into the mouth.

serves 6

Krupuk

The crisp, translucent crackers called *krupuk* are found in every Indonesian and Malaysian kitchen—and in other Southeast Asian pantries as well. Although many different varieties exist—fish (*krupuk palembang*), tapioca (*krupuk miller*), malingo nut (*emping malinjo*)—*krupuk udang*, made from shrimp, are the most common. They come in the form of brittle disks in various colors, and they puff into tasty, featherlight wafers when deep-fried. Most are only as large as a potato chip and are used as garnishes or snacks, but others expand to the size of a dinner plate.

I was once in Kukup, a small fishing village built on stilts in Johor, Malaysia, where the locals made their own dough for *krupuk*. It was a very dense mixture, which they shaped into logs and then cut crosswise into thin slices. They spread the slices over a bamboo mat and left them under the hot tropical sun until they were bone dry. Nowadays, alas, very few people make their own dough. Instead the dried chips are bought at the store and fried up at home (page 250).

Malaysia

Dal

spicy yellow lentil stew

In traditional Indian cooking, dal refers to any dried peas or beans and to the many dishes made from them. In Malaysia and Singapore, dal refers to a spicy stew made of yellow lentils (toovar dal) that typically accompanies Indian breads. The cooking time will vary with the age of the lentil.

1 cup (7 oz/220 g) dried yellow lentils (see note)
2 cups (16 fl oz/500 ml) water
½ teaspoon ground turmeric
1 teaspoon plus 2 tablespoons ghee or vegetable oil
1 teaspoon black mustard seeds
2 dried red chiles, cut up
1 yellow onion, sliced
2 cloves garlic, minced
2 slices fresh ginger, peeled and minced
20 fresh or dried curry leaves
1 teaspoon garam masala
2 small tomatoes, quartered lengthwise
½ teaspoon salt, or to taste

❧ Pick over the lentils, discarding any misshapen lentils or stones. Rinse the lentils until the water runs clear, then drain.

❧ In a saucepan over high heat, combine the lentils, water, turmeric, and the 1 teaspoon ghee or oil. Bring to a boil, stirring occasionally. Reduce the heat to medium, cover, and simmer until the lentils are soft and tender, about 30 minutes.

❧ In a frying pan over medium-high heat, warm the remaining 2 tablespoons ghee or oil. When hot, add the mustard seeds and fry until they turn gray, spatter, and pop, about 2 minutes. Add the chiles, onion, garlic, ginger, and curry leaves and sauté until the onion is soft and golden, about 5 minutes. Stir in the *garam masala* and tomatoes and cook for 1 minute.

❧ Pour the onion mixture into the pan of cooked lentils, add the salt, and simmer for 5 minutes to blend the flavors. Transfer to a serving dish and serve.

serves 4

Thailand

Tom Yum Goong

lemongrass soup with shrimp

In Thailand, tom yum goong is often served in a round metal urn shaped like a bundt cake pan. The urn rests atop a brazier and has a cone-shaped chimney extending from the center. My first taste of this aromatic soup was a rustic village version: large, sweet, succulent shrimp were surrounded by a thick sea of crushed pieces of lemongrass and galangal, chiles, and kaffir lime leaves. I had to burrow my spoon through the water jungle of ingredients for a taste of the delicious broth. Although most restaurants serve the broth strained, rejecting the home-style presentation, I still carry the imprint of that simple, yet extraordinary soup in my memory whenever I sit down to a bowl of tom yum goong.

Lemongrass carries a wonderful citrusy scent that, along with the kaffir lime leaves, beautifully balances the heat of the roasted chile paste in this signature Thai preparation. Related to the equally lemony citronella, lemongrass is one of the ingredients that give Thai dishes their characteristic aromatic quality. An added benefit: Thai cooks believe lemongrass combats head colds, making this sour, sharp soup a curative as well.

¾ lb (375 g) large shrimp (prawns) in the shell

2 tablespoons vegetable oil

4 lemongrass stalks, tender midsection only, smashed and cut into 2-inch (5-cm) lengths

6 slices fresh galangal or 3 slices dried galangal

6 green Thai chiles or 8 green serrano chiles, cut in half crosswise

6 cups (48 fl oz/1.5 l) chicken stock

8 kaffir lime leaves, spines removed

1–2 tablespoons roasted chile paste (page 245), or to taste

1 cup (7 oz/220 g) drained canned straw mushrooms

4-inch (10-cm) piece bamboo shoot, thinly sliced

3 tablespoons fish sauce, or to taste

¼ cup (2 fl oz/60 ml) fresh lime juice, or to taste

1 fresh red chile, sliced into rounds

¼ cup (¼ oz/7 g) fresh coriander (cilantro) leaves

☙ Peel and devein the shrimp, reserving the shells. Rinse the shrimp and set aside.

☙ In a large saucepan over medium-high heat, warm the vegetable oil. When the oil is hot, add the shrimp shells and fry them, stirring, until they turn bright orange, about 1 minute. Toss in the lemongrass, galangal, green chiles, chicken stock, and 4 of the lime leaves. Raise the heat to high and bring to a boil. Reduce the heat to medium and simmer, uncovered, for 15 minutes to develop the flavors. Remove from the heat and pour the stock through a sieve placed over a clean saucepan. Discard the contents of the sieve.

☙ Add the chile paste, straw mushrooms, and sliced bamboo shoot to the saucepan, stir well, and bring to a boil over medium heat. When it is boiling, add the shrimp and the remaining 4 lime leaves and cook until the shrimp turn bright orange-pink, 1–2 minutes. Season with the fish sauce and lime juice, then taste and adjust the seasoning.

☙ Ladle the soup into warmed bowls and garnish with the red chile slices and coriander leaves.

serves 6

Malaysia

Aloo

curried potatoes and peas

Typically, Malaysians buy their garam masala, an indispensable Indian spice blend, premixed from a neighborhood spice merchant.

3 tablespoons ghee or vegetable oil

1½ teaspoons peeled and minced fresh ginger

1 or 2 green jalapeño chiles, chopped

10–12 fresh or dried curry leaves

½ teaspoon black mustard seeds

½ teaspoon cumin seeds

1 yellow onion, coarsely chopped

1 lb (500 g) baking potatoes, peeled and cut into 1-inch (2.5-cm) cubes

1½ teaspoons ground coriander

½ teaspoon salt

¼ teaspoon ground turmeric

1 cup (8 fl oz/250 ml) water

½ cup (2½ oz/75 g) peas

½ teaspoon garam masala

1 small tomato, cut into 1-inch (2.5-cm) cubes

¼ cup (⅓ oz/10 g) chopped fresh coriander (cilantro)

In a large saucepan over medium-high heat, warm the ghee or oil. When hot, add the ginger, chiles, curry leaves, and mustard and cumin seeds and sauté until the seeds pop and turn gray, about 30 seconds. Add the onion and cook, stirring, until soft and translucent, about 2 minutes. Add the potatoes and cook, stirring, until light brown, about 5 minutes. Add the ground coriander, salt, turmeric, and water; stir to mix well. Reduce the heat to a gentle boil, cover partially, and cook, stirring occasionally, until the potatoes are almost fully cooked and the liquid has nearly evaporated, 12–15 minutes.

Mix in the peas, cover, and cook for 1 minute longer. Sprinkle with *garam masala* and add the tomato and chopped coriander. Toss gently to mix. Transfer to a serving bowl and serve immediately.

serves 6

Laos

Tom Ponh

fish and eggplant purée in lettuce leaves

A popular dish in Laos, this fish purée typifies the complex herbaceous flavors present in the traditional foods of Indochina. I prefer the rich taste imparted by grilling the fish over a charcoal fire, although some cooks boil the fish for this recipe.

1 lb (500 g) catfish or other whitefish fillets such as cod or snapper

vegetable oil for brushing

1 large globe eggplant (aubergine) or 4 large Asian (slender) eggplants, 1¼ lb (625 g) total weight

6 cloves garlic, unpeeled

2 shallots, unpeeled

2 tablespoons fish sauce, or to taste

3 red Fresno or serrano chiles, seeded and finely chopped

2 green (spring) onions, including 1 inch (2.5 cm) of the green tops, minced

3 tablespoons chopped fresh mint

2 tablespoons chopped fresh Thai basil

2 tablespoons fresh coriander (cilantro) leaves

2 fresh dill sprigs, chopped

1 teaspoon salt, or to taste

DIPPING SAUCE

1 fresh red chile, seeded and finely minced

3 tablespoons fish sauce

¼ cup (2 fl oz/60 ml) fresh lime juice

1 tablespoon sugar

¼ cup (2 fl oz/60 ml) water

SALAD AND HERBS

1 head red-leaf or butter (Boston) lettuce, leaves separated

1 handful fresh Thai basil leaves

1 handful fresh coriander (cilantro) leaves

1 handful fresh polygonum leaves (page 248)

1 handful fresh mint leaves

1 cucumber, peeled, seeded, and cut into thin strips ⅛ inch (3 mm) wide and 2 inches (5 cm) long

♛ Prepare a medium-hot fire in a charcoal grill.

♛ Brush the fish fillets with oil. Place the fish on the grill rack and grill, turning once, until opaque throughout, about 5 minutes total per ½ inch (12 mm) at the thickest point of the fillets. Transfer the fish to a platter and let cool. Break up the cooled fish into chunks; set aside.

♛ Using a skewer, puncture the eggplant(s) in several places and set over the charcoal fire. Grill, turning occasionally, until the skin(s) blacken and the flesh is very tender, about 20 minutes for the globe eggplant and 10 minutes for the Asian eggplants. Remove from the grill and let cool. Cut in half lengthwise and scoop out the tender flesh; set aside.

♛ Meanwhile, thread the garlic cloves and shallots on a metal skewer and set over the charcoal fire. Grill, turning occasionally, until charred and tender, 10–15 minutes. Remove from the grill and set aside to cool. Peel the garlic and shallots.

♛ In a food processor, combine the fish chunks, eggplant flesh, 4 of the garlic cloves, the shallots, fish sauce, chiles, green onions, mint, basil, coriander leaves, and dill. Process until a smooth purée forms. If it is too thick, thin the purée with a little water to the consistency of a thick dip. Add the salt and taste and adjust the seasonings. Transfer to a serving bowl.

♛ To make the dipping sauce, in a mortar, combine the remaining 2 grilled garlic cloves and the chile and pound to a purée. Stir in the fish sauce, lime juice, sugar, and water. Pour into a saucer.

♛ Arrange the lettuce, basil, coriander, polygonum, and mint leaves, and the cucumber strips around the edges of a large platter and place the bowl of fish-eggplant purée in the middle.

♛ Each diner takes a lettuce leaf, scatters a few herb leaves and strips of cucumber in the center, adds a dollop of the purée, rolls up the lettuce leaf, dips the roll into the sauce, and eats it out of hand.

serves 4–6

Myanmar (Burma)

Mohingha

curried fish and noodle soup

Soup is common breakfast fare throughout Asia. Each country has its favorite, and Myanmar is no exception. Mohingha is quintessential hawker food, and most home cooks rarely make the dish, relying instead on favorite local vendors. Catfish makes the best stock, but other fish, such as snapper, cod, or halibut, may be used. In Myanmar, where banana trees are plentiful, slices from the heart of the trunk are added. Bamboo shoots make an acceptable substitute.

2 lb (1 kg) catfish fillets

1 teaspoon salt

½ teaspoon ground turmeric

2 lemongrass stalks, smashed and each one tied into a knot

4 cups (32 fl oz/1 l) water

SPICE PASTE

3 yellow onions, cut into 1-inch (2.5-cm) pieces

1-inch (2.5-cm) piece fresh ginger, peeled and roughly chopped

6 cloves garlic

1 lemongrass stalk, tender midsection only, chopped

2 fresh red chiles, seeded and roughly chopped

1 teaspoon dried shrimp paste

½ teaspoon ground turmeric

3 tablespoons peanut oil

4 cups (32 fl oz/1 l) thin coconut milk (page 245)

1 cup (4 oz/125 g) thinly sliced bamboo shoot

2 tablespoons chickpea (garbanzo bean) flour or toasted rice powder mixed with ¼ cup (2 fl oz/60 ml) water to make a smooth paste

2 tablespoons fish sauce

salt to taste

2 tablespoons fresh lemon juice, or to taste

¾ lb (375 g) thin fresh egg noodles or dried rice vermicelli

ACCOMPANIMENTS

6 hard-boiled eggs, peeled and cut into wedges

2 lemons, cut into wedges

1 cup (1 oz/30 g) fresh coriander (cilantro) leaves

1 white onion, finely sliced

½ cup (1½ oz/45 g) fried shallots (see sidebar, page 79)

✾ Cut the fish fillets into 1-inch (2.5-cm) cubes. Put into a bowl and toss with the salt and turmeric to mix well. Set aside to marinate for 15 minutes. Put the fish, lemongrass, and water into a saucepan and bring to a gentle boil over high heat. Reduce the heat to low and simmer for 5 minutes. Using a slotted spoon, transfer the fish to a bowl and set aside. Reserve the stock, discarding the lemongrass.

✾ To make the spice paste, in a mortar or blender, combine the onions, ginger, garlic, lemongrass, chiles, dried shrimp paste, and turmeric and pound or process to a smooth paste.

✾ In a large saucepan over medium-high heat, warm the peanut oil until it is almost smoking. Carefully add the spice paste—it will spatter in the hot oil—and stir immediately to incorporate it with the oil. Reduce the heat to low, cover, and simmer gently, stirring every few minutes. If the mixture seems too dry and without oil, stir in some water, re-cover, and continue simmering until the oil returns and appears at the edge of the paste. This step should take 10–12 minutes total. Uncover, raise the heat to high, and add the reserved fish stock, thin coconut milk, and bamboo shoot. Bring to a boil, reduce the heat to low, and simmer, uncovered, until the bamboo shoot is tender, about 5 minutes. Raise the heat to high, add the chickpea or rice powder paste, and stir until the stock begins to thicken, 1–2 minutes. Add the fish sauce and fish pieces and simmer together for 5 minutes to blend the flavors. Season with salt and lemon juice. Remove from the heat and keep warm.

✾ Meanwhile, if using egg noodles, bring a large saucepan three-fourths full of water to a boil. Add the noodles and cook, stirring, until the water boils a second time. Cook until the noodles are tender, 1–2 minutes longer. Drain in a colander, rinse with warm water, and drain again. If using rice vermicelli, soak in warm water for 15 minutes, drain, and then boil for 1 minute and drain.

✾ Arrange the egg and lemon wedges, coriander, onion slices, and fried shallots on a platter. Divide the noodles among individual bowls. Ladle the hot soup over the noodles and serve immediately. Each diner squeezes a lemon wedge into his or her bowl and adds accompaniments as desired.

serves 6

Malaysia

Satay Ayam dan Kambing

grilled skewered chicken and lamb
with spicy peanut sauce

Centuries ago in Java, skewers of bite-sized meats marinated with spices were cooked over charcoal fires. An adaptation of the Arab trader's kabob, satay spread across the more than thirteen thousand islands that the Indonesian archipelago comprises, with nearly every island cooking up its own distinctive recipe. The best satay is inevitably prepared by the numerous street vendors who cut and weave a variety of meats onto sticks and set them over a well-seasoned grill. The spiced morsels are eaten dunked into a sauce made of spices, chiles, kecap manis (sweet soy sauce), and often peanuts. Inland, chicken, beef, and goat meat are used and enjoyed by the predominately Muslim population.

Near the coast, fresh seafood turns up on sticks. Muslims are prohibited from eating pork, but among the Chinese population and on the island of Bali, which is primarily Hindu and Christian, pork satay is common. The Balinese also enjoy chunks of grilled duck, although their specialty is satay penyu, made with marinated cubed turtle meat.

The neighboring countries of Malaysia, Singapore, and Thailand caught on to the satay craze, and each added its own culinary magic. In Singapore, the Satay Club, an open-air hawker center offering Malay-style satay, is a popular retreat with locals. Malay cooks use a more complex blend of seasonings, including galangal, dried shrimp paste, and such Indian spices as cumin, coriander, and turmeric, to make their kuah kacang, or "peanut sauce." The Thais take the concept further by adding just the right amount of red curry paste and fish sauce and marrying it all together with coconut milk.

Malay cooks judge the quality of a peanut or other sauce by the color of the oil that floats on the surface. It should have the characteristic tint of the color extracted from the sauce ingredients. Without color, the sauce will taste raw and harsh. Some Westerners find the amount of oil used excessive. If you are among them, add the prescribed amount and then spoon off the excess oil after the sauce is cooked.

SATAY

1½ tablespoons palm sugar or dark brown sugar

1 tablespoon ground coriander

1 tablespoon ground cumin

2 teaspoons peeled and minced fresh ginger

1 teaspoon minced garlic

1 teaspoon ground turmeric

1 teaspoon salt

1 lb (500 g) boneless, skinless chicken thigh or breast meat, cut into ¾-inch (2-cm) cubes

1 lb (500 g) boneless lamb, cut into ¾-inch (2-cm) cubes

PEANUT SAUCE

8 dried red chiles, cracked, seeded, soaked in warm water for 15 minutes, and drained

2-inch (5-cm) piece fresh ginger, peeled and chopped

2-inch (5-cm) piece fresh galangal, peeled and chopped

5 large shallots, quartered lengthwise

6 cloves garlic, halved

2 lemongrass stalks, tender midsection only, chopped

1 slice dried shrimp paste, ⅛ inch (3 mm) thick

1 tablespoon ground coriander

1 teaspoon ground cumin

1 teaspoon ground turmeric

½ teaspoon ground fennel

½ cup (4 fl oz/125 ml) vegetable oil

⅓ cup (3 fl oz/80 ml) tamarind water (see sidebar, page 114)

1½ cups (7½ oz/235 g) unsalted roasted peanuts, coarsely ground

2 tablespoons palm sugar or dark brown sugar

2 teaspoons salt

1½ cups (12 fl oz/375 ml) water

BASTING OIL

⅓ cup (3 fl oz/80 ml) coconut cream (page 245)

1 tablespoon vegetable oil

1 tablespoon brown sugar

ACCOMPANIMENTS

lontong, cut into ½-inch (12-mm) cubes (optional; page 249)

1 English (hothouse) cucumber, peeled and cut into irregular ¼-inch (6-mm) wedges

1 red (Spanish) onion, cut into ¼-inch (6-mm) wedges

Soak 20 bamboo skewers in water to cover for 30 minutes.

To make the *satay*, in a bowl, stir together the palm or brown sugar, coriander, cumin, ginger, garlic, turmeric, and salt. Divide the mixture equally between 2 bowls. Add the chicken to one bowl and the lamb to the other; mix to coat the meat well. Thread 3 or 4 pieces of chicken onto the pointed end of each bamboo skewer. They can touch but should not press against each other. Repeat with the lamb. Cover and refrigerate for a few hours or preferably overnight.

To make the peanut sauce, in a blender or food processor, combine the drained chiles, ginger, galangal, shallots, garlic, lemongrass, and shrimp paste. Process to form a very smooth spice paste *(rempah)*. If needed, add a few tablespoons of water to facilitate the blending. Add the ground coriander, cumin, turmeric, and fennel and process until well mixed.

In a saucepan over medium heat, warm the vegetable oil. Add the spice paste and fry, stirring continuously, until a thick, fragrant, emulsified mixture forms, about 2 minutes. Reduce the heat to medium-low and continue frying, stirring occasionally, until oil beads appear on the surface, about 10 minutes longer. Stir in the tamarind water, peanuts, palm or brown sugar, salt, and water, reduce the heat to low, and simmer gently for 45 minutes. The sauce is done when beads of oil dot the surface and it is the consistency of thick cream. (The sauce can be made up to 3 days in advance, covered, and refrigerated, then reheated.)

Prepare a fire in a charcoal grill. To make the basting oil, in a bowl, stir together the coconut cream, vegetable oil, and brown sugar.

When the coals are white and glowing, place the skewers on the grill rack about 2 inches (5 cm) above the coals. Brush the meats with the basting oil and grill, turning once, to brown both sides and cook the meats through, about 2 minutes on each side.

Meanwhile, reheat the peanut sauce over medium-low heat and pour into a serving bowl. Arrange the skewers on a platter and place the *lontong* cubes (if using), cucumber, and onion alongside. Serve at once with the peanut sauce.

serves 10

Singapore

Poh Pia

fresh vegetable spring rolls

Every country in Southeast Asia has its own version of the spring roll, and fresh ones—that is, not fried—are particularly popular in Singapore and Malaysia, where the Nonya kitchen flourishes. The filling for this recipe is inspired by the poh pia *served at Singapore-born Chris Yeo's Straits Café in San Francisco.*

FILLING

2 tablespoons vegetable oil

1 teaspoon chopped garlic

3 shallots, thinly sliced

¼ lb (125 g) shrimp (prawns), peeled, deveined, and cut into ¼-inch (6-mm) pieces

2 carrots, peeled and finely julienned

1 small jicama, 7–8 oz (220–250 g), peeled and finely julienned

1 cup (4 oz/125 g) julienned bamboo shoot

1 cup (3 oz/90 g) finely shredded cabbage

1 tablespoon distilled white vinegar

1 teaspoon sugar

¼ teaspoon salt

¼ cup (2 fl oz/60 ml) water

3 eggs, lightly beaten (optional)

1–2 teaspoons vegetable oil, if using eggs

1 package (1 lb/500 g) lumpia wrappers or fresh spring roll wrappers

3 Chinese sausages, steamed and coarsely chopped (optional)

1 small English (hothouse) cucumber, peeled, seeded, and julienned

3 green (spring) onions, white part only, finely slivered

2 red Fresno or serrano chiles, seeded and finely slivered

16 fresh coriander (cilantro) sprigs

1 cup (8 fl oz/250 ml) hoisin sauce

⅓ cup (3 fl oz/80 ml) Sriracha sauce (page 251)

✤ To make the filling, preheat a wok over medium-high heat and add the oil. When it is hot, add the garlic and shallots and stir-fry until the shallots are translucent, 1–2 minutes. Add the shrimp and stir-fry until they turn bright orange-pink, about 2 minutes. Raise the heat to high, add the carrots, jicama, bamboo shoot, and cabbage, and stir-fry until the vegetables are tender, about 5 minutes. Add the vinegar, sugar, salt, and water, stir well, cover, and simmer gently until the vegetables are cooked but still crisp, about 5 minutes longer. Pour the vegetables into a colander to drain and let cool.

✤ While the filling cools, prepare the remaining ingredients: If you are using the eggs, place a 9-inch (23-cm) frying pan over medium-high heat and heat until hot. To test, sprinkle with drops of water. If they turn to beads and dance across the surface, the pan is ready. Add 1 teaspoon oil to the pan and wipe up the excess with a paper towel. (Too much oil will not work for this recipe.) Reduce the heat to low. Pour in about one-third of the beaten egg, then swirl the pan to spread it evenly over the bottom. Let cook for 1 minute, or until the bottom is light brown and the edges start to shrink back. Carefully peel loose at the edge and turn out onto a cutting board. Roll up the omelet jelly-roll style and cut crosswise into very thin shreds. Toss and lift the pieces to fluff them and set aside. Cook the remaining egg in two batches and cut into shreds.

✤ Arrange the wrappers, the omelet shreds and sausage (if using), the cucumber, green onion, chiles, coriander sprigs, and filling on a platter. Pour the hoisin and Sriracha sauces into 2 dipping saucers.

✤ Invite your guests to wrap their own *poh pia:* To make a spring roll, lay 1 wrapper on a flat surface. Scatter a tablespoon of the vegetable filling across the lower third of the wrapper, top it with a small amount of egg shreds and Chinese sausage (if using), cucumber strips, green onions, chile slivers, and coriander sprigs. Top with some hoisin sauce and a dribble of Sriracha sauce. Roll up the bottom of the wrapper to enclose the filling and form a log. Fold in the sides to enclose the ends, then finish rolling until the log is totally enclosed. Leave the roll whole or cut in half crosswise and eat out of hand.

makes about 16 rolls; serves 16

Nonyas, in traditional batik sarongs and embroidered kebayas, leave a colorful trail in Singapore's modern marketplaces.

Thailand

Tom Kha Gai

chicken coconut soup

This spectacular soup is one of Thailand's best-known dishes. It is easy to make and includes many of the ingredients that distinguish classic Thai cooking: lemongrass, galangal, fish sauce, kaffir lime, chiles, and coconut milk. I like the soup made with chunks of chicken on the bone, but you may use boneless if you prefer. Do not eat the galangal, lemongrass, and lime leaves. They deliver a bouquet of flavors but are far too tough to consume.

1 whole chicken breast, chopped into 1-inch (2.5-cm) pieces on the bone

2 cups (16 fl oz/500 ml) chicken stock

3 cups (24 fl oz/750 ml) coconut milk (page 245)

10 slices fresh galangal or 5 slices dried galangal

4 stalks lemongrass, tender midsection only, smashed and cut into 2-inch (5-cm) lengths

6 green Thai chiles or 8 green serrano chiles, cut in half crosswise

8 kaffir lime leaves, spines removed

½ cup (3½ oz/105 g) drained canned straw mushrooms

½ cup (2 oz/60 g) sliced bamboo shoot

3 tablespoons fish sauce

¼ cup (2 fl oz/60 ml) fresh lime juice, or to taste

¼ cup (¼ oz/7 g) fresh coriander (cilantro) leaves

In a large saucepan, combine the chicken, stock, coconut milk, galangal, lemongrass, chiles, and lime leaves. Bring to a boil over high heat, then reduce the heat to maintain a gentle boil and cook, uncovered, for 20 minutes.

Add the mushrooms and bamboo shoot, stir well, raise the heat to high, and bring to a boil. Add the fish sauce and lime juice, then taste and adjust the seasonings. Ladle the soup into warmed bowls, garnish with the coriander, and serve.

serves 6

Coconut Cream and Coconut Milk

Cracking a coconut demands technique and practice. First, select a mature coconut with a brown husk. Shake it: you should hear juice sloshing inside. Soak the coconut in water for a minute, to tame the brown fibers, then locate the "three-dot-face" on one end of the nut. Using an ice pick or a slim screwdriver, perforate one or two of the dots and pour the juice trapped inside into a bowl. You can drink the juice or, like the Vietnamese and Indonesians, use it in cooking.

Spread newspapers on a solid surface, such as a kitchen floor or sidewalk, and place the coconut on them. Using the dull edge of a cleaver or a hammer, make several quick, determined whacks across the equator of the nut until it cracks. Continue to strike with the hammer, breaking it into smaller pieces. Then with a small knife, pry the meat from the shell and peel off the thin brown skin. Cut the meat into 1-inch (2.5-cm) pieces and pulverize it, a few pieces at a time, in a food processor. One coconut will yield about 3½ cups (1 lb/500 g) pulverized coconut.

To make coconut cream, put the pulverized coconut into a bowl and add 1½ cups (12 fl oz/375 ml) hot water. Let steep for 10 minutes, then pour through a fine-mesh sieve or piece of cheesecloth (muslin) over a bowl and press or squeeze the coconut to expel as much liquid as possible. Place the squeezed coconut in another bowl. This first pressing, about 1 cup (8 fl oz/250 ml), is coconut cream and is primarily used as oil for frying spice pastes. For coconut milk, the liquid used in curries and soups, add 3 cups (24 fl oz/750 ml) hot water to the same coconut, let steep for 15 minutes, and repeat the straining and squeezing. This step yields about 2½ cups (20 fl oz/625 ml) coconut milk. Repeat this step for thin coconut milk. Refrigerate the milk and cream and use within 3 days.

Many Southeast Asians are able to avoid the messiest part of this task by buying already-grated meat from market vendors, who prepare it on the spot with a machine. Once home, cooks have only to steep the coconut to make the various grades of milk and cream.

Poat Dot

grilled corn with sweet and salty oil

No matter what country I am in, I can't pass up grilled corn. Introduced to Southeast Asia by European traders, corn was immediately adopted by the locals and is nearly always eaten as street food rather than prepared at home. Here, the sweet-and-salty-flavored oil brushed over the kernels is unlike any sauce a Westerner would expect with this New World staple.

6 ears of corn, husks and silk removed

vegetable oil for brushing, plus 2 tablespoons

2 tablespoons fish sauce

2 tablespoons water

1½ tablespoons sugar

1 teaspoon salt

2 green (spring) onions, white parts only, thinly sliced

❦ Prepare a fire in a charcoal grill, or preheat an ungreased cast-iron frying pan over medium heat.

❦ Very lightly brush the corn with oil and set on the grill rack or in the frying pan. Cook, turning every 2–3 minutes, until the kernels are tender and nicely charred, 12–15 minutes total. Keep warm.

❦ Meanwhile, in a bowl, stir together the fish sauce, water, sugar, and salt until the sugar dissolves. In a small saucepan over medium heat, warm the 2 tablespoons oil until it is almost smoking. Carefully pour the fish sauce mixture into the hot oil. It will spatter a bit. Add the green onions and simmer until the sauce begins to thicken with large bubbles, about 30 seconds. Remove from the heat and let cool.

❦ As soon as all the corn is cooked, brush with the sauce. Serve hot.

serves 6

Thailand

Rhoom

stuffed gold purses

I've watched Thai women use a paring knife to cut nooks and crannies, waves and curves, as they shape fruits and vegetables into amazing sculptures. These delicate purses, although they don't require a knife, do need a meticulous hand and patience. They are manageable for an everyday cook, however, and the end results make the labor worthwhile. If garlic chives are unavailable, use green (spring) onion tops cut lengthwise into long, narrow strips.

PURSES

6 eggs, beaten

3 tablespoons water

1–2 tablespoons peanut oil or corn oil

FILLING

1 teaspoon peppercorns

2 cloves garlic

1 tablespoon chopped fresh coriander (cilantro) roots or stems

1 tablespoon peanut oil or corn oil

2 shallots, minced

¾ lb (375 g) finely ground (minced) pork butt or chicken thigh meat

1 tablespoon palm sugar or brown sugar

1½ tablespoons fish sauce

3 tablespoons unsalted dry-roasted peanuts, chopped

3 cloves pickled garlic, thinly sliced

3 red Fresno or serrano chiles, seeded and finely slivered

½ cup (½ oz / 15 g) fresh coriander (cilantro) leaves

18 garlic chives blanched for 5 seconds in boiling water, drained, and patted dry

Sriracha sauce (page 251)

☙ To make the purses, in a pie dish or other shallow plate, beat together the eggs and water until blended. Set a well-seasoned 5-inch (13-cm) crepe pan or nonstick frying pan over medium–high heat and heat until hot. To test, sprinkle with drops of water. If they dance across the surface, the pan is ready. Add a thin film of oil to the pan and wipe up any excess with a paper towel. Have the eggs near the frying pan.

☙ Lay your fingers flat in the plate of eggs and then carefully position them over the frying pan. Wave your fingers back and forth in one direction, dripping long threads of egg across the width of the pan. Dip your fingers in the eggs again, and again wave them back and forth across the pan, this time dripping egg threads in the opposite direction. Repeat until you have a net, or filigree, of egg threads. Cook until the egg net sets up and is golden brown, 2–3 minutes. Carefully lift an edge and peel the net from the pan. Place on a baking sheet and cover loosely with foil. Repeat to make 18 nets in all. Set aside.

☙ To make the filling, in a mortar or mini food processor, pound together or process the peppercorns, garlic, and coriander roots or stems to form a paste. Preheat a wok over medium-high heat and add the oil. When hot, stir in the garlic paste and shallots and stir-fry gently until fragrant, about 1 minute. Add the pork or chicken and stir-fry, breaking up any clumps of meat, until no pink remains and the mixture is crumbly and dry, 2–3 minutes. Raise the heat to high, add the palm or brown sugar and fish sauce, and cook until the sugar caramelizes and the mixture is sticky, 3–5 minutes. Stir in the chopped peanuts, transfer to a bowl, and set aside to cool.

☙ To fill the purses, place 1 egg net on a flat surface. Put a heaping tablespoonful of the filling in the middle. Top with a few slices of pickled garlic, a few slivers of red chile, and a few coriander leaves. Fold in the sides to form a small parcel and secure closed by tying 1 garlic chive around the middle. Repeat until all the parcels are made.

☙ Arrange the purses, seam side down, on a serving plate. Top each purse with a touch of Sriracha sauce. Serve warm or at room temperature.

makes 18 purses; serves 6

Thais are inveterate snackers, sometimes stopping at their favorite street-side vendors as many as four or five times a day.

Vietnam

Canh Chua Ca

hot sour fish soup with pineapple

The intensely sour flavor imparted by tamarind is what gives this everyday soup its distinctive character.

1 tablespoon vegetable oil

2 cloves garlic, minced

1 yellow onion, thinly sliced

3 lemongrass stalks, tender midsection only, smashed and cut into 2-inch (5-cm) lengths

3 slices fresh galangal or 2 slices dried galangal

¼ lb (125 g) fresh white mushrooms, brushed clean, stems removed, and caps halved

½ cup (2 oz/60 g) thinly sliced bamboo shoot

½ cup (3 oz/90 g) cubed pineapple

6 cups (48 fl oz/1.5 l) chicken or fish stock

⅓ cup (3 fl oz/80 ml) tamarind water
(see sidebar, page 114)

2–3 tablespoons fish sauce, or to taste

1½ tablespoons sugar

1 teaspoon salt

¾ lb (375 g) catfish fillets, cut into 1½-inch (4-cm) chunks

1 cup (2 oz/60 g) bean sprouts

1 green (spring) onion, thinly sliced

¼ cup (¼ oz/7 g) each fresh mint leaves and fresh coriander (cilantro) leaves

2 red Fresno or serrano chiles, sliced

♛ In a large saucepan over medium–high heat, warm the oil. Add the garlic, onion, lemongrass, and galangal and sauté until the onion is soft, 2–3 minutes. Do not allow to brown. Add the mushrooms, bamboo shoot, and pineapple and cook, stirring, for 1 minute.

♛ Raise the heat to high, add the stock, and bring to a boil. Stir in the tamarind water, fish sauce, sugar, and salt. Stir well, taste, and adjust the seasoning. Add the fish and boil gently until opaque throughout, about 5 minutes. Add the bean sprouts, green onion, and mint and ladle into individual bowls. Garnish with the coriander and chiles and serve.

serves 6–8

Thailand

Kai Look Kooey

"son-in-law" eggs

In Southeast Asia, eggs are prepared in exotic ways. A sunny-side-up egg is cooked in a shallow pool of hot oil so that the whites are crisp and lacy, or beaten eggs are mixed with tiny amounts of meat or seafood and pickled vegetables and steamed into a silky smooth savory custard. Perhaps the most interesting preparation, however, is shelled hard-boiled eggs that are deep-fried and then curried or served with a sauce. In this recipe, they are topped with a sweet-and-salty sauce, strewn with chiles and fried shallots, and served at room temperature. Accompanied with rice, the eggs can be served as a main dish.

The name of the recipe has always puzzled me. The most common explanation has something to do with a mother-in-law's disdain for her son-in-law. But my feeling is that the son-in-law must have been well liked to have these wonderful eggs made just for him. I continue to pursue the mystery.

⅓ cup (3 fl oz/80 ml) tamarind water (see sidebar, page 114)

¼ cup (2 oz/60 g) firmly packed palm sugar

3 tablespoons fish sauce

vegetable oil for deep-frying

6 hard-boiled eggs, peeled and patted dry

2 fresh red chiles, seeded and very thinly sliced

2 tablespoons fried shallots (see sidebar, page 79)

❦ In a saucepan over medium heat, combine the tamarind water, palm sugar, and fish sauce. Simmer, stirring, until syrupy, 5–8 minutes. Transfer to a bowl.

❦ To fry the eggs, pour oil to a depth of 3 inches (7.5 cm) in a heavy saucepan and heat to 360°F (182°C) on a deep-frying thermometer. Lower the eggs, 2 or 3 at a time, into the hot oil. Deep-fry the eggs, turning to brown evenly. When golden and blistered, after 3–5 minutes, drain on paper towels.

❦ Cut the eggs in half lengthwise and arrange on a platter. Pour the sauce over them and scatter the chiles and fried shallots on top.

serves 6

Vietnam

Bo La-Lot

grilled minced beef rolled in la-lot leaves

When a special occasion is at hand, and the Vietnamese have money in their pockets, they like to go out and eat the banquet known as bo bay mon, *or beef cooked seven ways. Seven is considered a fortuitous number, so the name of this celebratory meal carries good luck, although the actual number of courses served may vary. The banquet always opens with* bo nhung dam, *a Vietnamese-style beef fondue, and ends with beef rice soup. The parade of dishes in between may include a steamed beef pâté, a grilled beef salad, grilled beef with bacon, and* bo la-lot, *seasoned beef wrapped in* la-lot *leaves and grilled.*

The la-lot *plant, which is also called pepper leaf because it is related to the pepper plant, has shiny, heart-shaped leaves and small nuts that are chewed like tobacco. When the leaves are used as wrappers and grilled, their aniselike flavor and camphor aroma are released. They can be found in well-supplied Vietnamese and Thai markets. The Japanese* shiso *leaf, also known as perilla leaf, is similar in shape and makes an excellent substitute.*

¾ lb (375 g) lean beef round, finely ground (minced)

2 oz (60 g) pork fat, finely minced, or 1 tablespoon vegetable oil

2 tablespoons finely minced lemongrass (from midsection of 2 stalks)

2 large shallots, finely minced

4 cloves garlic, finely minced

1 tablespoon fish sauce

2 teaspoons sugar

1 teaspoon five-spice powder

1 teaspoon salt

¼ teaspoon ground pepper

¼ teaspoon ground turmeric

30 la-lot, shiso, or bottled grape leaves (see note)

vegetable oil for brushing rolls

ACCOMPANIMENTS

30 butter (Boston) lettuce leaves

30 fresh coriander (cilantro) sprigs

2 cups (2 oz/60 g) fresh mint leaves

2 cups (2 oz/60 g) fresh Thai basil leaves

nuoc cham *dipping sauce (page 249)*

☙ In a bowl, combine the beef, pork fat or oil, lemongrass, shallots, garlic, fish sauce, sugar, five-spice powder, salt, pepper, and turmeric. Mix well, cover, and marinate for 2 hours at room temperature or as long as overnight in the refrigerator.

☙ Place 6 bamboo skewers, each 6 inches (15 cm) long, in water to cover. Prepare a medium-hot fire in a charcoal grill, or preheat a broiler (griller).

☙ Rinse the *la-lot* or *shiso* leaves with cold water and pat dry with paper towels. If using grape leaves, rinse thoroughly in cold water to remove the brine, then trim off the stems. Place the leaves, shiny side down and with the stem end toward you, on a work surface. Put 1 tablespoon of the filling on the stem end of each leaf and mold it into a log 2 inches (5 cm) long. Fold over the end nearest you and roll tightly from the bottom to enclose the log but leave the ends open. (If using grape leaves, fold in the sides to enclose the roll completely.) Repeat until all the rolls are made.

☙ Drain the skewers and thread 5 rolls horizontally onto each skewer, allowing the rolls to touch. Set the skewers on a tray and brush the rolls with oil.

☙ Place the skewers on the grill rack about 5 inches (13 cm) above the fire or on a broiler pan under the broiler. Grill or broil, turning once, until crisp and browned on both sides, about 3 minutes on each side.

☙ To serve, arrange the lettuce leaves, coriander sprigs, and mint and basil leaves on a platter. To eat, put a roll on a lettuce leaf with some of the fresh herbs. Roll up the lettuce to enclose everything, dip it into the sauce, and eat out of hand.

makes 30 rolls; serves 8–10

The north, with its lush pasturelands, is home to Vietnam's small beef herds, while the delta-webbed south is the country's rice bowl.

Malaysia

Bakwan Kepiting

stuffed crab soup with bamboo shoots

My first taste of this soup was in the home of Violet Oon, a Nonya who is a popular Singaporean food writer and cooking teacher. In her elegant version of this Nonya classic, Oon stuffs the shells of small local crabs with shrimp, pork, crabmeat, and coriander; panfries them; and then serves them in a delicate broth of bamboo shoot and browned garlic bits. Inspired by Oon's dish, this recipe uses rock crabs or blue crabs. If small live crabs are unavailable, you can form the filling into tiny balls and make a tasty crab-ball soup. Once you become accustomed to the nuances of sambal blacan (see sidebar, page 180), you'll find that a touch mixed into the soup gives a delightful finish.

3 tablespoons peanut oil or corn oil, or as needed

8 large cloves garlic, finely chopped

6 live rock crabs or hard-shell blue crabs, each about ¾ lb (375 g) or 4½ inches (11.5 cm) across

FILLING

¼ lb (125 g) shrimp (prawns), peeled, deveined, and chopped

6 oz (185 g) ground (minced) pork butt

3 tablespoons finely chopped bamboo shoot

2 tablespoons finely grated carrot

1 green (spring) onion, including 1 inch (2.5 cm) of the tender green tops, minced

3 tablespoons chopped fresh coriander (cilantro)

1 egg, lightly beaten

1 tablespoon cornstarch (cornflour)

1 teaspoon light soy sauce

½ teaspoon sugar

¼ teaspoon salt

1½ cups (6 oz/185 g) julienned bamboo shoot

8 cups (64 fl oz/2 l) water or light chicken stock

2 teaspoons light soy sauce, or to taste

2 teaspoons salt

1 teaspoon sugar

big pinch of ground white pepper, or to taste

fresh coriander (cilantro) leaves

fried shallots (see sidebar, page 79)

❦ In a small saucepan over medium heat, warm the oil. When it is hot but not smoking, add the garlic and sauté until lightly browned, about 1 minute. Pour through a fine-mesh sieve placed over a small bowl. Transfer the captured garlic to paper towels to drain. Set aside. Reserve the garlic oil.

❦ Rinse the crabs with cold water. Bring a large pot three-fourths full of water to a boil. With a pair of long-handled tongs, pick up the crabs and drop them into the water. Boil for 2 minutes, then lift out the crabs and rinse under cold water to cool. Working with 1 crab at a time, remove the top shell. Scrub the outside and reserve. Clean the crab (page 245). Pick out the meat from the body and legs and put into a bowl. Set the shells aside.

❦ To make the filling, add the shrimp, pork, chopped bamboo shoot, carrot, green onion, chopped coriander, egg, cornstarch, soy sauce, sugar, salt, and 2 tablespoons of the fried garlic to the crabmeat and mix well. Stuff into the cleaned shells, but do not pack too firmly. Use any leftover filling to make meatballs, each ¾ inch (2 cm) in diameter, and set aside.

❦ Heat a wide, heavy pot or wok over medium heat and add the reserved garlic oil. When hot, put the stuffed shells, filling side down, into the pot or wok. If they do not fit comfortably, fry in batches. When the bottoms are golden brown, after about 3 minutes, use tongs to transfer the shells to a plate.

❦ Add the julienned bamboo shoot to the pot or wok and stir-fry for 1 minute. Return the stuffed shells, filling side up, to the pot or wok in a single layer and add enough water or stock to reach to the tops of the shells, but do not submerge them. (Reserve the remaining liquid to add later.) Bring to a rolling boil over high heat. Reduce the heat so the liquid boils gently and simmer for about 8 minutes. To test for doneness, press down on the filling; it should feel firm to the touch. Again using the tongs, transfer the shells to a plate and keep warm.

❦ Add the remaining liquid to the pot or wok and bring to a boil. Add the reserved meatballs and boil until they float to the surface, 3–5 minutes. Season to taste with soy sauce, salt, sugar, and white pepper.

❦ To serve, put 1 stuffed crab shell, filling side up, into each individual shallow soup bowl. Ladle the hot soup, including some bamboo shoot and meatballs, into each bowl. Garnish with coriander leaves and sprinkle with fried shallots. Serve immediately.

serves 6

Rice Paper

While riding through the countryside outside of Ho Chi Minh City, I spotted rows of rice-paper rounds drying on bamboo trays in the strong afternoon sun. It was a home-style rice paper "factory," with a single woman at work, and I stopped to watch.

She poured a thin film of rice-flour batter over a piece of muslin stretched across a vat filled with boiling water. As one round was being steam-cooked, she turned to a second "drum steamer" and repeated the process. When the first round was done, she slipped a large, flat wooden paddle under it and lifted the enormous circle of wet rice paper onto a woven bamboo tray. She carried it outdoors and propped it at an angle facing the sun to dry. Each dried round, perhaps two hundred of which would be made by this hardworking woman that day, would carry the "watermark" of the bamboo tray.

Beyond this makeshift factory, for as far as the eye could see, thousands of white disks were drying in the sun. Such sizable output is necessary, though, for the Vietnamese use rice-paper rounds, made by hand and by machine, in huge numbers as coverings for their ubiquitous fresh and fried spring rolls and for wrapping pieces of grilled meat or seafood, herbs, and garnishes into easy-to-eat packets at the table.

Vietnam

Chao Tom

sugarcane shrimp

Sugarcane, a tropical grass native to Asia, is a major source of sugar. It also is used to make a refreshing beverage. The fibrous stalks are crushed between steel rollers, and the released juice is served over ice. In Vietnam, sugarcane juice is even simmered with garlic and enjoyed as a hot winter beverage. But the most delightful sight is watching children chewing and sucking on short lengths of the sweet stalks.

The stalks can also be split lengthwise and used as skewers. A signature Vietnamese dish, sugarcane shrimp is seasoned shrimp purée molded around the center of a sugarcane skewer, then grilled. It is eaten by easing the purée off the cane, combining it with lettuce, mint, cucumber, and coriander, and then rolling them up in rice paper and dipping the bundle into a sauce.

Fresh sugarcane is used for the skewers in this recipe. If unavailable, look for canned sticks packed in syrup, sold in Asian markets. The pork fat not only keeps the shrimp mixture moist but also makes it more flavorful. Toasted rice powder is used in Southeast Asian cooking much as bread crumbs are in Western cooking, as a thickener and to add a toasty flavor.

3 sections sugarcane, each 6 inches (15 cm) long

1 teaspoon chopped garlic

1 tablespoon chopped shallot

1-oz (30-g) piece pork fat, chopped

1 lb (500 g) shrimp (prawns), peeled, deveined, and patted dry

1 tablespoon toasted rice powder

2 teaspoons sugar

1 teaspoon cornstarch (cornflour)

½ teaspoon baking powder

¼ teaspoon ground pepper

about ¼ cup (2 fl oz/60 ml) vegetable oil

ACCOMPANIMENTS

nouc cham *dipping sauce (page 249)*

12 dried round rice papers, 8 inches (20 cm) in diameter

12 red-leaf or butter (Boston) lettuce leaves

½ cup (½ oz/15 g) fresh coriander (cilantro) leaves

½ cup (½ oz/15 g) fresh mint leaves

½ English (hothouse) cucumber, peeled and finely slivered

☙ Using a sharp knife, split each sugarcane section in half lengthwise, then split each half in half again. You should have a total of 12 skewers each 6 inches (15 cm) long. Set aside.

☙ Prepare a fire in a charcoal grill. In a food processor, combine the garlic and shallot and process to mince finely. Transfer to a bowl. Add the pork fat to the processor and process to form a purée. Add the shrimp and process to form a coarse paste. Return the garlic and shallot to the processor and add the rice powder, sugar, cornstarch, baking powder, and pepper. Pulse a few times to mix.

☙ Oil the lattice bottom of a bamboo steamer. Oil your hands, scoop up 2 tablespoons of the shrimp paste, and mold it evenly around the middle section of a sugarcane stick, leaving 1 inch (2.5 cm) exposed on each end. Place on the oiled steamer. Repeat with the remaining shrimp paste and sugarcane sticks, placing them, without touching, in the steamer. Add water to a wok or other steaming pan and bring to a rolling boil. Place the bamboo steamer over the boiling water, cover, and steam until the shrimp paste is almost cooked, 3–5 minutes.

☙ Remove the steamer from over the water, then remove the sugarcane sticks. Pat dry. Place the sticks on the grill rack over the hot fire and grill, turning often, until they are nicely charred with grill marks, about 2 minutes. Transfer to a platter.

☙ To serve, pour the dipping sauce into a saucer. Place the rice paper rounds on a plate. Arrange the lettuce, coriander, and mint leaves and cucumber slivers on a platter. Set a wide bowl of warm water on the table.

☙ To eat, take a round of rice paper, slip it briefly into the warm water, and then lay it down on a plate and leave it for 30 seconds or longer until it is softened and feels like a wet tissue. Put a lettuce leaf on top and then a few mint and coriander leaves and slivers of cucumber. Strip away the shrimp paste from the sugarcane (it can still be hot or at room temperature) and lay it in the middle of the herbs. Fold in one end and then roll up the rice paper into a cylinder. Dip it into the sauce and eat. Chew on the sugarcane sticks for sweetness.

serves 6

Vietnam

Cha Gio

crispy spring rolls

In 1991, Vietnam-born Paul Kwan and fellow filmmaker Arnold Iger went to Vietnam to shoot The Anatomy of a Springroll, *a documentary that uses Paul's mother's legendary recipe for spring rolls as a means to look back on his family's life in Ho Chi Minh City. This is her recipe. Lac E. Minh's spring rolls are showered with accolades from everyone who has tried them. Look for jars of Vietnamese chile-garlic sauce in Southeast Asian markets.*

FILLING

10 dried Chinese black mushrooms, soaked in warm water for 30 minutes

1 oz (30 g) dried cloud ear mushrooms, soaked in warm water for 20 minutes

2 oz (60 g) bean thread noodles, soaked in warm water for 15 minutes

½ lb (250 g) ground (minced) pork butt

1 lb (500 g) shrimp (prawns), peeled, deveined, and coarsely chopped

1 yellow onion, minced

1 small jicama, about ½ lb (250 g), peeled, finely shredded, and squeezed of excess water

2 carrots, peeled and finely shredded

2 tablespoons fish sauce

1 tablespoon finely minced garlic

1 teaspoon ground pepper

1 teaspoon sugar

½ teaspoon sea salt

1 egg, lightly beaten

1 package (12 oz/375 g) dried round rice papers, 8 inches (20 cm) in diameter

DIPPING SAUCE

1 cup (8 oz/250 g) sugar

½ cup (4 fl oz/125 ml) distilled white vinegar

½ cup (4 fl oz/125 ml) water

5 tablespoons (2½ fl oz/75 ml) fish sauce

2 tablespoons finely minced garlic

1 tablespoon fresh lime juice

1 tablespoon chile-garlic sauce (see note)

2 red Fresno or serrano chiles, chopped (optional)

coarsely chopped unsalted roasted peanuts

peanut or vegetable oil for deep-frying

1 head red-leaf or butter (Boston) lettuce, leaves separated

leaves from 1 small bunch fresh mint

❧ To make the filling, drain the softened black mushrooms and cloud ear mushrooms and squeeze out the excess water. Remove and discard the stems from the black mushrooms. Thinly slice the caps. Remove the tough knots from the underside of the cloud ear mushrooms. Roll up the mushrooms and cut crosswise into long, thin shreds. Drain the bean thread noodles and cut into 2-inch (5-cm) lengths. Put both mushrooms and the noodles into a large bowl and add the pork, shrimp, onion, jicama, carrots, fish sauce, garlic, pepper, sugar, salt, and egg. Mix well and set aside.

❧ To form the spring rolls, lay 1 rice paper round on a flat surface. Using a pastry brush, brush the rice paper with warm water and leave it for 30 seconds or longer until it is softened and feels like wet tissue. Put a heaping tablespoon of the filling in a line across the lower third of the wrapper. Mold the filling to form a log 3 inches (7.5 cm) long by 1 inch (2.5 cm) wide. Fold the bottom edge of the rice paper over the log, then fold both sides toward the middle to enclose the ends. Roll up into a taut roll and place on a tray. Cover with a damp kitchen towel. Repeat until all of the filling is used.

❧ To make the dipping sauce, in a bowl, stir together the sugar and vinegar until the sugar dissolves. Add the water, fish sauce, garlic, lime juice, chile-garlic sauce, and the chiles, if using. Divide the sauce among small saucers. Garnish with the peanuts.

❧ To fry the rolls, preheat a wok or deep saucepan over medium-high heat until hot. Add oil to a depth of 2½ inches (6 cm) and heat slowly to 365°F (185°C) on a deep-frying thermometer.

❧ Slip a batch of the spring rolls, one at a time, into the hot oil. Do not crowd the pan. Fry until golden, about 5 minutes. Using a skimmer, transfer the spring rolls to paper towels to drain. Keep hot. Repeat until all the rolls are fried.

❧ To serve, arrange the lettuce leaves and mint leaves on a platter. Arrange the spring rolls, whole or cut in half, on a platter. To eat, place a spring roll on a lettuce leaf with some mint and roll up the leaf. Dip the roll into the sauce and eat out of hand.

makes about 3 dozen spring rolls; serves 12

Indonesia

Soto Ayam

spicy chicken soup

In Indonesia, a soto *is a substantial meat-broth dish, and* soto ayam, *its most popular example, comes in nearly as many versions as there are Indonesian cooks. It is delicious by itself for a light supper, but typically the hawkers serve it with potato* perkedel *(fritters),* lontong, *noodles, hard-boiled eggs, and bean sprouts. See the sidebar on page 203 for directions on toasting and grinding the spice seeds.*

SPICE PASTE

8 shallots, quartered

1-inch (2.5-cm) piece fresh ginger, peeled and quartered

5 cloves garlic, quartered

2 slices fresh galangal, peeled and chopped

2 tablespoons coriander seeds, toasted and ground

1 tablespoon cumin seeds, toasted and ground

1 tablespoon fennel seeds, toasted and ground

⅓ cup (3 fl oz/80 ml) vegetable oil

2 lemongrass stalks, tender midsection only, cut into 2-inch (5-cm) lengths and smashed

1 cinnamon stick

2 cardamom pods

3 whole cloves

2 whole star anise

1 small chicken, about 2½ lb (1.25 kg), cut into serving pieces

2½ qt (2.5 l) water

2 teaspoons sugar

1 teaspoon salt, or to taste

ground white pepper to taste

3 small potatoes, quartered

2 carrots, peeled and cut into 2-inch (5-cm) lengths

ACCOMPANIMENTS

½ lb (250 g) bean sprouts

1 cup (1 oz/30 g) celery leaves

12 cubes lontong *(1-inch/2.5-cm cubes) (optional; page 249)*

½ cup (½ oz/15 g) fresh coriander (cilantro) leaves

½ cup (1½ oz/45 g) fried shallots (see sidebar, page 79)

To make the spice paste, in a blender, combine the shallots, ginger, garlic, and galangal and process to a smooth paste. If necessary, add a little water to facilitate the blending. Add the ground coriander, cumin, and fennel and blend to mix well.

In a large saucepan over medium-high heat, warm the oil. Add the spice paste and fry, stirring frequently, until the oil and spices are emulsified and fragrant, about 3 minutes. Add the lemongrass, cinnamon stick, cardamom pods, cloves, and star anise and stir together for 1 minute until fragrant. Add the chicken and the water and bring to a boil. Skim off any foam or other impurities from the surface. When the liquid is clear, reduce the heat to medium-low and simmer, uncovered, for 1 hour.

Remove the pan from the heat and, using a slotted spoon, transfer the chicken pieces to a plate. Pour the stock through a fine-mesh sieve placed over a clean saucepan. Using a large spoon, scoop off and discard any fat from the surface. Place the pan over high heat and add the sugar, salt, and white pepper. Bring to a boil, add the potatoes and carrots, reduce the heat to medium, and simmer, uncovered, until the vegetables are tender, about 15 minutes.

Meanwhile, hand-shred the chicken meat, discarding the skin and bones, and set the meat aside.

To serve, put one-sixth of the shredded chicken, bean sprouts, and celery leaves and 2 *lontong* cubes (if using) into each soup bowl. Ladle 1½–2 cups (12–16 fl oz/375–500 ml) of the hot stock into each bowl. Garnish with the coriander leaves and fried shallots and serve immediately.

serves 61

Magnificent stone temples dotted Java's deep green jungles long before European builders drafted plans for the first Gothic cathedrals.

Thailand

Khao Tom Moo

rice soup with pork balls, coriander, and garlic oil

Whenever I dream of my next visit to Bangkok, I imagine my ideal breakfast schedule: two at the Oriental Hotel and the remaining mornings at local street vendors. I love sitting under the hotel's umbrella-covered veranda at the edge of the Chao Phraya River, overlooking the bustling water traffic. Within a few days, the attentive hotel staff knows a guest's habits. The waiter approaches, saying, "Khao tom moo this morning, madame?" The hotel serves a delicious Thai omelet with a spicy fish sauce dip, but today the waiter is correct: rice soup with tiny pork balls and garlic oil is what I want. It makes a wonderful lunch, too.

6 cups (48 fl oz/1.5 l) chicken stock

1 tablespoon preserved radish

2 tablespoons fish sauce, or to taste

⅛ teaspoon ground white pepper

¼ lb (125 g) ground (minced) pork butt or shoulder

1½ cups (7½ oz/235 g) cooked long-grain white rice, preferably jasmine rice

3 tablespoons coarsely chopped fresh coriander (cilantro)

3 tablespoons chopped green (spring) onion, including tender green tops

¼ cup (2 fl oz/60 ml) garlic oil (page 247)

☙ In a saucepan over high heat, combine the chicken stock, radish, fish sauce, and white pepper. Bring to a boil, then reduce to medium heat. Adjust the heat to maintain a gentle simmer.

☙ With your fingers, break off about 1 teaspoon of the pork and roll it into a tiny meatball. Repeat until all the pork is used. Drop the balls, a few at a time, into the simmering stock and cook for 1 minute. Add the rice and simmer until the rice is soft and the soup is slightly thickened, about 5 minutes.

☙ Ladle the soup into warmed bowls and top with the coriander, green onion, and garlic oil.

serves 6

Philippines

Ukoy

small shrimp and sweet potato fritters

In the Philippines, the locals enjoy afternoon snacks of cakes and other sweets, much like high tea. Called a merienda, *this tradition is a remnant of four centuries of Spanish rule. At an elaborate gathering, ukoy and poh pia (page 48) also will be served.*

Using very small shrimp (30 to 40 per pound/500 g) so that the shells can be eaten is essential to the taste and crispy texture of these fritters. The secret to making them is to place a thick mound of batter on an oiled plate, shape it with an oiled spoon, and then carefully slide it off into the hot oil.

1 cup (8 fl oz/250 ml) water

1 teaspoon salt

½ lb (250 g) small shrimp (prawns) in the shell (see note)

BATTER

1 cup (5 oz/155 g) all-purpose (plain) flour

½ cup (2 oz/60 g) rice flour

¼ cup (1 oz/30 g) cornstarch (cornflour)

1 teaspoon baking powder

1 teaspoon salt

1 egg, beaten

1 clove garlic, finely minced

6 green (spring) onions, including 1 inch (2.5 cm) of the tender green tops, thinly sliced

¼ lb (125 g) bean sprouts

boiling water, as needed

1 large sweet potato, ¾ lb (375 g), peeled and coarsely grated

SAUCE

1 clove garlic

1 teaspoon salt

½ cup (4 fl oz/125 ml) rice vinegar

big pinch of ground pepper

peanut or vegetable oil for deep-frying

☫ In a saucepan, combine the water and salt and bring to a boil. Add the shrimp and bring to a second boil. Cook until the shrimp turn bright orange-pink, about 1 minute. Using a slotted spoon, transfer the shrimp to a bowl. Pour the cooking liquid into a measuring pitcher and let cool. Add water as needed to make 1 cup (8 fl oz/250 ml).

☫ To make the batter, in a large bowl, combine the two flours, cornstarch, baking powder, and salt. In a small bowl, stir the egg until blended, then stir in the garlic, half of the green onions, and the reserved cooking liquid. Stir the egg mixture into the flour mixture until smooth. Add water to arrive at the consistency of a medium batter.

☫ Put the bean sprouts in a bowl and add boiling hot water to cover. Let stand for 15 seconds. Drain in a colander and rinse with cold water. Drain again and pat dry with paper towels. Add the bean sprouts and sweet potato to the batter. Mix well.

☫ To make the sauce, in a mortar, pound together the garlic and salt to form a paste. Add the vinegar and pepper and stir to blend. Transfer to a saucer.

☫ Preheat a large frying pan over medium-high heat. Add oil to a depth of 1 inch (2.5 cm) and heat to 365°F (185°C) on a deep-frying thermometer. Ladle ⅓ cup (3 fl oz/80 ml) of the batter onto an oiled plate. Sprinkle with green onions and top with 2 shrimp. Hold the plate close to the oil and slide the batter into it. Quickly form 2 or 3 more cakes and add to the oil. Fry the fritters, spooning the hot oil over them as they cook and turning once, until golden brown on both sides and cooked through, about 6 minutes total. Using a slotted spoon, transfer to paper towels to drain; keep warm. To serve, arrange the fritters, shrimp side up, on a platter and sprinkle the sauce over the tops.

makes about 20 fritters; serves 10

Vietnam

Pho

hanoi beef soup

Many Vietnamese begin the day with a flavorful, fragrant bowl of pho, slurping this morning health tonic in nearly every conceivable setting. Preparing pho is a time-consuming but easy production, so it is often taken at a street stall rather than made at home.
In the stalls, one has a seemingly endless choice of meats to add to the soup: sliced raw beef, sliced brisket, lean or marbled flank steak, beef tripe, tendon, meatballs, or dac biet, the house specialty, which includes a mixture of several items. To add a cool contrast to the steaming broth, there is a host of fresh raw vegetables and herbs—bean sprouts, basil, mint, coriander, saw-leaf herb—to toss into the soup.
A squeeze of lime juice balances all the flavors. In Vietnam, cooks use fresh rice noodles, which can be difficult to find elsewhere. If you can locate them, omit the soaking and warm them through in boiling water before adding them to the bowls.

BEEF STOCK

3 lb (1.5 kg) oxtails, chopped into 2-inch (5-cm) pieces

2–3 lb (1–1.5 kg) beef brisket

4 qt (4 l) water

4-inch (10-cm) piece fresh ginger, cut into 4 equal pieces, crushed

10 shallots, unpeeled

1 lb (500 g) daikon, cut into 2-inch (5-cm) chunks

2 carrots, each cut into thirds

7 whole star anise

5 whole cloves

2 cinnamon sticks

3 tablespoons fish sauce, or to taste

2 teaspoons sugar, or to taste

NOODLES AND ACCOMPANIMENTS

½ lb (250 g) beef sirloin, wrapped in plastic wrap and placed in the freezer for 1 hour

leaves from ½ bunch fresh coriander (cilantro)

½ bunch fresh Thai basil

12 fresh saw-leaf herb sprigs (page 250)

2 limes, cut into wedges

½ lb (250 g) flat dried rice noodles, ¼ inch (6 mm) wide, soaked in warm water for 20 minutes

1 white onion, thinly sliced

3 green (spring) onions, including 1 inch (2.5 cm) of tender green tops, thinly sliced

1 lb (500 g) bean sprouts

🌱 To make the stock, fill a large stockpot with water and bring to a boil. Add the oxtails and brisket, return to a boil, and boil for 3 minutes. Pour off the water to discard the impurities. Add the 4 qt (4 l) fresh water to the pot and bring to a boil.

🌱 Meanwhile, place a dry frying pan over high heat and add the ginger and shallots. Char them, turning occasionally to color evenly, 2–3 minutes. Remove from the heat and toss them into the stockpot. Add the daikon, carrots, star anise, cloves, and cinnamon sticks. When the water reaches a boil, reduce the heat to maintain a gentle simmer, cover partially, and cook for 1½ hours. Remove the brisket and set aside. Continue to simmer the stock for 1 hour more. It should be a light amber and richly fragrant.

🌱 When the brisket is cool, cut into thin slices across the grain; set aside. When the stock is done, strain through a sieve and skim the fat from the surface. Discard the oxtails or reserve for another use. Return the stock to the stockpot and season with the fish sauce and sugar. Bring to a gentle simmer.

🌱 Meanwhile, prepare the accompaniments: Remove the partially frozen beef from the freezer and cut across the grain into paper-thin slices as wide as possible. (Slant the knife's blade at an angle to the beef to produce a wide slice.) Arrange on a platter. On a separate platter, arrange the coriander leaves, basil, saw-leaf herb sprigs, and lime wedges.

🌱 Drain the noodles. Have ready the white onion, green onions, and bean sprouts. Bring a large saucepan filled with water to a boil. Ladle out some of the water into 6 deep soup bowls to heat them. Drop the noodles into the boiling water, stir well, and cook until just tender, 1–2 minutes. Test by biting into a noodle. Drain well. Pour off the water from the soup bowls. Divide the noodles evenly among the bowls. Put a few slices of the cooked brisket into each bowl. Top with a handful of the bean sprouts, some white onion slices, and a sprinkle of green onions. Ladle about 2 cups (16 fl oz/500 ml) hot stock into each bowl. Serve with the platters of raw beef and herbs. Each diner takes a few herbs and a little beef, puts them into his or her hot soup, and then squeezes lime juice over the top.

serves 6

Street Food

The best way to experience true Southeast Asian cooking is to spend time eating hawker fare, authentic dishes served up in plain stalls at bargain prices. Made according to home-style recipes passed down through generations, these street foods are the labor of legions of entrepreneurial cooks.

Old-timers in Singapore recall the days when hawkers commuted to work each day by negotiating the busy streets at the helm of their portable restaurants, wood-and-tin structures on bicycle wheels with small stools hanging from the sides and a faded canopy covering the "kitchen." Some even wore their places of business across their shoulders, balancing bamboo poles with pots and woks, bowls and plates dangling from each end. Those itinerant hawkers are gone now, replaced by the government's efficient, sanitary, highly convenient food centers, populated with large numbers of permanent stalls—literally hundreds in Chinatown's Kreta Ayer center—and tables gathered together under a single roof. Some locals lament the loss of the traveling hawker, but others appreciate the orderliness that the city-state's regulations have delivered.

Singapore has the most organized system of food stalls in Southeast Asia, but every community boasts clusters of talented street-based cooks. In the night markets of Chiang Mai, locals fuel up on *khao soi* (curry noodles), *khanom jiin* (noodles with spicy fish), and other dishes. In Hanoi, not far from the train station, in alleyways off Hang Bong Street, bureaucrats and students, families and pensioners perch on stools to consume bowls of herbal chicken soup and plates of fish cakes and *cha gio* (spring rolls). And just beyond central Yangon's (Rangoon's) cavernous Bogyoke Market stands an open-air market thick with steam rising from pots of *mohingha,* the typical Burmese breakfast.

Thailand

Tod Mun Pla

spicy fish cakes

This snack food is readily available from street hawkers in Thailand. Many versions exist, but this one, made with kaffir lime leaves, is a favorite. You can substitute the zest of 1 lime for the leaves, but the unique perfumy character of the kaffir lime will be missing.

1 lb (500 g) whitefish fillets, finely ground

1 tablespoon roasted chile paste (page 245) or red curry paste (page 246)

1 tablespoon fish sauce

1 tablespoon cornstarch (cornflour)

½ teaspoon salt

2 oz (60 g) green beans, ends trimmed and beans thinly sliced

6 kaffir lime leaves, spines removed and leaves finely slivered

peanut oil for deep-frying

Sriracha sauce (page 251) or Sweet-Sour Cucumber Relish (page 103)

In a bowl, combine the fish, chile paste or curry paste, fish sauce, cornstarch, salt, green beans, and lime leaves. Knead the mixture for 1 minute. Moisten your hands with water and divide the mixture into 20 balls. Flatten each ball into a patty about 2 inches (5 cm) in diameter and ½ inch (12 mm) thick.

Preheat a frying pan over medium-high heat. Add peanut oil to a depth of 1 inch (2.5 cm) and heat to 375°F (190°C) on a deep-frying thermometer. Slip a few patties into the hot oil and fry on the first side until golden brown, about 2 minutes. Turn the patties over and fry on the second side until golden, about 2 minutes longer. Using a slotted spatula or tongs, transfer to paper towels to drain.

Arrange the fish cakes on a platter and serve the Sriracha sauce or cucumber relish on the side.

serves 6

Thailand

Sakoo Sai Kai

stuffed tapioca dumplings

Asians are fond of soft, gelatinous, sticky foods. In Thailand, tapioca is enjoyed for this trio of features. Here, tapioca pearls are used as a coating for a sweet-savory meat-filled dumpling. Just before serving, the dumplings receive a drizzle of garlic oil, a favorite Thai condiment. Unless you have tried this dumpling in its homeland, it is difficult from reading the recipe to imagine how all the textures and flavors come together in a single delicious bite. This recipe is adapted from a version served at the Lemongrass restaurant, a modern but cozy neighborhood haunt in Bangkok.

FILLING

½ teaspoon peppercorns

5 cloves garlic

1 tablespoon chopped fresh coriander (cilantro) roots or stems

½ teaspoon salt

1 tablespoon peanut oil or corn oil

½ cup (2½ oz/75 g) minced shallots

½ lb (250 g) finely ground (minced) pork butt or chicken thigh meat

½ cup (2½ oz/75 g) chopped unsalted dry-roasted peanuts

¼ cup (1½ oz/45 g) preserved radish, minced

¼ cup (2 oz/60 g) firmly packed palm sugar or brown sugar

2 tablespoons fish sauce

2 tablespoons chopped fresh coriander (cilantro)

TAPIOCA COATING

2 cups (12 oz/375 g) small tapioca pearls

3 tablespoons tapioca flour

1½–2 cups (12–16 fl oz/375–500 ml) boiling water

1 banana leaf

garlic oil (page 247)

☙ To make the filling, in a mortar, pound together the peppercorns, garlic, coriander roots or stems, and salt to form a paste. Preheat a wok over medium heat and add the oil. When hot, stir in the garlic paste and stir-fry gently until fragrant, about 1 minute. Raise the heat to high, add the shallots and pork or chicken, and stir-fry, breaking up any clumps of meat, until no pink remains and the mixture is dry and crumbled, about 3 minutes. Add the peanuts, preserved radish, palm or brown sugar, and fish sauce, and continue to stir-fry over high heat until the sugar caramelizes and the mixture is sticky, 3–5 minutes. Remove from the heat, let cool, and stir in the chopped fresh coriander.

☙ To make the tapioca coating, in a large mixing bowl, combine the tapioca pearls and tapioca flour. Stirring constantly, gradually pour in enough boiling water to make a thick paste. Turn the dough out onto a flat work surface and knead for 2 minutes. It should be thick and sticky. If the dough becomes dry while you are kneading it, add a little more water. Let cool.

☙ You will need two bamboo steamer baskets or 2 heat-resistant shallow pie dishes that will fit comfortably into a tiered steamer. Cut out 2 banana leaf rounds each about ½ inch (12 mm) smaller in diameter than the basket or pie dish. Put the leaf rounds into the baskets or dishes and set aside.

☙ Dip your fingers into a bowl of cold water. Pinch off a 1½-inch (4-cm) piece of tapioca dough and roll it into a ball. Flatten it into a 3-inch (7.5-cm) round. Pack 1 teaspoon of filling into the center of the dough, then fold up the edges of the round to enclose the filling and form a ball. Place the ball on a banana-leaf round. Repeat to make 42–48 balls in all and place them, without touching, on the banana leaves. Cover the steamers with their lids.

☙ Add water to a wok or other pan for steaming and bring to a rolling boil. Place the steamers, stacked, over the water and steam until the dumplings are translucent and cooked through, 10–12 minutes.

☙ To serve, remove the baskets or dishes from over the water. Drizzle the dumplings with garlic oil and serve warm.

makes 3½–4 dozen; serves 12

Sinigang Na Hipon

sour shrimp and vegetable soup

Sinigang reflects nearly every Filipino's appreciation for sour flavors. The soup's tart character usually comes from various fruits, such as medium-ripe guavas and citrus fruits, and from fruit blossoms and lemongrass. Here, tamarind, another favorite souring agent, is used.

½ lb (250 g) large shrimp (prawns) in the shell

1-inch (2.5-cm) piece fresh ginger, crushed

6 cups (48 fl oz / 1.5 l) water

1 sweet potato, ½ lb (250 g), peeled and cut into ½-inch (12-mm) cubes

¼ lb (125 g) green beans, ends trimmed and cut into 1-inch (2.5-cm) lengths

1 small daikon, cut on the diagonal into slices ½ inch (12 mm) thick

1 yellow onion, cut into 8 wedges

2 green jalapeño chiles, halved lengthwise, seeded, and cut crosswise into thirds

2 tomatoes, cut into 8 wedges

¾ cup (6 fl oz / 180 ml) tamarind water (see sidebar, page 114)

2 tablespoons fish sauce

¼ lb (125 g) watercress sprigs or spinach leaves

salt and ground pepper to taste

hot steamed long-grain white rice

꙳ In a saucepan, bring the shrimp, ginger, and water to a boil over high heat. Reduce heat to medium-low and simmer until the shrimp turn orange-pink, 2–3 minutes. Transfer the shrimp to a bowl and let cool, then peel and devein. Set the shrimp aside.

꙳ Using a large spoon, skim the surface of the shrimp stock to remove any impurities. Return the pan to high heat and add the sweet potato, green beans, daikon, and onion wedges. Boil gently until the vegetables are almost cooked, about 5 minutes. Reduce the heat to medium and add the chiles, tomatoes, tamarind water, fish sauce, watercress or spinach, and shrimp. Simmer for 2 minutes to blend the flavors. Season with salt and pepper.

꙳ Ladle into warmed bowls. Place a large scoop of rice on each individual plate. Diners spoon the soup and vegetables onto the rice to eat.

serves 6

Singapore

Bak Kuh Teh

sparerib soup

A favorite breakfast or late-night soup, bak kuh teh *is a standard at Singaporean hawker stalls. The ribs are dipped into a chile-soy mixture and eaten over steamed rice, while fried Chinese crullers (baguettelike doughnuts) are dunked into the broth. The crullers, called* yu tiao, *can be purchased at Chinese markets.*

1 lb (500 g) pork back ribs, chopped into 1-inch (2.5-cm) lengths

6 cups (48 fl oz/1.5 l) water

2 cloves garlic, crushed

3 tablespoons dark soy sauce

4 whole star anise

1 cinnamon stick

1 teaspoon white peppercorns

½-inch (12-mm) chunk rock sugar or 1½ teaspoons sugar

1 teaspoon salt

ACCOMPANIMENTS

¼ cup (2 fl oz/60 ml) soy sauce

2 fresh red chiles, seeded and thinly sliced

2 Chinese crullers, thinly sliced on the diagonal into slices ½ inch (12 mm) thick (see note)

2 tablespoons fried shallots (see sidebar, right)

hot steamed long-grain white rice

In a 2-qt (2-l) clay pot or medium saucepan over medium-high heat, combine the ribs and water. Bring to a boil and boil gently for 3 minutes. Skim off and discard any foam from the surface. Add the garlic, soy sauce, star anise, cinnamon stick, peppercorns, sugar, and salt. Reduce the heat to medium-low and simmer, uncovered, until the pork is tender, about 45 minutes. Using a large spoon, scoop off and discard any fat from the surface.

To serve, divide the soy sauce and chiles evenly among 4 dipping saucers. Place the crullers on a plate. Scald 4 soup bowls, then ladle the broth along with 4–6 pieces of pork rib into each bowl. Scatter the fried shallots evenly on top. Serve with rice in small bowls alongside.

serves 4

Fried Shallots and Garlic

A bowl of crispy fried shallot flakes and another of fried garlic flakes are indispensable to the Southeast Asian cook. Indonesians scatter a generous handful of them over spicy *soto ayam* (chicken soup), the Burmese strew them over coconut-milk rice, Indian cooks in Singapore add a dusting to *pilaus* (pilafs), and Thai cooks even add them to sweet dishes. They are always sprinkled on a

dish at the last moment and deliver a crunch and an explosion of flavor with the first mouthful. Although easy to make, these crisp bits are difficult to keep around. My fingers seem to reach automatically into the bowl whenever I walk by.

To make shallot or garlic flakes, slice the cloves into very thin, very uniform slices, then separate the slices. Pour vegetable oil to a depth of about 1 inch (2.5 cm) in a small frying pan, place over medium heat, and heat to 325°F (165°C) on a deep-frying thermometer. Add the slices and fry until they turn light golden brown, about 5 minutes, reducing the heat if they color too quickly. Scoop them out with a slotted spoon, drain on a paper bag, let cool, and store in a jar in a cool cupboard.

Singapore

Murtabak

indian flat bread stuffed with spicy lamb

Whenever I am in Singapore, I head to the local murtabak hawker stand for entertainment and a treat. I am enthralled by the Indian cook who makes the bread for this delicious packet of spicy lamb. A true artisan, he takes a small lump of dough and transforms it into a sheet as thin as filo. The bread, called roti, is folded several times and grilled. To make murtabak, he wraps the uncooked dough around seasoned lamb before grilling it. Although the sight of roti being made may dissuade you from making it yourself, this recipe will work for the home cook who cannot duplicate the airborne theatrics of the masters.

Cut up murtabak into squares to serve as a hearty appetizer. Left whole and doused with curry sauce, it makes an excellent light lunch. In either case, serve it with milky Indian coffee.

Most of the Indians living in Singapore are Tamils, with origins in the southeastern Indian state of Tamil Nadu (formerly Madras), and they are traditionally vegetarians. For those vegetarians who do not also eschew eggs, the murtabak hawker fashions a roti packet with a filling of egg, onion, and sometimes peas.

Griddled Indian Layered Bread dough
(page 147)

FILLING

2 tablespoons ghee

4 shallots, minced

2 cloves garlic, minced

1 slice fresh ginger, peeled and finely minced

1 lb (500 g) ground (minced) lamb

2 tablespoons curry leaves (optional)

1 tablespoon Indian-style curry powder

1 teaspoon sugar

1 teaspoon salt

1 egg, lightly beaten

ghee or vegetable oil for frying

1 white onion, thinly sliced

✺ Prepare the bread dough up to the point where it has rested for 4 hours.

✺ To make the filling, in a wok over medium heat, warm the ghee. Add the shallots, garlic, and ginger and sauté until translucent, about 1 minute. Do not allow to brown. Add the lamb, curry leaves (if using), curry powder, sugar, and salt, breaking up any large clumps of meat. Continue to cook, stirring often, until the meat is no longer pink and all the liquid has evaporated, 5–8 minutes. The mixture should be dry and crumbly. Taste and adjust the seasonings. Remove from the heat and let cool, then mix in the egg.

✺ Preheat a griddle or large frying pan over medium-high heat. Add a thin film of ghee or oil.

✺ Working quickly, take 1 ball of dough and place it on a large work surface brushed with ghee or oil. With a rolling pin or your fingers, flatten the ball of dough. Roll or spread it out into a 12-inch (30-cm) or larger round. Scatter one-eighth of the onion slices and one-eighth of the meat mixture onto the middle of the round. Fold in all 4 sides so the edges overlap in the middle, completely enclosing the filling and making a 5-inch (13-cm) square packet.

✺ Place the square, folded side up, on the griddle. Fry until the bottom is nicely browned, about 3 minutes. Turn the square over and brown the second side, about 3 minutes longer. Transfer to a platter and keep warm while you fry the remaining packets.

✺ Cut each griddled bread into several pieces and arrange on a platter. Serve at once.

makes 8 stuffed breads; serves 8

Myanmar (Burma)

Be Ya Kyaw

yellow split-pea fritters

Snacking is a way of life for Asians, and these fritters are hard to pass up when you come upon an Indian street vendor in downtown Yangon (Rangoon) making them. Easy to assemble, these crisp, spicy fritters are perfect with a cool drink or as part of an afternoon tea.

1 cup (7 oz/220 g) dried yellow split peas

2 cups (10 oz/315 g) finely chopped yellow onion

½ cup (¾ oz/20 g) chopped fresh coriander (cilantro)

2 red Fresno or serrano chiles, finely minced

1 teapoon salt

½ teaspoon ground turmeric

corn or peanut oil for deep-frying

½ white onion, thinly sliced

1 lemon, halved

☙ Pick over the split peas, discarding any misshapen peas and stones, and put into a bowl. Cover with cold water and let soak overnight.

☙ The next day, drain the split peas and place in a food processor. Process to form a purée. Add the chopped onion, coriander, chiles, salt, and turmeric; pulse to work into a moist paste. Do not overprocess.

☙ Preheat a wok or large, deep frying pan over medium–high heat. Add oil to a depth of 2 inches (5 cm) and heat to 350°F (180°C) on a deep-frying thermometer. Meanwhile, moisten your hands, scoop up about 2 tablespoons of the purée, and form into a patty about 2½ inches (6 cm) in diameter and ½ inch (12 mm) thick. Repeat until all the purée is used.

☙ When the oil is ready, working in batches, slide the patties into the hot oil; do not crowd the pan. Fry, turning once, until golden brown on both sides, about 5 minutes total. Using a slotted spoon, transfer the fritters to paper towels to drain.

☙ Arrange on a platter, garnish with the onion slices, squeeze lemon juice on top, and serve.

makes about 2 dozen fritters; serves 8–12

Malaysia

Otak Otak

spicy fish mousse in banana leaves

Banana leaves are the aluminum foil of Southeast Asia. They are used to enclose foods so they can be easily packed for the road, and they make good wrappers for steamed, grilled, boiled, and roasted foods. The leaves are also used as plates and sometimes as makeshift umbrellas.

Otak otak, *which is made in Singapore and Malaysia, has countless variations. This one, a favorite Malaysian recipe, calls for mackerel, which is flavorful and beautifully matches the rich spice paste that is combined with the fish. I prefer the fish ground, although small fillets may be used, with the spice paste spread across the top before wrapping.*

SPICE PASTE

6 dried red chiles, cracked, seeded, soaked in warm water for 15 minutes, and drained

3 candlenuts or blanched almonds, soaked in warm water for 10 minutes and drained

2 lemongrass stalks, tender midsection only, chopped

2 slices fresh galangal, chopped, or 1 slice dried galangal, soaked in water for 20 minutes, drained, and chopped

4 cloves garlic, quartered

2 shallots, quartered

1 slice dried shrimp paste, ⅛ inch (3 mm) thick

½ teaspoon ground turmeric

1 cup (8 fl oz/250 ml) thick coconut milk (page 245)

1½ lb (750 g) mackerel fillet, finely ground (minced)

1 tablespoon sugar

1½ teaspoons salt

¼ teaspoon ground white pepper

2 kaffir lime leaves, spines removed and leaves cut into hairlike slivers

4 fresh polygonum leaves, finely chopped (optional; page 248)

24 pieces banana leaf, each 7 inches (18 cm) square

2 tablespoons vegetable oil, or as needed

3 red Fresno or serrano chiles, finely slivered

❧ To make the spice paste, in a mortar or blender, combine the chiles, candlenuts or almonds, lemongrass, galangal, garlic, shallots, shrimp paste, and turmeric. Pound or process to form a smooth paste. If needed, add a few tablespoons of the thick coconut milk to facilitate the blending. Transfer to a large bowl and mix in the remaining coconut milk.

❧ Prepare a fire in a charcoal grill.

❧ In a blender or food processor, combine the fish, sugar, salt, and white pepper and process to a paste. Add to the spice paste and mix well. Fold in the lime leaves and the polygonum leaves (if using).

❧ To wrap, bring a large pot of water to a boil. Dip a banana-leaf square into the boiling water for a few seconds to make it pliable, then dry with a kitchen towel. Place the leaf square, shiny side down, on a work surface with the veins running horizontally. Brush the top surface with a thin film of the oil. Spread 2–3 tablespoons of the fish purée along the middle of the leaf, forming a rectangular slab about 5 by 2 inches (13 by 5 cm) and leaving 1 inch (2.5 cm) uncovered on both ends. Scatter a few chile slivers on top. Fold in the bottom and top edges, overlapping them in the middle. Seal both ends with toothpicks. Set aside. Repeat until all the fish purée is wrapped in banana-leaf squares.

❧ When the coals are glowing, place the banana packets on the grill rack 3–4 inches (7.5–10 cm) above the coals and grill for about 3 minutes. Turn over the packets and grill for 3 minutes longer. Remove a packet from the grill, open it, and taste to see if the fish is cooked. If not, return to the grill for a few minutes longer.

❧ Transfer the packets to a platter and serve hot, warm, or at room temperature.

makes 24 packets; serves 12

Along Malaysia's long east coast, men set out in prahus, traditional small wooden boats, to catch fish for the market and the table.

VEGETABLES AND SALADS

Cooks choose from a vivid kaleidoscope — green, red, gold, yellow, purple, tan — of fresh vegetables.

Preceding spread: Vendors in Hanoi's marketplaces typically grow the fresh produce they sell, often transporting it in baskets hung from the ends of a pole slung across their shoulders. **Above:** Wat Si Chum, home to an immense stone image of a seated Buddha, is just one of several temples in Old Sukhothai, Thailand's first capital and the center of the famed Sukhothai kingdom, which rose in the mid-thirteenth century and flourished for some 150 years. **Bottom right:** The hollow cane of the bamboo plant— strong, waterproof, flexible, resistant to insects—is a natural and economical choice for building homes throughout Southeast Asia.

ASIAN COOKING IS KNOWN for its superb preparations of vegetables. Even many Western food writers believe that the Chinese have shown the rest of the world how to cook vegetables properly, leaving them tender and flavorful and their brilliant color intact. Southeast Asia owes many of its vegetable dishes, such as Malaysian stir-fried water spinach with *sambal* and Thai stir-fried broccoli with straw mushrooms, to this Chinese culinary legacy.

Salads, in contrast, are, for the most part, foreign to the Chinese, who rarely eat raw vegetables. Southeast Asian cooks, however, do combine uncooked vegetables (and sometimes fruits) with chopped or shredded meats, fish, or poultry; a scattering of fresh leafy herbs; finely julienned rhizomes; chopped peanuts; and a dressing. Sometimes noodles are tossed in as well. Although this sounds like an enor-

mous concoction, on the Southeast Asian dining table it fits on a small dish the size of a Western salad plate. It arrives with all the other dishes and is eaten communally. In Western parlance, this would be a salad.

Shopping for these vegetable-based dishes in Asia is always a delightful adventure. At the "wet" markets just about everything is available: fresh local produce, meats and poultry of all kinds, fresh—often live—seafood. In every Southeast Asian city and village, the wet markets teem with people in search of daily provisions, leaving little room to maneuver. Stop to stare a second too long, and a loaded hand truck may threaten to run you over. It is easy to get sprayed by live pompanos splashing in a steel pan, banged on the head by a line of hanging dried fish, or elbowed by another customer who is reaching for a bunch of Thai basil. If you don't watch out, your feet can get hosed down, or you might encounter an escaped lobster the size of a cat, as I did one day at the large, bustling market in Pattaya, in central Thailand.

As if the natural beauty of fresh produce alone is not enough to lure customers, shop-keepers painstakingly arrange banana blossoms, ginger buds, clumps of leafy herbs, or bushels of exotic fruits in spiraling circles

Above top: A riverside peanut seller, her goods displayed in an artful balancing act, is ready to measure out a canful of nuts for a hungry stroller along Tonle Sap, in central Phnom Penh. **Above bottom:** Marginata seedlings, nourished with only water and resting on delicate mesh screens, are cultivated in Indonesia for the lumber they will eventually provide. **Right:** A veritable rainbow of umbrellas blooms over the market stalls in Georgetown, on Penang, protecting shoppers, vendors, and goods from the searing Malaysian sun.

or towering pyramids. They pack chiles of varying sizes into baskets woven from banana leaves. Every spare inch of retail space not occupied by fresh ingredients is crammed with bottles and jars of sauces, condiments, and oils; dry goods; cooking utensils; and various odds and ends.

Perhaps the most intriguing marketplaces in Southeast Asia are the floating operations in and around Bangkok. Imagine a farmers' market set up in the middle of a water canal, or *klong,* with each stall a long wooden boat loaded down with just-harvested produce, fish and shellfish, dry goods, or even a small kitchen. In recent decades, most of the canals have been filled for roadbeds, and many of Bangkok's once-ubiquitous water markets have been pushed outside of the urban area to the countryside, where they now serve villagers rather than city dwellers. The beauty of this floating shopping mall is the colorful display of seasonal goods and, of course, the river life that thrives along the shore, with homes and other structures—a pharmacy, a clinic, a school—resting on wooden pillars above the water.

Above top: Plump, succulent shrimp (prawns) of all sizes are enjoyed tucked into spring rolls in Vietnam, tossed with pomelo in salads in Thailand, and cooked into a fiery lime-spiked *sambal* in Malaysia. **Above bottom:** Star fruit—named for the five-pointed shape it reveals in cross section and much beloved for its tart, crisp, juicy flesh—is just one example of the wealth of fresh fruits that flourish in the Southeast Asian soil. **Right:** A Shan woman sips a cup of traditional sesame-flavored tea at Pindaya, a small Burmese town.

On a visit to Denpasar, Bali's largest city, the market scene was nearly as exotic. I kept myself busy admiring mounds of the green and mature coconuts, round green eggplants (aubergines), lemongrass, chiles, spike-skinned fruits such as rambutan and jackfruit, snake-skinned salaks, papayas, mangoes, mangosteens, passion fruits, several varieties of bananas, and even grapes. Suddenly, a short distance away, some local women were creating a small commotion. I went over to uncover the cause and found the women rummaging through huge crates of vegetables native to the West: green beans, cabbage, cauliflower, potatoes, tomatoes, corn, and cucumbers. The way in which the vegetables were displayed did not suggest fancy imported produce, however. Introduced by early European explorers, these vegetables have been fully integrated into local cooking. In other words, while contemporary Western chefs may believe they invented East-West cooking, it actually began more than four hundred years ago during the European colonialization of the region.

Gado gado, for example, is a composed salad of Western vegetables (potatoes, cabbage, bean sprouts, beans, and cauliflower) dressed with a spicy peanut sauce and topped with *krupuk* (shrimp chips). Yet, despite its "imported" components, *gado gado* is an utterly Indonesian dish. At the same time, it is a plate that reflects an important chapter in local history.

Every Southeast Asian market has a spot reserved for itinerant food vendors who hawk fried noodles and noodles in soup, pounded salads, curried one-dish meals, breads, grilled corn, banana fritters, and juices in a spectacular selection that might include star fruit, watermelon, papaya, mango, guava, carrot, and sugarcane, to name only a handful of the possibilities. The scene is a swirl of purposeful activity, and even the heat and humidity add to the enjoyment of certain foods. Indeed, Indonesian *urap,* a chilled spicy "salad" of bean sprouts, green beans, and toasted coconut, seems to taste best under the weight of a tropical sun. My latest addiction is Cambodian *nyuom traiyong chaek,* a "salad" of shredded banana blossoms and chicken that marries

perfectly with the local sunshine and a cold glass of freshly squeezed sugarcane juice.

Some Malaysian salads are an acquired taste. One that I was unsure about the first time I encountered it was the Indian hawker specialty called *rojak*. It is a mix of fruits and hard and soft vegetables dressed with a roughly pounded sauce of dried shrimp paste, black prawn paste, tamarind, lime juice, palm sugar, and peanuts. Eventually, I saw this creation as a combination of many of my favorite vegetables and fruits, and now whenever I see it I can never resist it.

Yet another acquired taste, at least in its original form, is the spicy northeast Thai salad known as *larb*. Traditionally, it is made from the meat of the water buffalo, which is minced; mixed with lemongrass, chile, toasted rice powder, fish sauce, mint, and other flavorings; and served raw, much like French steak tartare. The choice of meat has been expanded to include beef, pork, and poultry, however, all of which are briefly poached before combining with the other ingredients. This highly seasoned salad has spread beyond its original

home, to tables from Chiang Mai to Phuket, and is now regularly served at weddings (the name means "good luck") and as a snack food, often as an accompaniment to the excellent local beer.

The line separating salads and snacks is equally fluid in Myanmar (Burma), as the recipe for pickled ginger mix on page 122 illustrates. The Burmese consider no dinner table complete without at least two salads, the ingredients for which are drawn from a long list: green mangoes and papayas, raw and cooked eggplants, cabbage, daikon, cucumbers, yard-long beans, and chickpeas (garbanzo beans), as well as chicken, shrimp, pork, fish, and even pig's ears, the latter typically mixed with sliced cucumbers and chile sauce.

Another interesting salad, and one that some culinary observers feel carries French influence, is Vietnamese *dia rau song*. Usually translated simply as "table salad," it is composed primarily of whole lettuce leaves, finely shredded carrots, bean sprouts, and cucumbers brightened with sprigs of mint, basil, coriander (cilantro), and other herbs. It is an inevitable part of nearly every meal, especially those that include grilled or fried dishes.

Just as essential to Southeast Asian tables are various pickles, relishes, and *sambals.* Many dishes depend on these intensely flavored preparations for the eater to appreciate their tastes fully. For example, Malaysian *ayam pong-tay,* braised chicken prepared with fermented soybean paste, is delicious on its own, but when *sambal blacan,* a potent mix of dried shrimp paste, chiles, and lime, is eaten along with it, it reaches its potential. Without the *sambal,* you would feel unsatisfied—a situation not unlike having a hamburger and a bun and nothing more.

Various vegetables and fruits, and some meats and seafoods, are packed into brines, creating flavors that may be salty, sweet, sour, spicy, or a combination of two or more of these characteristics. At home, these preserved concoctions are occasionally served as a side dish or before the meal as a kind of appetizer. In open-air markets, countless vendors sell them, setting up attractive showcases for the colorful jars and bottles. Even once you have bought a jar, you may be reluctant to open it, knowing that you will ruin the meticulously arranged mosaic of ingredients.

Many home cooks in Southeast Asia's large cities are keen on the new air-conditioned supermarkets that sell *sambals* and prepacked vegetables and fruits in a modern setting. But for me, the old-fashioned wet markets are where you find the true heart of Southeast Asian cuisine. Yes, they may be somewhat disheveled and chaotic, sticky hot and crowded, but they are the real Asia—the Asia without disguises.

Left: Rice fields around Negara, in western Bali, are the site of traditional—and raucous—water buffalo races held yearly in celebration of the completed harvest. **Above top:** Even the most crowded urban streets of Southeast Asia are lent a communal feel with the presence of countless outdoor market stalls and throngs of shoppers. **Above bottom:** In the Philippines, the most unique means of transportation are jeepneys—basically jeeps with extended rear ends that have been roofed and outfitted with two benches. The owners colorfully paint and decorate their vehicles to catch the eye of potential fares.

Thailand

Yam Woon Sen

glass noodle salad with shrimp, chicken, and mint

Woon sen, or glass noodles, are made from mung bean flour and are sold as bean thread noodles, bean thread vermicelli, transparent noodles, or mirror noodles. They have little flavor, but they are great for soaking up sauces. In salads such as this one, they add an intriguing texture and a refreshing "icy" appearance. Thai iced tea—the rich blend of tea, cinnamon, star anise, and vanilla served in tall glasses with evaporated milk—is the perfect accompaniment.

½ cup (4 fl oz/125 ml) chicken stock

6 oz (185 g) boneless, skinless chicken breast meat, minced

salt and ground pepper to taste

6 oz (185 g) shrimp (prawns), peeled and deveined

¼ lb (125 g) bean thread noodles, soaked in warm water for 15 minutes and drained

DRESSING

juice of 2 limes (about 6 tablespoons/3 fl oz/ 90 ml)

3 tablespoons fish sauce

2 teaspoons sugar

1 tablespoon roasted chile paste (page 245)

2 large red Fresno or serrano chiles, seeded and finely chopped

1 green (spring) onion, including 1 inch (2.5 cm) of the tender green tops, chopped

3 tablespoons coarsely chopped fresh coriander (cilantro)

1 tablespoon finely shredded fresh mint

4 large red-leaf lettuce leaves, finely shredded

2 tablespoons fried shallots (see sidebar, page 79)

❧ In a saucepan over medium heat, bring the stock to a gentle boil. Add the chicken and cook, breaking up the clumps of meat, until the meat turns opaque and has a crumbled texture, about 3 minutes. Using a wire skimmer, transfer the chicken to a bowl. Season with salt and pepper and let cool.

❧ Raise the heat to medium-high, add the shrimp to the boiling stock, and boil until they turn bright orange-pink, about 30 seconds. Drain well and let cool, then add to the bowl with the chicken.

❧ Bring a saucepan three-fourths full of water to a boil over high heat. Add the noodles and cook until they are clear, about 1 minute. Pour into a colander and rinse under cold running water. Drain well and transfer to a bowl.

❧ To make the dressing, in a large bowl, combine the lime juice, fish sauce, sugar, roasted chile paste, and chiles. Stir together until the sugar dissolves.

❧ Add the chicken-shrimp mixture and the noodles to the dressing and toss to mix. Mix in the green onion, fresh coriander, and mint.

❧ Line a large salad bowl with the shredded lettuce and mound the noodle salad on top. Garnish with the fried shallots. Serve at room temperature.

serves 4

In Thailand, the decorative carving of vegetables and fruits renders melons into boats, tomatoes into roses, a knob of ginger into a sea creature.

Malaysia

Kangkong Tumis Ayer

stir-fried water spinach with sambal

Sometimes referred to as morning glory and properly known as water convolvulus, water spinach is a leafy green with hollow stems that can be found in most Asian markets. It takes well to a light stir-fry with only a little garlic, but it is marvelous in this Malaysian recipe as well, where it shows itself off against an aromatic backdrop of pounded chiles, dried shrimp paste, and garlic.

¾ lb (375 g) water spinach

2 fresh red chiles, seeded

2 cloves garlic, quartered

1 large shallot, chopped

1 slice dried shrimp paste, ⅛ inch (3 mm) thick

2–3 tablespoons vegetable oil, or as needed

1 teaspoon sugar

¼ teaspoon salt

1–2 teaspoons light soy sauce

♔ Cut off and discard the tough hollow stems from the water spinach. Cut the tender tips and leaves into 4-inch (10-cm) lengths. Rinse thoroughly to rid the greens of sand and grit, then drain and dry.

♔ In a mortar or blender, combine the chiles, garlic, shallot, and shrimp paste and pound or process until a smooth paste forms.

♔ Preheat a wok or deep frying pan over medium heat. When the pan is hot, add 2 tablespoons oil and swirl to coat the pan. When the oil is hot, add the chile paste and stir-fry until fragrant, about 30 seconds. Raise the heat to high and add the water spinach in batches, letting each batch wilt slightly before adding the next batch. Stir and toss rapidly until all the greens wilt. If the pan becomes dry, add more oil as needed. Add the sugar, salt, and soy sauce to taste, stirring until well mixed. If liquid collects in the bottom of the pan, push the spinach to the sides of the pan and reduce the liquid over high heat until it thickens enough to coat the greens.

♔ Transfer to a serving plate and serve hot.

serves 4

Indonesia

Tahu Goreng

fried bean curd with peanut sauce

Fresh bean curd, also known as tofu, is a Chinese ingredient that has been readily adopted by the Southeast Asian cook. In this Indonesian salad, bean curd is deep-fried and then cut into small cubes that have a wonderfully crisp outside and a moist and cool inside. The rich, chile-laced peanut sauce perfectly balances the many flavors and textures of the dish.

½ lb (250 g) bean sprouts

vegetable oil for deep-frying

½ lb (250 g) firm bean curd (tofu)

PEANUT SAUCE

2 red Fresno or serrano chiles, seeded and chopped

1 shallot, quartered

1 clove garlic

⅛ teaspoon salt

2 tablespoons palm sugar or brown sugar

⅓ cup (3 fl oz/80 ml) tamarind water (see sidebar, page 114)

1 tablespoon sweet soy sauce

1 tablespoon fresh lemon juice, or to taste

4 tablespoons (2 oz/60 g) unsalted dry-roasted peanuts, crushed

3–4 tablespoons (1½–2 fl oz/45–60 ml) water

1 small English (hothouse) cucumber, peeled and finely shredded

½ carrot, peeled and finely shredded

❦ Bring a large saucepan three-fourths full of water to a boil. Drop the bean sprouts into the boiling water, blanch for 30 seconds, drain, and place under cold running water until cool. Drain thoroughly and set aside.

❦ Pour oil to a depth of 2 inches (5 cm) in a saucepan or wok and heat to 375°F (190°C) on a deep-frying thermometer.

❦ While the oil is heating, pat the bean curd dry. Ideally, the bean curd will be in 2 blocks, each 2½–3 inches (6–7.5 cm) square by 1 inch (2.5 cm) thick. Cut each square into 3 rectangles. If the block is 2 inches (5 cm) square, cut the block in half horizontally so that it is no thicker than 1 inch (2.5 cm), then cut into thirds.

❦ When the oil is ready, lower the rectangles, one block at a time, into the oil and deep-fry, turning once, until golden brown, 4–5 minutes total. Using a slotted spatula, transfer the bean curd to paper towels to drain. Repeat with the second block. Cut the bean curd into 1-inch (2.5-cm) cubes; set aside.

❦ To make the peanut sauce, in a mortar or blender, combine the chiles, shallot, garlic, and salt and pound or process to a paste. (If using a blender, add a little water to facilitate blending.) Add the palm or brown sugar, tamarind water, sweet soy sauce, lemon juice, and 2 tablespoons of the peanuts and pound or process to a coarse paste. Transfer the mixture to a bowl and stir in the remaining 2 tablespoons peanuts. Add the water as needed to dilute to the consistency of light (single) cream. Taste and adjust the seasonings.

❦ To assemble the salad, scatter the shredded cucumber and carrot on a platter. Put the bean curd cubes on top, and then scatter the bean sprouts over them. Pour the peanut sauce over the salad. Serve at room temperature.

serves 4–6

Herbs

Every Vietnamese meal includes a *dia rau song*, a fresh vegetable platter that accompanies one or more of the dishes being served. It carries several whole lettuce leaves; an assortment of crisp raw vegetables such as bean sprouts, carrots, and cucumbers; and an abundance of fresh herbs such as mint, coriander (cilantro), and basil. The diner layers the lettuce leaf with the vegetables and herbs and then tops it with a strip of grilled meat, a tiny spring roll, a shard from a *banh xeo* (page 196), or other small bite. Finally, he or she rolls up the leaf into a bundle, plunges it into a dipping sauce, and then eats it.

Fresh herbs are also ubiquitous in a Nonya meal. I still recall a lovely dinner I ate at the Singaporean home of a superb Nonya cook who served an unusual rice salad. An enormous mound of fried rice was covered with a blanket of wispy threads of more than twenty green-leaved herbs. Indeed, every Southeast Asian kitchen relies upon a gardenful of herbs, whether it be that of a Thai cook preparing *tom kha gai* (chicken coconut soup, page 50), a Burmese cook composing a curry, or an Indonesian cook assembling a *rempah*.

Vietnam

Goi Xoai

green mango and grilled shrimp salad

The first time I saw a green mango salad put together by a street hawker I was intrigued by his exotic technique. He held the peeled mango in one hand and a short-bladed cleaver in the other. First he made a series of small, repetitious parallel chops in one section of the fruit. Then he positioned the blade at the top of the first cuts and made a single horizontal cut across them, releasing a pile of thin, irregular julienned slivers with pointed ends. He repeated the technique around the entire fruit until the seed was reached. The slivers were immediately tossed into a mortar and bruised with a pestle to mix with the dressing. When you are served a green mango salad, check for the pointed ends. If you see them, the mango was grated by hand. If they are absent, it was done by machine.

½ lb (250 g) large shrimp (prawns), peeled and deveined

1 tablespoon vegetable oil

½ teaspoon coarse salt

ground pepper to taste

2 green mangoes, peeled and grated, preferably by hand

1 carrot, peeled and finely grated

1 tablespoon chopped fresh polygonum (page 248), Thai basil, or coriander (cilantro) leaves

1 red Fresno or serrano chile, chopped

¼ cup (2 fl oz/60 ml) nuoc cham *dipping sauce (page 249)*

2 tablespoons fried shallots (see sidebar, page 79)

☙ Prepare a hot fire in a charcoal grill. In a bowl, toss the shrimp with the oil, salt, and pepper to taste.

☙ Place the shrimp over the hottest part of the fire and grill, turning as needed, until they turn bright orange-pink and feel firm to the touch, about 2 minutes. Transfer to a plate and set aside to cool.

☙ In a large bowl, combine the mangoes, the carrot, the chopped polygonum, basil, or coriander, the chile, and the dipping sauce and toss well. Alternatively, lightly pound the vegetables with the salad dressing in a mortar.

☙ Arrange the salad on a platter and top with the shrimp. Sprinkle with the shallots and serve.

serves 4–6

Indonesia

Urap

spicy green beans, bean sprouts, and coconut salad

I remember the first time I tasted this salad, in a quiet bungalow at Sanur Beach on Bali. I fell in love with it and the island. Perhaps I was won over by the cool sea breeze wrestling with the warm sun, or the swishing sounds of giant palms competing with the hypnotic tempo of wooden mallets striking the bronze bars on a gamelan. The urap *arrived as a side dish to my grilled banana leaf–wrapped spicy fish. The combination of crunchy textures, the sizzling bites of chile, and the cooling watercress, spinach, and green beans seduced me with the first bite.*

This salad is often served as part of a selamantan, *a feast held to celebrate meaningful occasions.* Urap, *deep-fried meats,* sambal goreng *(dry stir-fried vegetables), and* lawar *(special Balinese festive dishes of chopped vegetables) are artfully arranged around a banana leaf–lined platter with a glistening mound of yellow rice steamed in coconut milk at the center. In Malaysia and Thailand, versions of* urap *use regional vegetables and seasonings. Serve the salad cold or at room temperature.*

⅓ lb (155 g) yard-long beans or green beans, trimmed and cut into 1-inch (2.5-cm) lengths

⅓ lb (155 g) bean sprouts

½ lb (250 g) spinach, tough stems removed

1 bunch watercress, tough stems removed

DRESSING

1 slice dried shrimp paste, ⅛ inch (3 mm) thick

2 cloves garlic, quartered

2 thin slices fresh galangal, peeled and chopped

1 large red Fresno or serrano chile, seeded and coarsely chopped

3 kaffir lime leaves, spines removed and leaves minced

1 teaspoon sugar

¼ teaspoon salt

3 tablespoons grated fresh or unsweetened dried coconut

2 tablespoons fresh lime juice

1 tablespoon vegetable oil

2 tablespoons fried shallots (see sidebar, page 79)

❦ Bring a large saucepan three-fourths full of salted water to a boil. Add the beans and blanch for 2 minutes, then scoop out with a wire skimmer and place under cold running water to halt the cooking. Drain well and set aside. Repeat with the bean sprouts, spinach, and watercress, blanching them one at a time: the bean sprouts for 10 seconds, the spinach for 1 minute, and the watercress for 30 seconds. Rinse each one with cold water, wrap in a kitchen towel, and squeeze out as much excess water as possible. Gather the spinach into a bunch and cut into thirds. Repeat with the watercress. Put all the vegetables into a large bowl and set aside.

❦ To make the dressing, wrap the dried shrimp paste in aluminum foil and place the packet directly on a stove-top burner turned on to medium-high heat. Toast it, turning it once or twice, until fragrant, 1–2 minutes. Remove the packet and open it; if the shrimp paste crumbles, it is ready. Let cool.

❦ In a mortar, combine the toasted shrimp paste, garlic, galangal, chile, and lime leaves. Pound until a smooth paste forms. Mix in the sugar, salt, coconut, lime juice, and oil. Add to the vegetables, mix well, cover, and refrigerate until ready to serve.

❦ Just before serving, transfer the salad to a serving platter and scatter the fried shallots on top.

serves 6

Vietnam

Goi Ga

torn chicken and cabbage salad

A Vietnamese menu does not exist that does not include this chicken and cabbage salad. Best described as Vietnamese coleslaw, this healthful salad is oil-free except for the tasty garnish of shrimp chips.

DRESSING

1 red Fresno or serrano chile, seeded and minced

1 clove garlic, finely minced

1½ tablespoons sugar, or to taste

3 tablespoons fresh lime juice

2 tablespoons fish sauce

1 whole chicken breast, about ¾ lb (375 g)

4 cups (8 oz/250 g) finely shredded green cabbage

½ carrot, peeled and finely shredded

½ cup (¾ oz/20 g) finely slivered fresh mint

2 tablespoons finely slivered fresh polygonum (page 248) or fresh coriander (cilantro) leaves

2 tablespoons chopped unsalted roasted peanuts

fried shrimp chips (page 250)

☙ To make the dressing, in a bowl, combine the chile, garlic, sugar, lime juice, and fish sauce. Stir together until the sugar has dissolved. Set aside.

☙ Place the chicken in a saucepan and add water to cover. Bring to a simmer over medium-high heat, adjust the heat to maintain a gentle simmer, and cook until opaque throughout, about 20 minutes. Transfer the chicken to a plate, let cool, then remove the skin and bones. With your fingers, tear the meat along the grain into long, thin shreds and place in a large bowl. Discard the cooking liquid or reserve for another use.

☙ Add the cabbage, carrot, mint, polygonum or coriander, and dressing and toss gently to mix well.

☙ Arrange the salad on a platter. Sprinkle with the peanuts, garnish with the shrimp chips, and serve.

serves 6

Malaysia

Sambal Brinjal

grilled eggplant with spicy sambal

Nonyas, women of Chinese and Malaysian heritage, take their cooking seriously. Coached in the culinary arts as children, they are traditionally taught to make sambals using a batu lesong, or mortar and pestle. For some cooks, there is even a strict order in which ingredients are pounded: chiles first and then dried shrimp paste, in order to permeate the chiles with the shrimp flavor. If you abide by these rules, I am told, you will attain the ultimate flavor. If you are short on time, however, you can use a blender, just as many modern Asian women do. This eggplant dish, with its spicy sambal, makes a wonderful opener or main dish.

2 red Fresno or serrano chiles, seeded and cut crosswise into thirds

¼ teaspoon salt

1 slice dried shrimp paste, ⅛ inch (3 mm) thick

4 shallots, quartered

2 cloves garlic, halved

1½ tablespoons dried shrimp, soaked in warm water for 15 minutes

6 Asian (slender) eggplants (aubergines), halved lengthwise

4 tablespoons (2 fl oz/60 ml) vegetable oil

1½ teaspoons white vinegar

1½ teaspoons sugar

☙ Prepare a fire in a charcoal grill.

☙ In a mortar or blender, combine the chiles, salt, dried shrimp paste, shallots, and garlic and pound or process to form a fine paste. Transfer to a bowl and set aside.

☙ Drain the shrimp and pound them in the mortar to a coarse powder. Set aside.

☙ When the fire is ready, brush the eggplants on both sides with 2 tablespoons of the oil, and place, cut sides down, on the grill rack. Grill until the bottoms are charred, 3–5 minutes. Turn over and cook on the second sides until charred, 3–5 minutes longer. The eggplants are done when they can be easily pierced to the center with a knife. Transfer, cut sides up, to a serving plate. Cover to keep warm.

☙ Preheat a wok or small frying pan over medium-high heat. When the pan is hot, add 2 tablespoons oil and swirl to coat the pan. When the oil is hot, add the garlic-shallot paste and stir-fry until fragrant, about 1 minute. Raise the heat to high and add the pounded shrimp, vinegar, and sugar. Fry gently until the mixture is golden brown and dry, 1–2 minutes.

☙ Remove the pan from the heat and spread an equal amount of the mixture on top of each eggplant half. Serve warm or at room temperature.

serves 6

Thailand

Nam Jim Tua

sweet-sour cucumber relish

Side dishes, condiments, and pickles are essential to the cuisines of Southeast Asia. In Thailand, for example, satay is served not only with the traditional spicy peanut sauce, but also with this highly seasoned relish. It is particularly refreshing with deep-fried foods.

½ cup (4 fl oz/125 ml) rice vinegar

¼ cup (2 oz/60 g) sugar

1 teaspoon salt

½ English (hothouse) cucumber

½ carrot

1 large shallot or ¼ red (Spanish) onion, thinly sliced

3 red or green Fresno or serrano chiles, seeded (if desired) and finely chopped

fresh coriander (cilantro) leaves

¼ cup (1½ oz/45 g) chopped unsalted dry-roasted peanuts

☙ In a small saucepan over medium heat, combine the vinegar, sugar, and salt. Bring to a gentle boil, stirring to dissolve the sugar and salt. Remove from the heat and set aside to cool.

☙ Peel the cucumber and carrot. Cut both in half lengthwise, then again cut each half in half lengthwise. Finally, cut the 8 "sticks" crosswise into slices ⅛ inch (3 mm) thick. Just before serving, in a bowl, combine the cucumber, carrot, shallot or onion, chiles, and the vinegar dressing. Toss gently to mix.

☙ To serve, divide the relish among small saucers and garnish with coriander leaves and peanuts.

makes about 1½ cups (12 fl oz/375 ml)

Thailand

Kanah Namman Hoi

chinese broccoli with straw mushrooms

Variously called Chinese broccoli or Chinese kale in English and gai lan *in Cantonese,* kanah *looks like a slender broccoli stalk with dark green leaves and small white blossoms. It has a more robust flavor than Western broccoli, however.*

1 lb (500 g) young, tender Chinese broccoli

2 tablespoons peanut oil or corn oil

4 cloves garlic, chopped

2 green serrano chiles, cut in half on the diagonal

½ cup (3½ oz / 105 g) drained canned straw mushrooms

2 tablespoons water

2 tablespoons oyster sauce

1 tablespoon fish sauce

1 teaspoon sugar

ground pepper to taste

❧ Trim the ends off the broccoli stalks. If the stalks are young and tender, they will not need peeling; if they seem a bit tough, peel away a thin outer layer. Cut each stalk crosswise into 2-inch (5-cm) lengths, including the stalks, leaves, and flowers.

❧ Bring a large saucepan three-fourths full of water to a boil. Add the broccoli and blanch until it turns bright green, about 30 seconds. Scoop out the broccoli, shake off the excess water, and set aside.

❧ Preheat a wok or large frying pan over medium-high heat. When hot, add the oil and swirl to coat the pan. When the oil is hot, add the garlic and stir-fry until golden, about 15 seconds. Raise the heat to high, add the chiles, broccoli, and mushrooms, and stir-fry until the vegetables are seared with the oil, about 30 seconds. Sprinkle in the water, oyster sauce, fish sauce, sugar, and pepper and stir-fry until the broccoli is tender but still crisp, about 3 minutes. Transfer to a serving dish and serve at once.

serves 6

Cambodia

Nyuom Traiyong Chaek

banana blossom and chicken salad

The banana blossom is a common salad ingredient in Southeast Asia, and the many salads that call for it have more similarities than differences. Typically, the salad is tossed with a blend of fish sauce, lime or lemon juice, garlic, and sugar—the quintessential Southeast Asian dressing. One version I tasted in Vietnam included thin slices of star fruit, which added a faint tartness. Whole shrimp (prawns) or hand-shredded poached chicken is a common addition, along with a host of leafy green herbs. Chopped peanuts are the traditional finishing touch.

But the main attraction of any of these salads is the banana blossom, with its delightful fibrous and crunchy texture and a grasslike flavor reminiscent of raw artichokes. To keep the blossoms from discoloring, treat them like artichokes, immersing the cut slivers in a bowl of water to which lemon juice has been added.

4 cups (32 fl oz/1 l) water

1 teaspoon salt

2 green (spring) onions, left whole and bruised

1 whole chicken breast, about ¾ lb (375 g)

juice of ½ lemon

1 large banana blossom, 1–1½ lb (500–750 g)

2 lb (1 kg) bean sprouts

DRESSING

1 clove garlic, pounded or finely minced

1½ teaspoons finely minced shallot

1½ tablespoons sugar

2 tablespoons fish sauce

1 tablespoon fresh lime juice

1 cup (1 oz/30 g) small fresh Thai basil leaves

½ cup (½ oz/15 g) small fresh mint leaves

¼ cup (1½ oz/45 g) chopped unsalted roasted peanuts

1 or 2 red jalapeño chiles, cut into thin slivers

❦ In a saucepan, combine the water, salt, and green onions and bring to a boil. Add the chicken, adjust the heat to maintain a gentle simmer, and cook until opaque throughout, about 20 minutes. Transfer the chicken to a plate, let cool, then remove the skin and bones. With your fingers, tear the meat along the grain into long, thin shreds and place in a large bowl.

❦ Fill a large bowl with water and add the lemon juice. Remove the tough outer red leaves of the banana blossom and discard. Discard the undeveloped tiny buds. Remove the large, tender leaves, stack them, and cut them crosswise into strips ⅛ inch (3 mm) wide. Submerge the strips in the lemon water. When you reach the tight heart, with its tiny buds, cut it in half lengthwise, then cut crosswise into thin strips. Add to the lemon water until ready to use.

❦ Pinch off the brown root tips from the bean sprouts. (This is for aesthetic reasons only; you can skip this step if you do not have time.)

❦ To make the dressing, in a mortar, pound together the garlic, shallot, and sugar to form a smooth paste. Stir in the fish sauce and lime juice.

❦ To serve, drain the banana blossom strips and, with your hands, squeeze out the excess water. Add them to the chicken along with the bean sprouts, basil, and mint. Toss together. Add the dressing and toss until well mixed.

❦ Transfer the salad to a serving platter and garnish with the peanuts and chile slivers. Serve at once.

serves 4–6

Yam Med Mamuang

cashew salad

Cashews are grown in abundance in the southern Thai province of Ranong, and this cashew-rich salad is one of the country's little-known culinary gems. Look for big whole cashews and fry them slowly in oil so that they cook evenly. If you prefer, you can toast them in the oven at 325°F (165°C) for 5–8 minutes. This is a perfect snack to serve with iced limeade or cold beer.

½ cup (4 fl oz/125 ml) vegetable oil

½ lb (250 g) raw large whole cashews

2 shallots, thinly sliced

1 green (spring) onion, including 1 inch (2.5 cm) of the tender green tops, thinly sliced

1 lemongrass stalk, tender midsection only, finely minced

1 tablespoon coarsely chopped Chinese celery leaves or regular celery leaves

1 tablespoon chopped fresh mint

1 red jalapeño chile, seeded and thinly sliced

DRESSING

2 tablespoons fresh lime juice

1½ teaspoons fish sauce

½ teaspoon sugar

¼ cup (¼ oz/7 g) fresh coriander (cilantro) leaves

☙ Pour the oil into a wok and place over medium heat. Slowly heat to 325°F (165°C) on a deep-frying thermometer. When the oil is hot, add the cashews and fry, stirring frequently, until light golden brown, about 5 minutes. Using a slotted spoon, transfer the nuts to a brown paper bag to drain.

☙ Place the still-warm cashews in a bowl and immediately add the shallots, green onion, lemongrass, celery leaves, mint, and chile. Toss to mix well.

☙ To make the dressing, in a small bowl, combine the lime juice, fish sauce, and sugar. Stir until the sugar dissolves. Pour the dressing over the salad and toss well. Turn the salad out onto a serving plate, garnish with the coriander leaves, and serve.

serves 4–6

Thailand

Yam Som

flaked pomelo and shrimp salad

The pomelo, a winter fruit native to Southeast Asia, looks like an enormous yellow grapefruit with a slightly pointed top. Pomelo segments are not as juicy as those of grapefruit, but they have a snappier texture.

½ lb (250 g) large shrimp (prawns), peeled and deveined

1 large pomelo or 2 sweet grapefruits

DRESSING

2 teaspoons roasted chile paste (optional; page 245)

2 tablespoons fresh lime juice

1 tablespoon fish sauce

2 teaspoons sugar

1 red jalapeño chile, seeded and thinly sliced

1 tablespoon chopped fresh mint

2 tablespoons fried shallots (see sidebar, page 79)

1 tablespoon fried garlic (see sidebar, page 79)

2 tablespoons roasted peanuts, crushed

¼ cup (¼ oz / 7 g) fresh coriander (cilantro) leaves

♨ Bring a large saucepan three-fourths full of salted water to a boil. Add the shrimp and boil until they turn orange-pink, 1–2 minutes. Drain and let cool.

♨ Peel the pomelo and divide it into segments. Remove the membrane from each segment and, using your fingers, break the flesh apart into smaller pieces, dropping them into a bowl. If using grapefruits, treat them in the same way, but place the pieces in a sieve to drain off the excess juice.

♨ To make the dressing, in a large bowl, combine the roasted chile paste (if using), lime juice, fish sauce, sugar, and chile. Stir until the sugar dissolves. Add the shrimp, pomelo or grapefruit, mint, fried shallots, fried garlic, and peanuts and toss to mix.

♨ Turn out onto a serving plate, garnish with the coriander, and serve.

serves 4–6

The Floating Markets of Thailand

In and around Bangkok, many of the local people spend much of their lives on a *klong*, or canal. Along these byways travels every water conveyance, from small paddled boats to midsized taxis to long rice barges, the last often so fully loaded that their prows barely rise above the water. The Chao Phraya River, which flows from Thailand's northern hills and winds through the heart of the country like a sinuous snake, fans out into a huge network of canals that extends to almost every village in the central plains. For locals whose homes are perched on stilts along the banks, this floating world is both the source of their livelihood and their shopping center.

Every morning, women in brightly colored dress and straw hats load up their home-grown vegetables, fruits, coconuts, and flowers in long, narrow boats. For them, these boats are the family car. Some are pushed along with a bamboo pole or paddles, while more fortunate sellers switch on gasoline-driven motors. Their daily destination is the central floating market at Thonburi, Bangkok's sister city across the river, or to such smaller—and less touristed—markets as Khu Wiang or Damnoen Saduak. There, they will peddle goods straight from their boats, while their singsong chants fill the air with promises of bargains.

In true entrepreneurial spirit, some boat owners have installed small kitchen burners in their crafts so that they might sell ready-to-eat foods. Not surprisingly, noodle dishes are at the top of most menus.

In the twentieth century, Bangkok, once called the Venice of the East because of its many canals, saw its waterways slowly filled in to accommodate the growing number of automobiles. With the arrival of the car has come the sacrifice of much of the city's traditional *klong* life. Yet the floating market is likely to remain a vital part of the landscape.

Cambodia

Pleah Sach Ko

raw beef salad with lemongrass

Raw beef salads are common in Cambodia, Laos, Thailand, and Vietnam. For some salads the beef is thinly sliced, while for others it is finely minced. It is usually mixed with crunchy raw vegetables and a garden of fresh herbs. This Cambodian dressing has a touch of diluted prahok, *or preserved fish paste. It is optional, although it adds depth to the dressing and is a uniquely Cambodian touch. Packed in jars,* prahok *can be found in most Southeast Asian markets.*

1 lb (500 g) round or rump steak, wrapped in plastic wrap and placed in the freezer for 1 hour

¼ cup (2 fl oz/60 ml) fresh lime juice

2 lemongrass stalks, tender midsection only, very thinly sliced

DRESSING

2 shallots, unpeeled

2 cloves garlic, unpeeled

8 fresh coriander (cilantro) sprigs

1 teaspoon galangal powder

½ cup (4 fl oz/125 ml) fresh lime juice

2–3 tablespoons fish sauce

1 tablespoon prahok juice (optional; page 248)

3 tablespoons sugar

¾ cup (4½ oz/140 g) unsalted roasted peanuts, coarsely chopped

2 shallots, very thinly sliced

1 small daikon or jicama, peeled and cut into very thin julienne

2 cups (4 oz/125 g) bean sprouts, brown root tips pinched off

½ red bell pepper (capsicum), cut into fine julienne

½ carrot, peeled and cut into fine julienne

½ cup (½ oz/15 g) small fresh mint leaves

½ cup (½ oz/15 g) small fresh Thai basil leaves

☙ Remove the partially frozen beef from the freezer and cut across the grain into paper-thin slices. In a bowl, combine the beef with the lime juice and lemongrass. Set aside to marinate and "cook" for 30 minutes.

☙ Meanwhile, make the dressing: Preheat a broiler (griller). Place the shallots and garlic cloves on a baking sheet and slip under the broiler 3–4 inches (7.5–10 cm) from the heat source. Broil (grill) the shallots and garlic, turning as necessary, until evenly charred on all sides, 3–5 minutes. Remove from the broiler, let cool, and remove the skins.

☙ Strip the leaves from the coriander stems and set the leaves aside to use for the garnish. In a mortar, combine the shallots, garlic cloves, coriander stems, and galangal powder and pound together to form a paste. Transfer the pounded mixture to a bowl. Add the lime juice, fish sauce to taste, the *prahok* juice (if using), the sugar, and half of the peanuts.

☙ Using your hands, squeeze the beef of excess liquid. You can reserve these juices, if desired, and stir them into the dressing. In a large bowl, toss together the beef, sliced shallots, daikon or jicama, bean sprouts, bell pepper, carrot, mint leaves, and basil leaves. Add the dressing and toss well.

☙ Transfer the salad to a serving platter and garnish with the remaining peanuts and reserved coriander leaves. Serve at once.

serves 6

On Cambodia's hottest days, many peasants often eat only plain rice for dinner to give their digestion a rest from the heat.

Malaysia

Rojak

fruit and vegetable salad
with spicy dressing

This salad of mixed fruits and vegetables is a street hawker's specialty in Malaysia and Indonesia. Many versions exist, and I have never seen it made the same way twice. It always seems to be a handful of this and two handfuls of that mixed in the ubiquitous wide tin or plastic bowl. Cooks use whatever fresh fruits and vegetables are in season, and the final flavor is at once hot, spicy, sweet, and sour, with an overall deep, rich base. A thick, treaclelike black prawn paste, called hay koh *in Hokkien, a southern Chinese dialect, and* petis udang *by Malaysians, permeates the dressing with a surprisingly mellow flavor.*

I can vouch that it takes a few practice sessions to understand and master this salad's complexity. Once you do, however, you will enjoy experimenting with other vegetables and fruits. Purchase the deep-fried bean curd in Chinese markets. Serve this Nonya-style rojak *with a glass of cold Asian beer.*

DRESSING

1 slice dried shrimp paste, ⅛ inch (3 mm) thick

3 red Fresno or serrano chiles, seeded

2 tablespoons black prawn paste

1 tablespoon palm sugar or brown sugar

juice of 1 lime

pinch of salt

¼ cup (2 fl oz/60 ml) tamarind water
(see sidebar, page 114)

¼ lb (125 g) bean sprouts

¼ lb (125 g) water spinach or regular spinach,
tough stems removed

¼ jicama

½ English (hothouse) cucumber

2 star fruits

½ small green mango

¼ pineapple

4 squares deep-fried bean curd (tofu), each
¾ inch (2 cm) square, cut into quarters

½ cup (3 oz/90 g) unsalted dry-roasted peanuts,
coarsely pounded

☙ To make the dressing, wrap the dried shrimp paste in a piece of aluminum foil and place the packet directly on a stove-top burner on medium-high heat. Toast it, turning it once or twice, until fragrant, 1–2 minutes. Remove the packet and open it; if the shrimp paste crumbles, it is ready. Let cool.

☙ In a mortar or blender, combine the toasted shrimp paste and chiles and pound or process until a smooth paste forms. Add the black prawn paste, palm or brown sugar, lime juice, salt, and tamarind water and pound or process to a smooth purée. Thin with water, if necessary, to the consistency of light (single) cream. Transfer to a bowl and set aside.

☙ Bring a saucepan three-fourths full of water to a boil. Add the bean sprouts, blanch for 30 seconds, scoop out with a wire skimmer, and rinse under cold running water until cool. Drain thoroughly and set aside. With the water still boiling, add the water spinach or regular spinach, blanch for 1–2 minutes or until wilted, drain, and rinse under cold running water until cool. Drain thoroughly and squeeze dry in a kitchen towel, then cut into 2-inch (5-cm) lengths. Set aside.

☙ Peel the jicama, cucumber, star fruits, mango, and pineapple and cut them into irregular-shaped wedges about ¼ inch (6 mm) thick. Scatter the fruits, vegetables, bean curd, and peanuts on a shallow platter. Pour the dressing over the salad and toss but do not overmix. Serve the salad at room temperature.

serves 6

Vietnam

Dua Cai Chua

pickled sour mustard greens

Every marketplace in Vietnam has a huge display of pickles. Packed into jars of all sizes, the intricately arranged fruits and vegetables form colorful, eye-catching patterns. Pickled foods are an essential element in the Vietnamese meal, whether served as a table relish before the repast, as an accompaniment to enhance and balance the flavors of other dishes, or combined with other ingredients to make a dish. The pickling brines vary in flavor. Some have a salty edge with just a hint of sweetness, and others are sweet with just a touch of salt. My preference is the brine for these sour mustard greens, a tart-sweet mix with a bit of salt—a perfect accompaniment to rich dishes such as the pork stewed with coconut juice on page 204.

In Vietnam, some cooks dry the mustard greens in the hot sun for several hours before brining. This results in a chewy and crunchy texture. Other cooks simply dry the greens long enough to rid them of any lingering moisture before covering them with the brine.

1 lb (500 g) Chinese mustard greens
4 cups (32 fl oz / 1 l) water
½ cup (4 fl oz / 125 ml) rice vinegar
⅓ cup (3 oz / 90 g) sugar, or to taste
1 teaspoon salt

☼ Trim off the ends of the mustard green stalks, then cut the greens, including the leaves, crosswise into 2-inch (5-cm) lengths. Cut the thick, broad stalks crosswise into slices ½ inch (12 mm) thick. Rinse thoroughly with cold water and drain well. Air-dry the mustard greens until all the moisture is evaporated and place them in a large glass jar.

☼ In a saucepan, combine the water, vinegar, sugar, and salt. Bring to a boil, stirring to dissolve the sugar, then remove from the heat. Let cool completely. Pour the cooled brine over the greens to cover. Let marinate at room temperature for 3 days, then refrigerate until ready to serve or for up to 3 months.

☼ To serve, remove the pickled greens from the brine and serve at room temperature.

makes 1 qt (1 l)

Tamarind

In the searing heat of a Ho Chi Minh City afternoon, residents sometimes take refuge under the spreading tamarind trees that line many of the streets. The sickle-shaped, thin-skinned fruit pods that hang from the branches are an invaluable ingredient throughout Southeast Asia. The pods contain a fruity, slightly citric sour pulp that is pressed into a liquid that is used in soups, salads, curries, meats, and fish dishes.

Tamarind water is easy to make and store. Look for tamarind pulp sold in blocks in Asian markets. To make about 1½ cups (12 fl oz/375 ml) tamarind water, cut up ½ pound (250 g) of the pulp into small pieces, place in a bowl, and add 2 cups (16 fl oz/500 ml) boiling water. Mash the pulp to separate the fibers and seeds, then let stand for 15 minutes, stirring two or three times. Pour the liquid through a fine-mesh sieve placed over a bowl, pushing against the pulp with the back of a spoon and scraping the underside of the sieve to dislodge the clinging purée. Transfer to a jar and refrigerate for up to 4 days or freeze in an ice-cube tray for up to 1 month. A tamarind concentrate, which dissolves instantly in hot water, is also available in some Asian markets and can be used in a pinch.

Malaysia
Sambal Bhindi Udang

stir-fried okra and shrimp with sambal

Here, okra is cooked just until tender with a little crunch and infused with a multidimensional flavoring typical of a Malaysian sambal. Use small, tender okra for the best results.

SPICE PASTE

2 tablespoons dried shrimp, soaked in warm water for 15 minutes

2 shallots, quartered

3 cloves garlic

2 red jalapeño chiles, seeded

1 slice dried shrimp paste, ⅛ inch (3 mm) thick

3 tablespoons vegetable oil

1 lb (500 g) okra, ends trimmed and cut into 1-inch (2.5-cm) pieces

¼ cup (2 fl oz/60 ml) tamarind water (see sidebar, left)

½ lb (250 g) large shrimp (prawns), peeled and deveined

1 small head pickled garlic, coarsely chopped (optional)

❦ To prepare the spice paste, drain the soaked dried shrimp, reserving 2 tablespoons of the water. In a blender, combine the shrimp, the 2 tablespoons water, the shallots, garlic, chiles, and dried shrimp paste. Process to a fine-grain paste. Set aside.

❦ Preheat a wok or frying pan over medium-high heat. When the pan is hot, add the oil and swirl to coat the pan. When the oil is hot, add the spice paste and fry, stirring frequently, until the mixture is emulsified, about 2 minutes. Reduce the heat to medium and cook, stirring occasionally, until beads of oil appear on the surface of the paste, about 8 minutes.

❦ Raise the heat to high and add the okra. Fry for 1 minute, tossing frequently. Stir in the tamarind water. If the mixture seems too dry, add a tablespoon or so of water to moisten it and continue cooking until the okra is tender but still crisp, 3–5 minutes. Add the shrimp and toss and stir until they turn bright orange-pink, about 1 minute.

❦ Transfer the okra and shrimp to a platter and top with the pickled garlic, if using. Serve immediately.

serves 6

Singapore

Yu Sang

chinese new year salad

In China, people do not commonly eat raw fish or raw vegetables, but Singaporean Chinese do. While this dish is usually prepared for Chinese New Year in Southeast Asia, it is so popular that I have been served it at other times of the year as well. When the salad is brought to the table, it is the custom for everyone to pick up their clean chopsticks and help toss it together. Be sure to use sashimi-grade fish. The pickled gingers, tea melons, and shallots can be found in a Chinese market.

¼ lb (125 g) very fresh tuna, striped bass, or red snapper fillets, wrapped in plastic wrap and placed in the freezer for 1 hour

1 tablespoon fresh lemon juice

1 teaspoon Asian sesame oil

big pinch of ground white pepper

DRESSING

½ cup (5 oz/155 g) Chinese plum sauce

1 tablespoon sugar, or to taste

¼ teaspoon salt

¼ cup (2 fl oz/60 ml) hot water

2 tablespoons fresh lime juice

SALAD

1 tablespoon sesame seeds

2 cups (8 oz/250 g) finely julienned daikon, squeezed of excess water

2 cups (8 oz/250 g) finely julienned carrot

3 green (spring) onions, white part only, finely shredded into 2-inch (5-cm) lengths

6 kaffir lime leaves, spines removed and leaves shredded into hairlike threads

½ cup (½ oz/15 g) fresh coriander (cilantro) leaves

4 Chinese sweet pickled shallots, thinly sliced

2 tablespoons well-drained, finely shredded pickled tea melons (2 or 3 pickled tea melons)

¼ cup (1½ oz/45 g) well-drained, finely shredded sweet pickled ginger

2 tablespoons finely slivered fresh young ginger

1 tablespoon well-drained, finely shredded pickled red ginger

¼ cup (1½ oz/45 g) unsalted roasted peanuts, lightly crushed

☙ Remove the partially frozen fish from the freezer and cut across the grain into paper-thin slices. Cover and refrigerate. Then, just before serving, combine the fish, lemon juice, sesame oil, and white pepper in a bowl and toss well.

☙ To make the dressing, in a bowl, combine the plum sauce, sugar, salt, and hot water. Stir to dissolve the sugar, then stir in the lime juice. Set aside.

☙ To assemble the salad, preheat a dry frying pan over medium heat. When the pan is hot, add the sesame seeds and stir frequently until the seeds are light golden brown and begin to pop, 2–3 minutes. Pour onto a small plate and let cool.

☙ In a large bowl, toss together the daikon, carrot, green onions, lime leaves, and half of the coriander leaves. Make a bed of the mixture on a platter. In a bowl, stir together the pickled shallots, tea melons, and the three gingers. Scatter the mixture over the daikon-carrot mixture. Mound the seasoned fish slices in the middle. Top with the peanuts and sesame seeds and then with the remaining coriander leaves. Pour the dressing evenly over the top.

☙ Place the salad in the middle of the table. Have everyone reach in with their chopsticks to help toss the salad.

serves 8–10

Many of the ancestors of the now-prosperous Singaporean Chinese— Hokkien, Cantonese, Chao Zhou, Hainanese, Hakka— arrived as indentured laborers from China.

Cambodia

Cha Traop Dot

wok-braised eggplant with chopped pork and shrimp

Cambodian cuisine shares many of the culinary flavors and ingredients of its neighbors, Thailand and Laos; uses Chinese cooking techniques and ingredients; and is inspired by the pungent seasonings of Indian cooking. This popular dish exemplifies that rich multicultural heritage.

4 Asian (slender) eggplants (aubergines) or 1 globe eggplant, about 1½ lb (750 g) total weight

2 tablespoons vegetable oil

4 cloves garlic, chopped

1 red Fresno or serrano chile, seeded and minced

½ lb (250 g) pork butt, chopped

½ lb (250 g) shrimp (prawns), peeled, deveined, and chopped

2 tablespoons fish sauce

1 tablespoon sugar

¼ teaspoon freshly ground pepper

2 green (spring) onions, chopped

☙ Prepare a fire in a charcoal grill. Puncture the eggplant(s) in several places. Place on the grill rack about 4 inches (10 cm) from the fire and grill slowly, turning occasionally, until the skin is blackened and the flesh is tender, 20–30 minutes for small eggplants and about 45 minutes for large. Let cool, then peel and tear the flesh into strips.

☙ Preheat a wok or frying pan over medium-high heat. When hot, add the vegetable oil, swirl to coat the pan, and heat until almost smoking. Add the garlic and sauté until light golden brown, about 30 seconds. Add the chile, pork, and shrimp and stir-fry, breaking up any clumps, until the pork turns white and the shrimp are bright orange-pink, 3–5 minutes. Stir in the fish sauce, sugar, and pepper. Raise the heat to high, add the eggplant, and cook until blended and slightly thickened, about 3 minutes.

☙ Add the green onions, mix well, and transfer to a serving plate. Serve immediately.

serves 4–6

Thailand

Yam Tua Poo

chopped winged bean salad

All the ingredients in this salad must be chopped into small, uniform pieces, as size is important to the overall flavor and texture of the dish. The salad is traditionally made with winged beans, a popular Thai bean with four lengthwise ribs. When cut cross-wise, the pieces look like they have wings, thus the name. Yard-long beans, sometimes called Chinese long beans, or regular green beans may be substituted.

1 tablespoon salt

1 boneless, skinless chicken breast, about 6 oz (185 g)

½ lb (250 g) winged beans, yard-long beans, or green beans, trimmed

¼ cup (1 oz/30 g) unsweetened grated dried coconut

1 red jalapeño chile, seeded and thinly sliced

DRESSING

⅓ cup (3 fl oz/80 ml) coconut cream (page 245)

2 teaspoons roasted chile paste (page 245)

2 tablespoons fresh lime juice

1 tablespoon fish sauce

1 tablespoon sugar

2 tablespoons fried shallots (see sidebar, page 79)

1½ tablespoons fried garlic (see sidebar, page 79)

3 tablespoons unsalted roasted peanuts, crushed

coconut cream for garnish (optional)

☸ Bring a small saucepan three-fourths full of water to a boil. Add ½ tablespoon of the salt and the chicken and bring to a second boil. Reduce the heat to medium-low, cover, and simmer the chicken until it is cooked through, about 10 minutes. Remove the chicken from the pan and discard the cooking liquid. Let cool, then cut into ¼-inch (6-mm) pieces.

☸ Bring a large saucepan three-fourths full of water to a boil. If using yard-long beans, cut into 6-inch (15-cm) lengths. Add the remaining ½ tablespoon salt and the beans and boil until tender but still very crisp, about 1 minute. Lift out with a wire skimmer and rinse well under cold running water to stop the cooking. Cut the beans into ¼-inch (6-mm) pieces and set aside.

☸ In a dry frying pan over medium heat, toast the coconut, stirring occasionally, until it turns a light golden brown, 1–2 minutes. Pour onto a plate and let cool. Set aside.

☸ In a large bowl, combine the cooled chicken, green beans, and chile. The salad can be made up to this point and refrigerated, covered, until ready to proceed with the recipe.

☸ To make the dressing, put the coconut cream into a bowl. Stir in the roasted chile paste, lime juice, fish sauce, and sugar, mixing until the sugar dissolves.

☸ Add the dressing to the chicken-bean mixture and toss to mix well. Sprinkle with the toasted coconut, fried shallots, fried garlic, and peanuts. Toss once or twice to mix.

☸ Turn out onto a serving platter. Garnish with a dollop of coconut cream, if desired, and serve.

serves 4–6

Pounded Salads

On any journey through the floating markets of Thailand, a kind of culinary music orchestrates the trip. It is the melody of vendors—pounding, stirring, cooking—preparing their edible wares for sale. One morning, as I skimmed along the busy waters, I heard the somewhat high-pitched clang of one object striking another. I searched the surrounding activity and soon discovered the source of the sound: a traditional Thai earthenware mortar, which has a deep and narrow bowl, was being struck rhythmically with a stout hardwood pestle. The vendor was lightly pounding—bruising really—shredded green papaya, dried shrimp, shallots, garlic, peanuts, fresh mint, and Thai basil, tenderizing the stiff ingredients and fusing them together into a salad. Thailand's waterborne vendors are remarkably astute cooks. They know just how hard and how long to pound, stopping precisely at the moment before a salad turns mushy.

Similar pounded salads using unripe papaya and mango are also popular in Laos, Cambodia, and Vietnam. Cambodian and Laotian cooks mix *prahok*, a creamy preserved fish paste with a flavor as pungent as overripe Brie, with the classic Southeast Asian "vinaigrette" of lime juice, fish sauce, garlic, shallots, and sugar. The Vietnamese version calls for the addition of a little *rau ram*, a pungent herb with pointed leaves and light red stems.

Laos

Tom Som

shredded green papaya, bean, and carrot salad

Typically, a green (unripe) papaya or mango is used as a raw "vegetable" in Southeast Asian salads, as illustrated by the Vietnamese mango and shrimp salad on page 98 and this Laotian classic.

¼ lb (125 g) yard-long beans or green beans, trimmed and cut into 1-inch (2.5-cm) lengths

1 small green papaya, about 1 lb (500 g), halved, seeded, and peeled

1 carrot, peeled

2 cloves garlic

3 small green serrano chiles

1 firm tomato, cut into 6 or 8 thin wedges

2 tablespoons fresh lime juice

1 tablespoon fish sauce

1 tablespoon sugar

1½ teaspoons prahok *juice (optional; page 248)*

1 cup (1 oz/30 g) fresh coriander (cilantro) leaves

2 kaffir lime leaves, spines removed and leaves finely shredded

½ cup (2½ oz/75 g) chopped unsalted roasted peanuts

☙ Bring a saucepan three-fourths full of water to a boil. Add the beans, blanch for 1 minute, drain, and rinse under cold running water until cool. Drain again and set aside.

☙ With a handheld grater or a Japanese mandoline fitted with the medium blade, shred the papaya into long, fine julienne. Repeat with the carrot.

☙ In a mortar, pound together the garlic and chiles to form a coarse paste. Add the beans and bruise them slightly to break down the fiber. Transfer the mixture to a large salad bowl. In small batches, pound the papaya and carrot slivers to bruise them lightly, then add them to the beans. Finally, lightly pound the tomato wedges and add to the bean-papaya mixture.

☙ In a small bowl, stir together the lime juice, fish sauce, sugar, and the *prahok* juice, if using, until the sugar dissolves. Pour over the vegetables and mix thoroughly. Transfer to a serving dish, garnish with the coriander, lime leaves, and peanuts, and serve.

serves 6

Myanmar (Burma)

Ghin Thoke

pickled ginger mix

The Burmese engage in long, lingering conversations, a national pastime that is generally accompanied with a snack. Ghin thoke, a variation of the Mandalay specialty lephet, *or pickled tea leaf salad, is a typical daytime repast, while* lephet *is preferred as an after-dinner treat and digestive, usually to accompany a lengthy political discussion. In Myanmar, these dessert-like snacks can be purchased at small shops, where they are enjoyed with hot tea.*

There seems to be no set rule for the number of ingredients that make up this "salad." I have seen recipes with as few as three essential ingredients—the sesame seeds, pickled young ginger, and fried garlic slivers—and others that contain as many as eight.

For a Western-style presentation, arrange the ingredients in separate tiny mounds on a plate and mix them together with a fork and spoon at the table in front of your guests. Or do as the Burmese do and put a little of the mix into individual bowls so guests can dip in with their fingers. Yellow split peas, called chana dal, *can be purchased already fried in Indian markets. Fried fava (broad) beans can be substituted. Pickled young ginger, called* kizami shoga *in Japanese, is available at Japanese and Chinese markets.*

½ *cup (3½ oz/105 g) yellow split peas*
vegetable oil for deep-frying
½ *cup (3 oz/90 g) raw or unsalted dry-roasted peanuts*
2 tablespoons peanut oil
1 tablespoon Asian sesame oil
2 cloves garlic, thinly sliced
2–3 tablespoons sesame seeds
¼ *cup (1½ oz/45 g) well-drained pickled young ginger*
1 red Fresno or serrano chile, seeded
¼ *cup (1 oz/30 g) dried small shrimp*
1 lime, halved

☙ Put the split peas into a saucepan and add water to cover by 1 inch (2.5 cm). Bring to a boil over high heat, reduce the heat to medium, and simmer for 10 minutes. Test a pea for doneness; it should be almost tender. Drain and dry well on paper towels.

☙ Pour vegetable oil to a depth of 1 inch (2.5 cm) in a saucepan and heat to 350°F (180°C) on a deep-frying thermometer. Add the split peas and fry until golden brown and crispy, about 1 minute. Using a slotted spoon, transfer the peas to paper towels to drain. If you are using raw peanuts, add them to the hot oil and fry them until they turn golden brown, about 3 minutes. Using the slotted spoon, transfer the peanuts to paper towels to drain.

☙ Pour the peanut oil and sesame oil into a small saucepan and heat to 325°F (165°C) on the deep-frying thermometer. Add the garlic and fry slowly, turning as necessary, until lightly golden, 2–3 minutes. Using the slotted spoon, transfer to paper towels to drain. Reserve the garlic-sesame oil in the pan.

☙ Preheat a dry frying pan over medium heat. When hot, add the sesame seeds and stir frequently until the seeds are light golden brown and begin to pop, 2–3 minutes. Pour onto a small plate and let cool.

☙ Cut the ginger into ¼-inch (6-mm) pieces or very fine slivers. Cut the chile into ¼-inch (6-mm) pieces or fine slivers.

☙ On a serving platter, put the chile pieces in the middle and arrange small piles of the split peas, peanuts, garlic, sesame seeds, ginger, and dried shrimp around the chile. Just before serving, at the table, drizzle on about 1 tablespoon of the reserved garlic-sesame oil and squeeze the lime over the entire platter. Toss and serve.

serves 4

Vietnam

Dua Gia

sour bean sprouts

Sour bean sprouts are excellent accompaniments to Vietnam's so-called caramel syrup dishes (see catfish simmered in a clay pot, page 186). The tangy vegetables round out the sweetness present in the bronze-colored, caramel-syrup sauce. Picking the strings and heads off the bean sprouts may be laborious and time-consuming, but you will find the effort worthwhile. The bean sprouts will taste extraordinarily fresh and clean, and they will look like polished white stems.

In Southeast Asia, bean sprouts are seldom encountered beyond Vietnam. The most commonly sprouted bean is the mung bean, which is likely native to the region or perhaps to India. But the sprouts are believed to be a Chinese notion—an economic means of producing food without land—that was transplanted to local tables. Bean sprouts also turn up in such popular Vietnamese dishes as banh xeo *(page 196) and are inevitably included with the herbs and chiles that accompany bowls of* pho *(page 70).*

3 cups (24 fl oz/750 ml) water

⅓ cup (3 fl oz/80 ml) white vinegar

1 tablespoon salt

1 teaspoon sugar

1 carrot, peeled

1 lb (500 g) bean sprouts

6 green (spring) onions, including 1 inch (2.5 cm) of the tender green tops, cut into 2-inch (5-cm) lengths

☙ In a saucepan, combine the water, vinegar, salt, and sugar. Bring to a boil and boil for 1 minute. Remove from the heat and let cool.

☙ Using a vegetable peeler, make thin shavings or lengthwise slices of the carrot 2–3 inches (5–7.5 cm) long. Put the carrot, bean sprouts, and green onions into a bowl and pour in the cooled brine. Set aside for at least 4 hours. (You can refrigerate them for up to 3 days, but they will lose some crunch.)

☙ Drain and serve at room temperature.

makes about 4 cups (2½ lb/1.25 kg)

RICE, NOODLES, AND BREADS

Locals believe that if there is rice for the table, everything will be fine.

Preceding spread: In one of Hanoi's many food markets, a rice seller hand-threshes her grain by tossing it in a shallow basket. **Below:** The headquarters of Cao Daism, an indigenous Vietnamese religion drawing primarily on the tenets of Taoism, Buddhism, and Confucianism, is the Cao Dai Great Temple at Long Than, about fifty miles (85 km) northwest of Ho Chi Minh City. There, followers dressed in white practice their faith through daily prayers, ritualistic chanting, prostration, and offerings of fruit, flowers, tea, incense, and other items. **Right top:** A colorful procession moves along the pale sands of a Balinese beach. **Right middle:** Sheaves of newly harvested rice await transport in eastern Bali. **Right bottom:** In a marketplace in Singapore, a stack of thin, round wrappers awaits its role in the making of *poh pia*, the Nonya version of Chinese spring rolls.

ONE CANNOT TALK ABOUT Southeast Asian rice, noodles, and breads without first acknowledging their genesis in China. Two general misconceptions plague this topic, however. For years, countless sources credited Marco Polo with discovering noodles in China and carrying the recipe back to Italy. But today, reputable scholars agree that techniques for preparing pasta were already well established in Italy by the time that the famous Venetian traveler began his journey. A second fallacy is that rice is a dietary staple throughout China—a belief held even by much of China's rice-eating population. In truth, the majority of the Chinese eat wheat products rather than rice. Southern China, with its monsoon rains and easily flooded plains, offers excellent conditions for rice cultivation. But the drier conditions and cooler climate north of the Yangtze River, a much larger area with a bigger population, are better suited to growing wheat. There, wheat is milled into flour, which is then transformed into noodles, dumplings, and breads, staples of the northern Chinese diet.

It is instead China's southern neighbors, the nations of Southeast Asia, that form the rice bowl of Asia, with a patchwork of paddies covering great stretches of every country, from Myanmar (Burma) to Thailand to Vietnam to Indonesia to the Philippines. A single snapshot illustrates the importance of rice in the region: Along the road to Ubud, the center of art and culture on the small, picturesque island of Bali, the commanding view of centuries-old rice terraces chiseled into the steep mountainous terrain has the look of a monumental staircase. At the base of this stunning sight, slender, elegant Balinese women on foot, baskets filled with wrapped rice snacks or the daily groceries balanced on their heads, share the thoroughfare with cars, trucks, dogs, goats, and chickens. They walk calmly and with assurance, gracefully avoiding all transport obstacles and never toppling their burden. For temple festivals and other celebrations, these same women steady a towering stack of trays on their heads, each level holding cakes, fruits, and rice balls. Called a *bebanten*, each load rises some four feet (1.3 m) into the sky.

With an estimated twenty thousand temples in Bali, each one with an anniversary celebrated every 210 days to commemorate its consecration, such festivals are a way of life. One day I saw the long, colorful flag of a *kampong* (village) entrance whipping in the air. The residents beckoned to me, inviting me to celebrate with them. Passing through the town, I spotted Bali's signature dish, *babi guling* (roast suckling pig), suspended over a glowing fire. On an overcrowded table were laid out *ayam goreng* (fried chicken), *bebek betutu* (Ubud-style smoked duck), *lawar* (a festive "salad" of mixed chopped vegetables, meats, and grated coconut), *sayur* (stewed vegetables in coconut milk), *ikan goreng* (fried whole fish with spices), and many *sambals*. But more important, interspersed among these plates were the symbolic rice dishes: *nasi kuning* (yellow rice surrounded with meat, vegetables, and seafood) cradled in a banana leaf bowl, *lontong* (rice steamed in banana leaves), *ketupat* (rice steamed in woven baskets), and *nasi putih* (plain white rice).

The central role played by rice in the Balinese meal repeats itself throughout Southeast Asia. People commonly believe that if all else fails, everything will still be fine if there is rice on the table, and everyone strives toward that goal. In Myanmar, for example, dozens of different rice varieties are grown, each distinguished by its taste, texture, color, aroma, and price. Not surprisingly, the costliest white rice, known as *nga kywe* and admired for its long, delicate grains, is found in the cupboards of the wealthiest citizens, while *nga sein,* with its tougher kernels, is consumed by the peasants. The region's steadily expanding population makes high yield among the most important characteristics of any rice variety, however, if supply is to meet the constantly growing demand. For decades, scientists at the International Rice Research Institute at Los Baños, on Luzon in the Philippines, have been developing new strains with higher yields to meet those needs. Yet even when presented with the opportunity to plant improved varieties guaranteed to put more rice on the table, some Southeast Asian farmers, long accustomed to the taste and planting peculiarities of the varieties they—and their ancestors—have always grown, resist the change.

Rice is taken so seriously in these countries that even the crust on the bottom of the pot is never thrown out. The Thais, for example, transform it into *khao tang,* a crispy rice cracker used for scooping up a chile sauce or other dip. Simply put, rice in Southeast Asia alone could fill a thick volume, from the various methods for cooking it—started in cold water, added to boiling water, steamed above boiling water—to the ways in which it is served and eaten—in bowls, in banana leaves, in baskets, with a spoon and fork, with chopsticks, with fingers—to the myriad dishes that are prepared for religious ceremonies.

Rice is also milled into flour for making some of the world's best noodles. Although wheat noodles are eaten in Southeast Asia, the breadth of rice noodle dishes is far greater. Rice noodles come dried, fresh, thin, coarse, flat, round, fat, and in broken sheets, and they are eaten for breakfast, for lunch, or for a snack from morning until midnight.

Left: One of Cambodia's most stunning sights, the Bayon, built by order of Jayavaram VII at the center of Angkor Thom, is a massive pyramid temple with four giant carved heads—reputedly images of the royal builder himself as bodhisattva—facing the four compass points. **Below top:** Outside nearly every *wat* (monastery) in Thailand, Buddhist monks in traditional flame-colored robes receive alms from local residents. **Below bottom:** A nationally protected nature preserve, southern Thailand's pristine Koh Phi Phi islands are a wonder of craggy limestone bluffs shooting out of crystalline waters—a paradise for swimmers, snorklers, divers, hikers, and birdwatchers.

Every Southeast Asian pantry holds a wealth of different types of noodles. In Vietnam, cooks reach for *bun,* or rice vermicelli; *banh canh,* fresh stubby clear noodles usually made from rice but sometimes from wheat or other starches; *bun tau,* or bean thread noodles; *hu tieu dai,* flat noodles made from tapioca starch; *mi soi,* thin egg noodles; and others. In Malaysia, hawkers at the many *makan malam*—"night market food stalls"— cook up bowls of *laksa* loaded with sticky rice vermicelli; stir-fry *kway teow* (wide rice noodles) with water spinach and squid; and combine *Hokkien mee,* sunny yellow noodles made from wheat flour and eggs, with chopped beef, beans sprouts, and a thick gravy spiked with shallots and chiles. In Thailand, where hardworking noodle vendors occupy countless small storefronts and market stalls, noodles of every size and shape, from white flat rice noodles to pale beige egg noodles to glasslike bean thread noodles, are dished up to hungry passers-by pulled in by the enticing aromas rising from the stove.

Although some people may publicly dismiss noodles as the poor man's one-dish meal, even those who snub them can be found consuming them with great satisfaction at hawker stalls. The most memorable bowls of *laksa* always seem to be prepared on a makeshift stove by an itinerant cook. The best *pad thai* I have ever eaten was served in an alley off a busy street in Bangkok, cooked up by a vendor I found through asking the doorman at my hotel where he ate his lunch.

Glutinous rice, also known as sticky or sweet rice, is the primary starch of Laos and northeastern Thailand, although ordinary rice is eaten there as well. As elsewhere, locally grown varieties range from glutinous to non-glutinous, with many distinctive types, each with a different degree of stickiness, falling in between. Laotians shape cooked glutinous rice into small cakes, deep-fry them, and eat them as savory treats. As with ordinary rice, glutinous rice is milled, and the flour is used for snacks and sweets, many of which are sold in markets and at simple food stalls.

The best Southeast Asian breads are found in similar modest locations. They are typically flat and grilled, panfried, deep-fried, or steamed. The most interesting and flavorful of them are the Indian breads, which are found primarily in Singapore, Malaysia, and Myanmar and which have both full-bodied taste and appealing texture. In general, Indians arrived in these countries first as soldiers and indentured laborers and later as clerks and traders. Most were from southern India, and they brought not only their village customs and religious deities, but also their herbs and spices, kabobs and curries, and, of course, their exceptional breads. I don't know whether it is the flour, the well-seasoned grill, or the accompanying curry sauce that produces such extraordinary taste. Perhaps it is the combination of all three. What I do know is that whenever I have only a few hours in Singapore or Malaysia, I know what I want to eat: *roti prata* and *thosai*. The tangy, salty, spicy redolent flavor of a curry

Left: Many Burmese boys spend at least a short time living as monks in a Buddhist monastery, although strict resistance to the temptation of worldly goods can prove difficult. **Below top:** The most important date on the Vietnamese calendar is the Lunar New Year celebration known as Tet, which is marked by family gatherings, the worship of ancestors, the preparation of traditional foods, and the raucous sound of firecrackers in the streets. **Below bottom:** A steaming bowl of *pho,* Hanoi's popular beef noodle soup, is a typical breakfast for young and old alike.

balanced against the coolness of a *raita* (yogurt-cucumber relish) gets all sopped up with the chewy, warm Indian bread.

One morning, when my husband and I had only a few hours in Singapore before our departure, we made a beeline for our favorite *roti* café. It is rustic and humble, with old-fashioned round marble tables that need more than one matchbook under a leg to keep them balanced. We wiped the crumbs from the tabletop, then sat down and ordered our *roti prata* and coffee. In just a few minutes, our waiter returned with two jugs, one of them filled with Indian coffee and the other one empty. With the full jug held at chest level, he poured a long, steady stream of hot coffee mixed with milk into the bottom of the

empty jug, which he held below his waist. As he poured, he simultaneously lifted his pouring hand high above his head. He then lifted the now-full jug chest high and poured again. He repeated the action until a crown of froth was created, producing a kind of Indian cappuccino. To my amazement, the floor never saw a drop of coffee.

Meanwhile, a large square of parchment paper was laid in the center of the table, and a stainless-steel condiment stand with three bowls of different curries was set to one side, along with the usual few thin tissues that were to serve as napkins. The *roti* arrived and was immediately plopped on the paper, and some curry sauce was poured on top. With my knee holding up the rickety table to prevent

Left: In the past, Dayak women on the island of Borneo traditionally tattooed their forearms and calves with intricate animal, plant, and spirit designs, and those of rank—the offspring of chiefs, for example—were permitted additional tattoos as well. Today, these decorative practices are found only among women living in the most remote areas of the island. **Below:** Outside Siem Reap's Ta Prohm temple, surrounded by fig trees and covered with creepers, a young Cambodian adds to the mysterious atmosphere of the structure with the sounds of his bamboo flute.

the sauce from rolling into my lap, we tore the bread into pieces and literally mopped up the escaping sauce. It is arguably the most marvelous breakfast in the world.

We weren't done yet, however. We walked two blocks to another simple storefront for our fix of *thosai,* a thin, crispy south Indian rice flour pancake, which, though related to *roti,* is not served in a *roti* shop. It comes with curry sauce, *aloo* (curried potatoes), and dal and some coconut chutney and *pachadi,* a grated carrot relish. At this stop we had *lassi,* a blended yogurt drink, instead of coffee.

We were now ready to say good-bye to Singapore and in a few days Southeast Asia, leaving behind a world of rice dishes, noodles, and breads that knows no equal.

Thailand

Pad Thai Goong

fried rice noodles with shrimp

Certain tastes—sweet, sour, salty, spicy, pickled—are always present in pad thai. *One of the national dishes of Thailand, this tangle of noodles, shrimp, and seasonings offers a trio of textures—crisp, crunchy, soft— in one dish. Be sure to choose the correct rice noodles, called* sen lek *in Thai. They are flat and roughly ¼ inch (6 mm) wide, about the size of linguine.*

3 tablespoons vegetable oil

¼ lb (125 g) medium-sized shrimp (prawns), peeled and deveined

2 tablespoons chopped garlic

2 tablespoons chopped shallot

2 extra-large eggs

1 tablespoon small dried shrimp, chopped into ¼-inch (6-mm) pieces if large

1 tablespoon coarsely chopped preserved white radish

½ lb (250 g) dried flat rice noodles (see note), soaked in warm water for 20 minutes and drained

2 tablespoons sugar

3 tablespoons fish sauce

3 tablespoons tamarind water (see sidebar, page 114)

2 tablespoons fresh lime juice

½ teaspoon dried red chile flakes

½ lb (250 g) bean sprouts

2 green (spring) onions, including 1 inch (2.5 cm) of the tender green tops, cut into 1-inch (2.5-cm) lengths

½ cup (3 oz/90 g) coarsely chopped unsalted dry-roasted peanuts

GARNISH

several fresh coriander (cilantro) sprigs

1 fresh red chile, thinly sliced

1 lime, cut into wedges

☸ Preheat a wok over medium-high heat. When the pan is hot, add 1 tablespoon of the vegetable oil and swirl to coat the pan. When the oil is hot, add the fresh shrimp and toss and stir until they curl and turn bright orange-pink, about 30 seconds. Transfer to a bowl and set aside.

☸ Add the remaining 2 tablespoons oil to the wok. When the oil is hot, add the garlic and shallot and stir-fry until they turn golden brown, about 30 seconds. Raise the heat to high and crack the eggs into the wok. With the tip of a spatula, gently break up the egg yolks, but do not beat. Let them fry without stirring until they start to set, about 1 minute. Then add the dried shrimp, preserved radish, and noodles and, using tongs or 2 spatulas, break up the eggs and toss everything together like a salad, about 1 minute. Add each of the following ingredients, one by one, tossing and stirring between each addition to mix: Start with the sugar, followed by the fish sauce, tamarind water, lime juice, dried chile flakes, half of the bean sprouts, all of the green onions, half of the peanuts, and all of the reserved stir-fried shrimp. Toss quickly and gently like a salad to coat each noodle strand, about 15 seconds. As soon as the strands begin to stick to one another, the noodles are cooked.

☸ Transfer the noodles to a platter and garnish with the remaining peanuts and bean sprouts, the coriander sprigs, the chile slices, and the lime wedges. Serve immediately. Each diner squeezes a bit of lime juice over his or her serving.

serves 2 as a main course or 4 as an appetizer

Bangkok residents typically eat noodles as a snack, buying them from a hawker on a boat-clogged klong or at a stall off Sukhumvit Road.

Singapore

Pappadam

crisp indian dal wafers

Asians love crisp fried foods, so it's no wonder that the Indian pappadam *has been so well received in Southeast Asia. The wafers, which are bone dry and brittle, are made from* urad dal, *split dried beans (actually seeds). Slipped into hot oil, they expand into large, thin, crisp disks. They can be served as bread at an Indian meal, but they are best as a snack with an icy cold Asian beer.*

There are two ways to cook a pappadam: *either deep-fried in hot oil or passed over a gas flame or an electric burner. Both methods are explained here.*

vegetable oil for deep-frying (optional)

12 pappadam *wafers*

❦ To fry *pappadam*, pour the oil to a depth of 1 inch (2.5 cm) in a deep frying pan and heat to 375°F (190°C) on a deep-frying thermometer. Slip a wafer into the hot oil. With tongs or a flat wire skimmer, press down on the wafer to submerge it in the oil. It should sizzle and expand within seconds. When it turns light khaki and the surface is covered with tiny bubbles, transfer it to paper towels to drain. Repeat until all the wafers are fried. Once they have cooled, store the wafers in an airtight tin. They will stay crisp for several hours.

❦ To toast *pappadam* over a flame or an electric burner, turn on a gas burner or preheat an electric burner on high heat. Grasp a wafer with tongs and hold it about 1 inch (2.5 cm) above the flame or burner. Pass it over the burner and move it around so that the whole wafer is evenly exposed to the heat on one side. It should expand and turn khaki within 20 seconds. Turn the wafer over and repeat on the second side. The entire cooking should take less than 1 minute. Store as directed above.

serves 6

Malaysia

Mee Goreng

yellow noodles with shrimp, tomatoes, and potatoes

In Indonesia mee goreng is considered the local fried noodle dish, but in Malaysia and Singapore it is a specialty of Indian cooks, who have their own version of stir-fried noodles with Chinese and Western ingredients. The noodles originated in China and migrated with the Chinese to Southeast Asia. The Malays added chiles; the Indonesians threw in the European potato, tomato, and cabbage; and local Indian cooks perfected the final version in Malaysia's many hawker centers. Hokkien noodles are fresh, thick, yellow rods introduced here by Hokkiens, natives of southern China who settled in the area.

½ lb (250 g) fresh Hokkien yellow noodles or Chinese egg noodles

3 tablespoons vegetable oil, or as needed

½ teaspoon salt

3 cloves garlic, chopped

2 oz (60 g) boneless, skinless chicken breast or thigh, cut into ¼-inch (6-mm) pieces

2 eggs

¼ lb (125 g) large shrimp (prawns), peeled and deveined

1 cup (3 oz/90 g) shredded cabbage

3 pieces deep-fried bean curd (tofu), each about 1½ inches (4 cm) square, cut into slices ¼ inch (6 mm) thick

1 tablespoon sambal ulek

2 tablespoons tomato ketchup or tomato sauce

1 tablespoon sweet soy sauce, or to taste

1 tablespoon light soy sauce, or to taste

1 potato, boiled, peeled, cooled, and cut into ½-inch (12-mm) cubes

¼ lb (125 g) bean sprouts

1 firm tomato, cut into ½-inch (12-mm) cubes

2 green (spring) onions, including 2 inches (5 cm) of the green tops, cut into 1-inch (2.5-cm) lengths

1 English (hothouse) cucumber, peeled and thinly sliced

fried shallots (see sidebar, page 79)

2 lemons, cut into wedges

☙ If using Hokkien noodles, put them into a bowl, add hot water to cover, and let stand for 1 minute. Drain the noodles and set aside. If using fresh Chinese noodles, bring a large saucepan three-fourths full of water to a boil, add the noodles, stir well, and bring to a second boil. Cook for 1 minute. Pour the noodles into a colander and rinse with cold running water. Drain thoroughly and set aside.

☙ Preheat a wok over medium-high heat. When the pan is hot, add the oil, salt, and garlic and stir-fry until lightly browned, about 1 minute. Add the chicken and stir-fry until the pieces turn opaque and are firm to the touch, about 2 minutes. Crack the eggs into the wok and, with the tip of a spatula, gently break up the yolks, but do not beat. Let them fry without stirring until set, about 1 minute. Add the shrimp and stir-fry until they turn bright orange-pink, about 2 minutes.

☙ Raise the heat to high and add the cabbage, fried bean curd, and noodles. Using tongs or 2 spatulas, toss quickly and gently like a salad to mix. Add the *sambal ulek*, ketchup or tomato sauce, and the soy sauces and toss to coat the noodles evenly with the sauce. Add the potato, bean sprouts, tomato, and green onions and stir-fry to mix. Taste and adjust the seasoning with the sweet soy sauce and light soy sauce. Transfer the noodles to a platter.

☙ Garnish with the cucumber, fried shallots, and lemon wedges. Serve immediately.

serves 2 as a main dish or 4 as a side dish

Malaysia

Nasi Kunyit

festive golden rice

Nasi kunyit *is glutinous rice steamed in coconut milk and colored gold with turmeric. In Malaysia, pandanus leaf is added to the rice. A Nonya from Penang would also add dried slices of* asam gelugor, *an orange, fluted tomato-like fruit that imparts a sour note. The rice is usually served molded into a cone and surrounded with curried meats, spicy salads,* sambals, *and shrimp chips.*

2½ cups (17½ oz/545 g) glutinous rice

1½ cups (12 fl oz/375 ml) water

1 cup (8 fl oz/250 ml) thick coconut milk (page 245)

1 lemongrass stalk, tender midsection only, cut in half crosswise and smashed

1 teaspoon ground turmeric

1 teaspoon salt

1 banana leaf (optional)

2 pandanus leaves (optional; page 248)

☙ Wash the rice thoroughly in several changes of cold water until the rinsing water runs clear. Drain, place in a bowl, add cold water to cover by 1 inch (2.5 cm), and let stand for a few hours or, preferably, overnight. Drain and set aside.

☙ In a saucepan over medium-high heat, combine the water, coconut milk, lemongrass, turmeric, and salt and bring to a boil, stirring occasionally. Add the rice and cook, stirring occasionally, until the rice absorbs most of the liquid, 3–5 minutes. Remove from the heat.

☙ Cut the banana leaf or a piece of aluminum foil to fit the bottom of a bamboo steamer or other steamer tray. Prick several holes all over the leaf or foil, adding a few extra holes in the center. With a wet wooden spoon, transfer the rice to the lined tray. Place the pandanus leaves, if using, on top.

☙ Bring water in a wok or steamer to a boil, top with the bamboo steamer or tray, cover, and steam until the rice is tender, about 20 minutes. Discard the pandanus leaves and lemongrass, transfer the rice to a platter, and shape it into a cone. Serve immediately.

serves 6–8

Indonesia

Serundeng

spicy grated coconut and peanut relish

Small side dishes and condiments are essential to the Indonesian table. The dainty portions of pounded sambals, *spiced coconut, pickled vegetables, and various sauces that flank the larger dishes add sparkle to simple preparations and round out the flavors of spicy plates.*

1 slice dried shrimp paste, ⅛ inch (3 mm) thick

1 cup (4 oz/125 g) unsweetened grated dried coconut

1 cup (5 oz/155 g) finely minced yellow onion

1 large clove garlic, pressed through a garlic press

1½ teaspoons finely minced fresh ginger

1 tablespoon vegetable oil

2 kaffir lime leaves, spines removed

1 teaspoon ground coriander

1 teaspoon ground cumin

1 teaspoon sugar

1 teapoon salt

1 tablespoon fresh lemon juice

1 cup (4 oz/125 g) unsalted roasted peanuts

☙ Wrap the shrimp paste in aluminum foil. Turn on a gas or electric burner to medium-high and place the foil packet on it. Heat, turning once or twice, until fragrant, about 3 minutes. Open the packet, and if the shrimp paste crumbles, it is ready. Transfer to a bowl and crush the paste with a fork. Add the coconut, onion, garlic, and ginger and mix well.

☙ Preheat a wok or large frying pan over medium-low heat and add the oil. When it is hot, add the coconut mixture and fry, stirring continuously, until light golden brown, about 5 minutes. Add the lime leaves, coriander, cumin, sugar, and salt and fry, stirring frequently over low heat, until the mixture is dry and crisp. This may take 10–15 minutes longer. Do not rush this step. Stir in the lemon juice and cook for 1 minute longer. Remove from the heat.

☙ Discard the lime leaves. Transfer the coconut mixture to a bowl and let cool. Mix in the peanuts and serve, or refrigerate for up to 1 week.

makes about 2 cups (8 oz/250 g)

Noodles

The world of Southeast Asian noodles can be dizzyingly complex, and a walk past the displays of fresh and dried noodles in an Asian market is guaranteed to both intrigue and confuse all but the most savvy Southeast Asian cooks.

Many noodles used in the region are made with rice flour. In Thailand, for example, the popular dish known as *pad thai* (page 135) calls for flat, narrow dried rice noodles, the size of linguine, while the equally familiar *mee krob* (page 162) uses thin, wiry dried rice vermicelli. So, too, does Philippine *pancit* (page 156), a noodle dish that traces its origin to Chinese chow mein. Traditionally, flat fresh rice noodles ¼ inch (6 mm) wide go into Vietnamese *pho* (page 70), while similar noodles about twice that width are known in Malaysia as *kway teow*, where they are often fried and tossed with pork, shrimp (prawns), squid, bean sprouts, chiles, and soy sauce. Finally, Nonya *laksa asam* (page 150), a thick, sour fish and noodle soup, uses rice noodles that look like a kind of white spaghetti.

Indian cooks in the region fancy the yellow Hokkien *mee*, a wheat-flour noodle from southern China, for making their famous multinational *mee goreng* (page 137), a dish that employs elements from Malaysian, Indonesian, and Chinese cooking. Thin dried cellophane noodles, also known as mung bean noodles, are added to soups in Thailand, Vietnam, Indonesia, and elsewhere in the region.

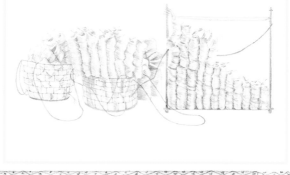

Hokkien Mee

hokkien braised yellow noodles and rice noodles

Many Singaporean Chinese are Hokkien immigrants from Xiamen (formerly Amoy), a small Chinese island just off the country's southern coast, and from Fujian, a province in southeast China. Their rustic cooking style is hearty and robust.

½-lb (250-g) piece fresh bacon, pork shoulder, or pork butt

3 cups (24 fl oz/750 ml) water

2-inch (5-cm) piece fresh ginger, bruised

2 cloves garlic, bruised

½ teaspoon salt

¼ lb (125 g) large shrimp (prawns)

½ lb (250 g) squid, cleaned (page 251)

NOODLES

¼ lb (125 g) dried rice vermicelli, soaked in warm water for 15 minutes

½ lb (250 g) fresh Hokkien yellow noodles or Chinese egg noodles

3 tablespoons pork lard or vegetable oil

½ teaspoon salt

5 cloves garlic, chopped

1 yellow onion, thinly sliced vertically

2 eggs

1 tablespoon light soy sauce

2 tablespoons fish sauce

¼ teaspoon sugar

large pinch of ground white pepper

¼ lb (125 g) bean sprouts

12 fresh garlic chives, cut into 3-inch (7.5-cm) lengths

ACCOMPANIMENTS

sambal blacan *(see sidebar, page 180)*

2 limes, cut into wedges

✾ To make the stock, in a saucepan, combine the bacon or pork, water, ginger, garlic, and salt. Bring to a boil, reduce the heat to medium, and boil gently until the meat is cooked through, about 40 minutes.

♛ Using tongs, transfer the bacon or pork to a cutting board; let cool. Return the stock to a boil. Drop in the shrimp and cook until they turn bright orange-pink, about 2 minutes. Scoop out the shrimp with the skimmer, place in a bowl, and let cool until they can be handled. Cut the squid bodies crosswise into rings ¼ inch (6 mm) wide. Drop the squid rings and whole tentacles into the stock. As soon as they turn opaque, after about 30 seconds, scoop them out and set aside. Peel and devein the shrimp and return the shells to the stock. Set the shrimp aside. Reduce the stock over high heat to about 1 cup (8 fl oz/ 250 ml). Strain the stock through a fine-mesh sieve and discard the shells. Cover and keep hot. Thinly slice the bacon or pork and set aside.

♛ To ready the noodles, drain the rice vermicelli. If using Hokkien noodles, put them into a bowl, add hot water to cover, and let stand for 1 minute. Drain. If using fresh Chinese noodles, bring a large saucepan three-fourths full of water to a boil. Add the noodles, stir well, and bring to a second boil. Cook for 1 minute. Drain, rinse with cold running water, and drain again.

♛ Preheat a wok over medium–high heat. When the pan is hot, add the lard or oil, salt, and garlic and stir-fry until a light golden brown, about 30 seconds. Raise the heat to high, add the onion and bacon or pork, and stir-fry until the onion and meat begin to brown, about 2 minutes. Push the ingredients up the sides of the wok. Crack the eggs into the middle of the wok and break up the yolks with the tip of a spatula. Leave the eggs alone to cook without stirring until they begin to set, about 1 minute. Stir the eggs together with the onion and meat.

♛ Add the noodles and the rice vermicelli and, using extra-long chopsticks or tongs, toss the noodles to mix. With the wok still very hot, add about ½ cup (4 fl oz/125 ml) of the hot stock, the soy sauce, fish sauce, sugar, and white pepper. Toss and stir the noodles with the stock until it is fully absorbed, about 3 minutes. If the noodles are not fully cooked, add a little more stock, but only as much as the noodles will absorb without getting mushy. Add the bean sprouts and toss well. When the bean sprouts begin to wilt, add the shrimp, the squid, and the chives and toss until heated through, about 2 minutes.

♛ Transfer to warmed individual plates. Accompany with the *sambal* and lime wedges.

serves 3 or 4

Singapore

Char Kway Teow

fried rice noodles with seafood

It is best to cook only a relatively small amount of kway teow at a time, no more than enough for three or four servings. The noodles, which are flat and about ½ inch (12 mm) wide, are too difficult to stir-fry in larger quantities. To serve more guests, do as the street vendors do and make a second batch. You will need a well-seasoned wok or one with a nonstick surface, as the fresh noodles tend to stick to the pan.

Ready-cooked fish cakes are available fried, steamed, or baked in a variety of shapes, including patties, slabs, and balls. They come from many ethnic styles— Chinese (Chao Zhou, Hakka), Japanese, Vietnamese, Korean—and have seasoning and textural differences. The fish cake best suited for this recipe is the fried or steamed dense slab type, which is stocked in the refrigerated section of Asian food markets.

1 Chinese sausage

1 lb (500 g) fresh flat rice noodles

½ lb (250 g) pencil-thin Chinese broccoli

2–4 tablespoons peanut oil or vegetable oil

1 teaspoon salt

1 tablespoon minced garlic

1 tablespoon sambal ulek *or Sriracha sauce (page 251)*

¼ lb (125 g) boneless, skinless chicken breast, cut crosswise into slices ¼ inch (6 mm) thick

¼ lb (125 g) shrimp (prawns), peeled and deveined

2 oz (60 g) prepared fried or steamed fish cake, thinly sliced (see note)

6 oz (185 g) bean sprouts

1 tablespoon fish sauce or light soy sauce

2 tablespoons dark soy sauce or sweet soy sauce

½ teaspoon sugar

1 egg

¼ cup (⅓ oz/10 g) cut-up garlic chives or green (spring) onion tops (1-inch/2.5-cm lengths)

☙ Put the sausage on a plate in a bamboo steamer or steamer tray, place over boiling water, cover, and steam until the sausage is plump, about 5 minutes. Remove the sausage, let cool, then cut on the diagonal into thin slices. If the noodles have been refrigerated or are hard, put them on the plate and steam

for 5 minutes, then turn them over and steam for 3 minutes longer. Separate the strands by gently pulling them apart.

☙ Cut the broccoli stalks, including the leaves and flowers, into 1½-inch (4-cm) lengths. If they are thicker than a pencil, cut them in half lengthwise. Bring a saucepan three-fourths full of water to a boil, add the broccoli, and blanch for 2 minutes. Drain and set aside.

☙ Preheat a wok over medium–high heat. When the wok is hot, add 2 tablespoons of the oil, the salt, and the garlic and stir-fry until the garlic is light golden brown, about 2 minutes. Raise the heat to high and add the *sambal ulek* or Sriracha sauce. Stir for a few seconds, then add the following ingredients, tossing and stirring between each addition: chicken, shrimp, broccoli, fish cake, and sausage. Continue tossing and stirring until the chicken and shrimp are cooked, about 2 minutes.

☙ Push the ingredients up the sides of the wok and add oil if needed to measure about 1 tablespoon. Add the noodles and bean sprouts to the center of the wok and sprinkle with the fish sauce or light soy sauce, dark or sweet soy sauce, and sugar. Using tongs or 2 spatulas, toss quickly and gently to mix the noodles with the meats. Taste and adjust the seasoning with fish sauce, soy sauce, and sugar.

☙ Push the ingredients up the sides of the wok again and add a teaspoon of oil to the pan. Crack the egg into the center and, using the tip of a spatula, gently break up the egg yolk, but do not beat. Fry without stirring until set, about 30 seconds. Add the garlic chives or green onion tops and toss together with the egg and noodles just enough to mix. There should be specks of egg scattered throughout the noodles. Transfer to a serving platter and serve.

serves 2

Rice noodles—flat, round, long, stubby, thick, thin— are ubiquitous in Southeast Asia, whether in soup, braised, stir-fried, or deep-fried.

Singapore

Thosai

indian rice-flour bread

Traditionally, these breads (sometimes spelled dosai*) are enormous, often measuring eighteen inches (45 cm) across, but this recipe is manageable for the home cook. Serve the breads with* aloo *(page 41),* dal *(page 38), or* opor ayam *(page 218).*

½ cup (3½ oz/105 g) urad dal, *well rinsed*

1¼ cups (9 oz/280 g) basmati rice or other long-grain white rice

about 2 cups (16 fl oz/500 ml) warm water

2 teaspoons salt

½ cup (4 fl oz/125 ml) ghee or vegetable oil

☙ Place the dal and rice in separate bowls, add water to cover by 2 inches (5 cm), and soak for 6 hours. Drain the dal and place in a blender. Process, slowly adding ¾ cup (6 fl oz/180 ml) of the warm water, a few tablespoons at a time. Blend until smooth and frothy, about 5 minutes. Transfer to a bowl.

☙ Drain the rice and process, slowly adding about ¾ cup (6 fl oz/180 ml) of the warm water, a few tablespoons at a time. Blend until a pastelike batter forms, 3–4 minutes. Add the rice to the dal, stir to mix, and cover with a kitchen towel. Set in a warm spot for 20–24 hours. When the mixture has a mild fermented scent and is covered with tiny bubbles, it is ready. Add the salt and dilute with just enough warm water (¾–1 cup/6–8 fl oz/180–250 ml) to form the consistency of a light cake batter.

☙ Preheat a 10-inch (25-cm) nonstick frying pan over medium heat. Add a very thin film of ghee or oil to the pan. Wipe off the excess. Pour in about ⅓ cup (3 fl oz/80 ml) of the batter and use the bottom of a ladle to spread it in a circular motion over the bottom of the pan. Dribble some ghee or oil over the surface, cover, and cook until the underside is covered with golden brown specks and the top is dry, about 2 minutes. Using a thin metal spatula, turn the bread over carefully and cook, uncovered, until crisp and browned, about 1 minute longer. Fold in half, transfer to a plate, and keep warm. Repeat with the remaining batter. Serve warm.

makes about 12 breads

Thailand

Khao Soi

chiang mai curry soup noodles

Khao soi is a specialty of the northern Thailand town of Chiang Mai, which lies close to the border with Myanmar (Burma). It is a rich and highly seasoned preparation that reflects the influence of its neighbor. Made with a thin egg noodle called ba mee, *the dish calls for Madras curry powder, a popular Burmese ingredient, along with Thai red curry paste. Although* khao soi *has plenty of flavor and texture of its own, the toppings and accompaniments are traditional and are important to the enjoyment of the dish.*

peanut oil for frying, plus 2 tablespoons

1⅛ lb (560 g) fresh thin Chinese egg noodles

3 cloves garlic, minced

2 tablespoons red curry paste (page 246)

2 teaspoons Madras curry powder

½ teaspoon ground turmeric

½ cup (4 fl oz/125 ml) coconut cream (page 245)

¾ lb (375 g) boneless, skinless chicken thighs, cut into ¼-inch (6-mm) chunks

4 cups (32 fl oz/1 l) chicken stock

3 cups (24 fl oz/750 ml) coconut milk (page 245)

2 tablespoons fish sauce, or to taste

1 teaspoon palm sugar or brown sugar

2 tablespoons fresh lemon juice

3 tablespoons chopped pickled Chinese cabbage, rinsed with cold water and drained

½ cup (1½ oz/45 g) chopped green (spring) onion, including 1 inch (2.5 cm) of the tender green tops

½ English (hothouse) cucumber, peeled and thinly sliced

fried shallots (see sidebar, page 79)

2 lemons, cut into wedges

☙ Pour the peanut oil to a depth of 2 inches (5 cm) in a saucepan and heat the oil to 375°F (190°C) on a deep-frying thermometer. Separate out 2 oz (60 g) of the noodles (about a handful) and drop them into the hot oil. Fry until golden brown, about 1 minute. Using a wire skimmer, transfer to paper towels to drain. Set aside.

☙ Bring a large saucepan three-fourths full of water to a boil. Drop the remaining 1 lb (500 g) noodles into the water, stir well, and bring to a second boil. Cook for 1 minute. Pour the noodles into a colander and rinse with cold running water until cool. Drain thoroughly and set aside.

☙ In a large saucepan over medium heat, heat the 2 tablespoons peanut oil. Add the garlic and stir-fry until light golden brown, about 2 minutes. Add the red curry paste, curry powder, and turmeric and fry, stirring, until the oil is fragrant and has a rich yellow hue, about 2 minutes. Add the coconut cream, raise the heat to medium-high, and cook, stirring frequently, until the cream boils gently and oil beads appear on the surface, 5–8 minutes. Add the chicken and stir to coat the pieces with the paste. Raise the heat to high, add the chicken stock, the coconut milk, the fish sauce, and the palm sugar or brown sugar, and bring to a boil. Reduce the heat to medium-low and simmer, uncovered, until fragrant and the flavors are blended, about 10 minutes. Stir in the lemon juice and remove from the heat.

☙ To serve, scald 6 bowls with hot water and divide the boiled noodles evenly among them. Ladle the soup over the noodles. Scatter an equal amount of pickled cabbage, green onion, cucumber slices, fried shallots, and fried noodles over each serving. Put a lemon wedge on the edge of each bowl. Serve immediately. Each diner squeezes lemon juice over his or her serving.

serves 6

Singapore

Roti Prata

griddled indian layered bread

Years of practice are necessary to master the technique for making roti *(see sidebar at right), so I have simplified the method for the home cook.*

3½ cups (17½ oz/545 g) bread (hard-wheat) flour

1 teaspoon salt

5 tablespoons (2½ oz/75 ml) plus about ½ cup (4 fl oz/125 ml) ghee

1¼–1½ cups (10–12 fl oz/310–375 ml) milk, heated to lukewarm

☙ In a bowl, sift together the flour and salt. Stir in the 5 tablespoons (2½ fl oz/75 ml) ghee until crumbly. Slowly stir in enough of the milk to form a soft, spongy, slightly sticky dough. Turn out onto a lightly floured surface and knead, dusting with flour to prevent sticking, until a smooth ball forms, about 10 minutes. Transfer to a bowl, cover with a towel, and let rest in a warm spot for 30 minutes.

☙ Turn the dough out onto a work surface and cut into 8 equal pieces. Shape each piece into a ball, brush with some of the remaining ghee, and set the balls, not touching, on a tray. Cover with a damp kitchen towel and let the dough rest for 4 hours.

☙ Oil a work surface, preferably a marble slab, with some of the ghee, then oil your palms. Flatten 1 ball of dough and stretch it slowly into a paper-thin round 9–12 inches (23–30 cm) in diameter. Fold the edges into the middle, forming a 4-inch (10-cm) envelope shape. Wrap in plastic wrap. Repeat with the remaining balls. Set aside for 1 hour.

☙ Again lightly oil the work surface with ghee. Unwrap 1 piece of dough and place it on the prepared surface. Flatten out the dough into a 6-inch (15-cm) round with oiled hands or rolling pin.

☙ Preheat a cast-iron griddle or frying pan over medium heat. To test the temperature, sprinkle with a little water. If it forms beads that dance and then disappear, the pan is ready. Add about 1 tablespoon ghee, and, when it is hot, add a dough round. Fry, turning once, until golden and crisp on both sides, about 4 minutes total. The bottom should be puffy and speckled. Transfer to paper towels to drain. Fry the remaining rounds and serve.

makes 8 breads

The Roti Master

At Indian coffeeshops in Singapore and Malaysia, the *roti* cook turns out one of the cheapest, tastiest snacks in all of Southeast Asia. *Roti* is a flat, plate-sized, layered Indian bread that is torn into pieces and dipped into a simple curry sauce for breakfast or lunch and eaten under or alongside chicken, fish, or lamb curry for dinner.

The *roti* cook is the consummate performer, a true culinary artist who loves showing off his skill. He takes a small lump of dough, throws it into the air, slaps it against the counter, and whirls and rotates it until it is a paper-thin sheet eighteen inches to two feet (45–60 cm) across and without a single tear. He then quickly folds it, creating the distinctive layers, and cooks it on an oiled griddle. If before the folding he adds a bit of onion and an egg and sometimes minced lamb, he is making *murtabak* (page 80), a slightly more elaborate but still inexpensive snack.

There is no professional school for learning this art of *roti* making, only strong family ties. And I worry that the art may soon be lost, for each time I travel to Singapore and Malaysia, I find fewer *roti* makers at work.

Khao Pad Bai Kraprow

fried rice with thai basil

Fried rice originated in China as a way to use up leftover cooked rice. Wherever fried rice is prepared in Asia, local cooks add regional ingredients and seasonings. This means that Thai cooks mix in garlic, chile, and basil with delicious results. The versatility of this dish welcomes a variety of vegetables, while other seafood or meats can be substituted for the shrimp.

2 tablespoons vegetable oil

¼ teaspoon salt

2 cloves garlic, minced

2 small red Fresno or serrano chiles, seeded and chopped

¼ lb (125 g) shrimp (prawns), peeled and deveined

4 cups (1¼ lb/625 g) cold cooked long-grain white rice, crushed gently to break up any clumps

1 tablespoon light soy sauce

1 tablespoon fish sauce

¼ teaspoon sugar

2 green (spring) onions, including 1 inch (2.5 cm) of the tender green tops, chopped

½ cup (¾ oz/20 g) firmly packed fresh Thai basil

¼ cup (⅓ oz/10 g) coarsely chopped fresh coriander (cilantro)

❧ Preheat a wok or deep frying pan over medium-high heat. When the pan is hot, add the oil, salt, and garlic and stir-fry until the garlic is light golden brown, about 30 seconds. Add the chiles and shrimp and stir-fry until the shrimp begin to turn bright orange-pink, about 30 seconds.

❧ Add the rice, breaking up any remaining clumps, and stir-fry until heated through, about 2 minutes. Add the soy sauce, fish sauce, and sugar and stir-fry to combine thoroughly. Add the green onions and basil leaves and stir-fry just until the leaves begin to wilt, about 30 seconds. Transfer the rice to a serving plate and garnish with the chopped coriander. Serve immediately.

serves 4

Malaysia

Laksa Asam

rice noodles with
tamarind mackerel "gravy"

Laksa could be described as a soup, since you need a spoon to eat it. At the same time, it is so hearty and thick that local cooks refer to the liquid surrounding the noodles as "gravy." Local rake-gilled mackerel is used in Malaysia, although other mackerel varieties are good substitutes. Daun kesum, also known as laksa *leaves, are the dark green pungent foliage of the polygonum plant. Fresh ginger buds, known as* bungan siantan, *are the buds of a particular ginger variety. Their flavor is so unusual that no substitute is possible. Leave them out if they are not available.*

This tamarind-based laksa *is from Penang, a small island off the coast of Malaysia that is home to a mixed population of Malay, Chinese, and Indian descent. The thick black prawn paste, a favorite flavoring of the Hokkien Chinese who have long lived in the region, looks like molasses and is made from shrimp, salt, sugar, flour, and water. It is a distinguishing feature of Penang* laksa.

STOCK

1½ lb (750 g) whole mackerel, cut into thirds crosswise

6 cups (48 fl oz/1.5 l) water

GRAVY

6 candlenuts or blanched almonds, soaked in warm water for 10 minutes and drained

8 dried red chiles, cracked, seeded, soaked in warm water for 10 minutes, and drained

4 fresh red chiles

3 lemongrass stalks, tender midsection only, chopped

4 shallots, quartered

4 cloves garlic

½-inch (12-mm) piece fresh turmeric or 1 teaspoon ground turmeric

1 teaspoon dried shrimp paste

2 cups (16 fl oz/500 ml) tamarind water (see sidebar, page 114)

6 fresh polygonum sprigs (page 248)

1 tablespooon sugar

2 teaspoons salt

2 lb (1 kg) fresh laksa noodles or 1 lb (500 g) dried rice vermicelli, soaked in warm water for 15 minutes and drained

GARNISHES

1 English (hothouse) cucumber, sliced

¼ fresh pineapple, cut into strips 2 inches (5 cm) long by ⅛ inch (3 mm) thick

1 ginger bud, shredded (optional)

1 cup (1 oz/30 g) fresh mint leaves

6 fresh polygonum sprigs

2 limes, cut into wedges

black prawn paste (see note)

❦ To make the stock, in a saucepan, combine the fish and water and bring to a boil. Reduce the heat immediately and cook at a gentle boil until the fish is opaque throughout, about 15 minutes. Using a slotted utensil, transfer the fish to a plate and let cool. Pour the stock through a fine-mesh sieve and reserve. When the fish is cool, tear it into fine flakes, discarding the bones and skin.

❦ To make the gravy, combine the drained candlenuts or almonds and drained chiles in a blender. Add the fresh chiles, lemongrass, shallots, garlic, turmeric, and dried shrimp paste and blend until a smooth paste forms. Pour the blended mixture into a large saucepan and add 1 cup (8 fl oz/250 ml) of the reserved fish stock. Place over high heat, bring to a gentle boil and cook, stirring frequently, until the mixture starts to break up, about 5 minutes. Add the tamarind water, the 6 polygonum sprigs, and 2 cups (16 fl oz/500 ml) of the reserved fish stock. Adjust the heat and cook at a gentle boil for 15 minutes. Remove the polygonum sprigs and discard. Add the flaked fish, sugar, and salt. The gravy should be the consistency of light (single) cream. If it is too thick, add the remaining fish stock.

❦ To serve, bring a saucepan three-fourths full of water to a boil. Add the noodles and stir them to loosen and heat through, about 5 minutes for the *laksa* noodles and 3 minutes for the rice vermicelli. Meanwhile, scald 6 deep soup bowls, then drain the noodles and divide them among the bowls. Garnish each bowl with some cucumber slices, pineapple strips, ginger bud shreds (if using,) and mint leaves, and top with a polygonum sprig. Ladle the gravy over the noodles and serve immediately with the lime wedges and dipping saucers of prawn paste on the side.

serves 6

The Cultivation of Rice

Rice is the single most important foodstuff in the daily diet of Southeast Asians, and, not surprisingly, every country in the region cultivates this indispensable grain. The visually striking, seemingly endless paddies of the Mekong River delta in Vietnam and the Chao Phraya basin of Thailand are well known beyond their national borders as prime real estate for rice growing—land so productive that rice, except in years of bad weather, is an important export for both countries.

But for me, rice paddies and fields, no matter what their size, are an impressive sight. On Bali, the paddies rise in staircases carved into the sides of mountains. Shielded from the sun by broad conical straw hats, wiry farmers, their backs slightly bent from years of planting and harvesting rice, make their way along the terraces, checking the progress of the deep jade shoots.

In contrast, at the southern end of the mighty Irrawaddy River, the lifeblood of Myanmar (Burma), a great flat delta spreads out in every direction. Until the mid-nineteenth century, this land was covered with jungle, but the relative predictability of the monsoon rains made it ideal rice-growing country, and by the mid-twentieth century Myanmar was the world's largest rice exporter. That position was lost in the early 1960s, but the delta's patchwork of paddies remains a testament to the centrality of rice in the nation's diet.

One of the most photographed of all rice-growing regions is Banawe, in the northern reaches of the Philippine island of Luzon. The narrow rice terraces climb a series of rugged mountains over an area of some one hundred square miles (259 sq km), causing even the most cynical observer to be swept away by their beauty.

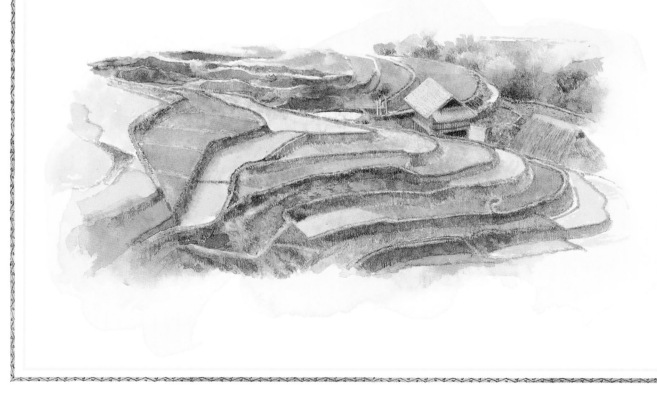

Thailand

Khao Phat Supparot

pineapple fried jasmine rice

Although any long-grain white rice can be used for Thai fried rice, jasmine rice is considered the best. Thais love the scent of a particular variety of jasmine flower called mali. *While so-called jasmine rice does not carry the true scent of that bloom, or of any fragrant flower, it does release a seductive perfume. It is because of the kernels' heady fragrance that the rice has been awarded the highest compliment by being given the name of the much-admired flower. In Thailand, it is also labeled fragrant rice or scented rice.*

Crab paste in soybean sauce, which is sold in jars in Thai or Southeast Asian markets, adds a rich, savory essence to the dish.

1 pineapple

2 tablespoons vegetable oil

½ teaspoon salt

3 cloves garlic, coarsely chopped

¼ lb (125 g) shrimp (prawns), peeled and deveined

1 boneless, skinless chicken breast half, cut into ¼-inch (6-mm) dice

2 eggs

1½ tablespoons crab paste in soybean sauce (see note)

2 tablespoons tomato ketchup

3 green (spring) onions, including 1 inch (2.5 cm) of the tender green tops, thinly sliced

4 cups (1¼ lb/625 g) cold cooked long-grain jasmine rice, crushed gently to break up any clumps

2 tablespoons fish sauce

fresh coriander (cilantro) leaves

1 tablespoon fried shallots (see sidebar, page 79)

☙ Preheat an oven to 400°F (200°C).

☙ Cut the pineapple in half lengthwise. Hollow out each half, leaving the shells intact and setting the pineapple pulp aside. Put the shells hollow side up on a baking sheet and place in the oven for 10 minutes while you stir-fry the rice. Remove from the oven when the excess moisture has dried out and set the shells aside.

☙ Meanwhile, coarsely chop enough of the reserved pineapple pulp to measure 1 cup (6 oz/185 g). Set aside. Reserve the remaining pulp for another use.

☙ Preheat a wok or deep frying pan over medium-high heat. When the pan is hot, add the oil, salt, and garlic and stir-fry until the garlic is a light golden brown, about 30 seconds. Raise the heat to high, add the shrimp and chicken, and stir-fry until the shrimp turn bright orange-pink and the chicken is cooked through, about 2 minutes.

☙ Crack the eggs into the pan over the shrimp and chicken and break up the yolks with the tip of a spatula. Leave the eggs alone to cook without stirring until set, about 30 seconds. When the whites turn opaque, add the crab paste and ketchup, stir once or twice, then toss in the green onions, cooked rice, and fish sauce. Break up any remaining clumps of rice and stir-fry to mix and evenly season the rice and to heat it through, about 2 minutes. Add the reserved chopped pineapple pulp and toss and stir to heat through, about 1 minute.

☙ Transfer the rice mixture to the pineapple shells, heaping it attractively. Garnish with coriander leaves and fried shallots. Serve immediately.

serves 4

Vietnam

Bun Bo

lemongrass beef and onions
over rice vermicelli

*This noodle salad is a signature dish of Vietnam.
As is the case with many Vietnamese dishes, once the
elements have been assembled, each diner mixes the
dish at the table to his or her liking.*

¾ lb (375 g) dried rice vermicelli, soaked in
warm water for 15 minutes

1 lb (500 g) beef chuck or flank, thinly sliced
against the grain

3 lemongrass stalks, tender midsection only,
finely minced

5 cloves garlic, chopped

1½ tablespoons fish sauce

½ teaspoon sugar

ground pepper to taste

SALAD

4 cups (8 oz/250 g) finely shredded red-
or green-leaf lettuce or romaine (cos) lettuce

½ English (hothouse) cucumber, peeled and
finely julienned

2 cups (4 oz/125 g) bean sprouts

1 carrot, peeled and finely grated

½ cup (¾ oz/20 g) coarsely chopped fresh
Thai basil

½ cup (¾ oz/20 g) finely shredded fresh
mint leaves

3 tablespoons vegetable oil, or as needed

1 large red (Spanish) onion, very thinly sliced

½ cup (3 oz/90 g) chopped unsalted roasted
peanuts

fried shallots (see sidebar, page 79)

nuoc cham *dipping sauce (page 249)*

❦ Bring a large saucepan three-fourths full of water
to a boil. Drain the noodles, add to the boiling water,
stir well, and boil until tender, 2–3 minutes. Pour into
a colander, rinse thoroughly with cold running
water, and drain again. Set aside.

❦ In a bowl, combine the beef, lemongrass, half of
the garlic, the fish sauce, sugar and pepper. Mix well,
cover, and set aside.

❦ To make the salad, in a large bowl, toss together
the lettuce, cucumber, bean sprouts, carrot, basil, and
mint. Divide the mixture evenly among 4 shallow
bowls. Top each salad with an equal amount of the
noodles. Set aside.

❦ Preheat a wok or deep frying pan over medium-
high heat. When the pan is hot, add the 3 tablespoons
oil and the remaining garlic and stir-fry until light
golden brown, about 30 seconds. Add the onion and
stir-fry until the layers separate, about 30 seconds
longer. Push the onion and garlic up the sides of the
pan. Add additional oil if the pan is dry. When the oil
is hot, add a batch of the beef mixture and spread it
over the bottom of the pan. Cook without stirring
until the beef is nicely seared on the bottom, about
1 minute. Turn over and sear the second side, about
1 minute longer. Transfer the beef and onion to a
plate. Fry the remaining beef mixture in batches.

❦ When all of the beef is seared, return it to the wok
and toss for a few seconds to reheat. Spoon one-
fourth of the beef-onion mixture over each salad.
Garnish with the peanuts and fried shallots. Pour the
dipping sauce into individual bowls.

❦ To eat, each diner spoons the dipping sauce over
his or her portion to taste, then, with chopsticks,
tosses together the noodles, salad, and topping.

serves 4

*Rice, fish, pineapples, and
bananas are farmed
extensively in the Mekong
Delta, where an ancient
system of canals is still
used to control the water.*

Philippines
Pancit Bijon Guisado

rice noodles with mixed meats and vegetables

On every festive occasion, my Filipino neighbors bring over a platter of pancit bijon. It has all the earmarks of a typical Chinese noodle dish, and indeed the Chinese who settled in the Philippines introduced the now-familiar preparation. Yet there is also a distinctive taste that separates it from its Middle Kingdom origins. I love its robust seasonings, but not until I spent time in the Philippines did I realize how much fish sauce defines this dish. It imparts a pleasantly salty, fishy flavor that makes the noodles unmistakably Southeast Asian. My other discovery about pancit and about Filipino cooking in general is the lavish use of garlic, which always draws me like a magnet.

½ lb (250 g) dried rice vermicelli, soaked in warm water for 15 minutes

2 tablespoons vegetable oil

½ teaspoon salt

2 tablespoons minced garlic

1 yellow onion, thinly sliced

2 celery stalks, thinly sliced on the diagonal

6 oz (185 g) boneless, skinless chicken breast, thinly sliced

2 Chinese sausages, thinly sliced

1 carrot, peeled and julienned

1 small red bell pepper (capsicum), seeded and sliced into long, narrow strips

1 cup (3 oz/90 g) finely shredded cabbage

6 oz (185 g) large shrimp (prawns), peeled and deveined

2 tablespoons fish sauce

1 tablespoon soy sauce

½ cup (4 fl oz/125 ml) chicken stock

2 green (spring) onions, including 1 inch (2.5 cm) of the tender green tops, chopped

fresh coriander (cilantro) leaves

1 lemon, cut into wedges

♨ Drain the noodles and set aside.

♨ Preheat a wok over medium-high heat. When the pan is hot, add the vegetable oil, salt, and garlic and stir-fry until the garlic is light golden brown, about 1 minute. Add the yellow onion and celery and stir-fry until the vegetables soften and the onion is translucent, about 3 minutes. Add the chicken and Chinese sausages and stir-fry until the chicken begins to turn opaque, about 2 minutes longer. Add the carrot, bell pepper, and cabbage and stir-fry for 1 minute longer. Toss in the shrimp and stir-fry until they turn bright orange-pink, 1–2 minutes. Sprinkle in the fish sauce and soy sauce and stir and toss to mix well. Add the stock and again toss to mix.

♨ Add the drained noodles and, using tongs or 2 spatulas, toss with the vegetables until thoroughly mixed and the stock has been completely absorbed by the noodles, 3–5 minutes. Taste and adjust the seasoning with fish sauce and soy sauce.

♨ Transfer the noodle mixture to a large platter and top with the green onions and coriander leaves. Garnish with the lemon wedges. Each diner adds a squeeze of lemon juice to his or her serving.

serves 6

Myanmar (Burma)

Ohn Htamin

rice cooked in coconut milk with fried shallots

Like most Asian cooks, the Burmese always rinse rice in cold water before cooking it. Washing removes the starches that cling to the grains and would make them unpleasantly sticky. Although this rice dish may seem simple, cooking the rice in coconut milk makes it addictively delicious. The generous sprinkling of fried shallots, a typical garnish in Southeast Asia, makes it even better. Serve as an accompaniment to Burmese curries and other dishes.

2½ cups (17½ oz / 545 g) long-grain white rice

3 cups (24 fl oz / 750 ml) thin coconut milk (page 245)

½ teaspoon salt

¼ teaspoon sugar

2 tablespoons fried shallots (see sidebar, page 79)

꙰ Wash the rice thoroughly with several changes of cold water until the rinsing water runs clear. Drain.

꙰ Select a heavy saucepan in which the rice takes up about one-third of the capacity but not more than half of the capacity. Place the rice in the pan and add the coconut milk, salt, sugar, and enough water to reach 1 inch (2.5 cm) above the surface of the rice. Bring the rice to a boil over high heat. Stir a few times to mix and to prevent the rice from the sticking to the pan bottom. Continue boiling until most of the liquid has reduced, leaving little craters on the surface of the rice. Cover tightly, reduce the heat to very low, and cook until tender, about 20 minutes.

꙰ Remove the pan from the heat and let stand, covered and undisturbed, for 10 minutes. With a wet wooden rice paddle or spoon, fluff up the rice. Transfer to a platter. Scatter the fried shallots over the top and serve immediately.

serves 6

Vietnam

Bun Rieu

crabmeat noodle soup with tomato, bean sprouts, and mint

*The flavors of this noodle soup are light, tomatoey,
and filled with reminders of home cooking. In
Vietnam, cooks arduously prepare the crab dumplings
by pulverizing whole mud crabs—shell, meat, and
all—in a mortar and then mixing the result with
water and straining it to extract the crab stock.
Vietnamese-born chef Dennis Wong, of San Francisco's
Le Soleil restaurant, has simplified the method,
making it perfect for the home cook who has neither
the mud crabs nor the time. Shredded banana blossoms
are the typical topping, but here Wong uses easier-
to-find cabbage or lettuce. He also suggests finely
shredded stems of water spinach as a topping.*

*Crab paste with soybean oil is a prepared condiment
made in Thailand and sold in jars in Asian stores.
Vietnamese fresh chile paste, called* tuong ot tuoi *and
packed in jars, is fiery hot, so warn your guests.*

*1 lb (500 g) dried rice vermicelli, soaked in warm
water for 15 minutes*

*⅔ cup (2½ oz/75 g) dried shrimp, soaked in
warm water for 30 minutes*

*½ lb (250 g) fresh-cooked lump crabmeat, picked
over for shell fragments*

3 eggs, lightly beaten

*3 tablespoons crab paste with soybean oil
(see note)*

1 teaspoon sugar

¼ teaspoon salt

2 tablespoons vegetable oil

*6 green (spring) onions, white part only, cut into
1-inch (2.5-cm) lengths*

4 tomatoes, cut into wedges

3 tablespoons tomato paste

8 cups (64 fl oz/2 l) chicken stock

2 tablespoons fish sauce

ACCOMPANIMENTS

3 cups (6 oz / 185 g) finely shredded romaine (cos) or red-leaf lettuce or (9 oz / 280 g) finely shredded cabbage

3 cups (6 oz / 185 g) bean sprouts

1 cup (1 oz / 30 g) fresh coriander (cilantro) leaves

1 cup (1 oz / 30 g) fresh mint leaves

2 green (spring) onions, white parts cut into 2-inch (5-cm) lengths and finely julienned, and 1 inch (2.5 cm) of the tender green tops chopped

6 teaspoons Vietnamese fresh chile paste (see note), sambal ulek, or Sriracha sauce (page 251)

6 teaspoons shrimp sauce (page 250)

2 lemons, cut into wedges

❧ Bring a large saucepan three-fourths full of water to a boil. Drain the noodles, add them to the boiling water, and boil until tender with still a little bite, about 1 minute. Pour into a colander, rinse thoroughly with cold water, and drain again. Set aside.

❧ Drain the dried shrimp, place in a blender, and process to a fine consistency. Transfer the ground shrimp to a large bowl and add the crabmeat, eggs, crab paste with soybean oil, sugar, and salt. Set aside.

❧ In a saucepan over medium-high heat, warm the vegetable oil. When the oil is hot, add the green onions and stir-fry until the oil becomes fragrant, about 10 seconds. Add the tomatoes and stir-fry for 15 seconds. Then add the tomato paste, chicken stock, and fish sauce and bring to a boil. Spoon the crabmeat mixture in small batches, a few seconds apart, into the stock until all of it has been added. Poach the crabmeat mixture until it is slightly firm and floats to the surface, 2–3 minutes. Stir to break up any clumps of crabmeat. Taste and adjust the seasonings with fish sauce, sugar, and salt.

❧ Scald 6 deep soup bowls. Divide the noodles evenly among the bowls, then ladle the hot stock and crabmeat over the noodles, again dividing evenly. Scatter an equal amount of shredded lettuce or cabbage, bean sprouts, coriander and mint leaves, and green onions over the noodles. Divide the chile paste or sauce and shrimp sauce evenly among 6 individual dipping saucers and set out with the lemon wedges. To eat, each diner mixes the sauces with the soup and adds a squeeze of lemon juice.

serves 6

A Chile Lexicon

When the chile arrived in Southeast Asia, introduced by the Portuguese in the sixteenth century, it revolutionized cooking.

One of the most common chiles found in the region is the Dutch Red. The size and shape of a slender finger, it appears in Asian markets in both its green and ripened red stages. Fresnos, serranos, or jalapeños are good substitutes, with the Fresno and jalapeño gentler on the palate.

Several popular dried red chiles of varying lengths and girths are used. They are typically sold packed into plastic bags in Asian markets. All of them deliver a serious jolt. They are cracked open and shaken to release the seeds, then soaked in warm water to soften before pounding in a mortar with other spices and seasonings. Dried red chiles give Thai red curry paste its distinctive color and pungent flavor.

For sheer hotness, tiny fresh chiles, called Thai, bird's eye, or bird chiles *(prik khee nu)*, are popular. In Thailand, these fiery capsules are included on relish plates and nibbled during the meal. When sampling, keep in mind the chile rule of thumb: the smaller the chile, the hotter the taste. The same holds true for girth: the slender ones tend to be sizzlers.

Indonesia

Nasi Goreng

javanese fried rice

Topping fried rice with a crisp fried egg is a Javanese tradition—an embellishment I cannot resist. Indonesian cooks crack the eggs into sizzling hot oil, which crisps and browns the whites, creating golden, lacy edges. A meal in itself in Asia, fried rice is served throughout the day, for breakfast, lunch, or a snack.

3 large shallots, quartered lengthwise

3 cloves garlic, quartered lengthwise

2 large fresh red chiles, seeded and chopped

½ teaspoon salt

3 tablespoons vegetable oil

1 boneless, skinless chicken breast half, cut into ¼-inch (6-mm) dice

¼ lb (125 g) large shrimp (prawns), peeled, deveined, and patted dry

4 cups (1¼ lb/625 g) cold cooked long-grain white rice, crushed gently to break up clumps

2 tablespoons sweet soy sauce

1½ teaspoons light soy sauce

large pinch of ground white pepper

2 cups (4 oz/125 g) shredded cabbage

¼ lb (125 g) green beans, trimmed and cut into 1-inch (2.5-cm) lengths, blanched in boiling water for 1 minute, and drained

¼ lb (125 g) bean sprouts

2 green (spring) onions, including 1 inch (2.5 cm) of the tender green tops, chopped

ACCOMPANIMENTS

vegetable oil for frying

4 eggs

salt and ground black pepper to taste

1 large tomato, thinly sliced

½ English (hothouse) cucumber, peeled and thinly sliced

4 fried shrimp chips (page 250)

fresh coriander (cilantro) leaves

fried shallots (see sidebar, page 79)

❀ In a blender, combine the shallots, garlic, chiles, and salt and blend until a smooth purée forms. If necessary, add a little water to facilitate the blending.

❀ Preheat a wok or deep frying pan over medium-high heat. When the pan is hot, add 2 tablespoons of the vegetable oil and swirl to coat the pan. When the oil is hot, add the chicken and shrimp. Stir-fry until the chicken is opaque and the shrimp turn bright orange-pink, about 2 minutes. Transfer to a plate.

❀ Return the pan to medium heat and add the remaining 1 tablespoon oil. Add the shallot-garlic purée and cook, stirring frequently, until the purée becomes a thick, dry paste, about 5 minutes. Raise the heat to high and add the rice, breaking up any remaining clumps. Toss and stir to coat the rice evenly with the paste. Add the sweet and light soy sauces and white pepper and again toss to evenly coat the rice. Add the cabbage, green beans, bean sprouts, and green onions and stir-fry until the vegetables are tender but still crisp, about 5 minutes.

❀ Return the reserved chicken-shrimp mixture to the pan and toss to mix. Remove the pan from the heat and cover loosely to keep warm.

❀ To prepare the accompaniments, pour enough vegetable oil into a wok or frying pan to form a generous film on the bottom and place over high heat. When the oil is hot, carefully crack 1 egg into the pan. Season with salt and black pepper. When the edges turn lacy and golden brown, the egg is done; this should take 1–2 minutes. Using a slotted spoon or spatula, transfer the egg to paper towels to drain. Repeat with the remaining 3 eggs.

❀ To serve, distribute the warm fried rice evenly among individual serving plates. Arrange a few tomato slices and cucumber slices along one side of each serving, then slip the edge of a shrimp chip under the rice on the opposite side. Scatter some fresh coriander leaves and fried shallots on the top. Place 1 fried egg, yolk side up, in the center of each serving, and serve immediately.

serves 4

Rice farmers who sow their seeds in the rich volcanic soil of tropical Java harvest two, and sometimes three, crops a year.

The Wok

The wok, known under various local names, is used from one end of Asia to the other. Invented in China thousands of years ago, it was designed to rest over a primitive wood fire. Made of thin tempered iron, it needed to absorb heat efficiently so that foods would cook quickly because of limited fuel.

Today, this practical pan is the most popular cooking utensil in Southeast Asian kitchens. I've seen it in an Indonesian village, cradled in the well of a wood-burning stove not unlike those of ancient China. Itinerant street hawkers fix them to the gas burner on their mobile kitchen carts, and waterborne cooks on Thailand's canals balance them in their boats. The wok is the primary cooking utensil both in the street stalls of Vietnam and in high-rise luxury apartments in Singapore.

Over the centuries, while the cooking of Southeast Asia has evolved, the basic design of the wok has remained the same, and its role in the kitchen has continued to be as varied as the profile of the pan itself is singular. It is excellent for stir-frying, of course, but it is also ideal for deep-frying split-pea fritters in Mandalay, steaming dumplings in Singapore, frying *rempahs* in Kuala Lumpur, simmering a *gaeng* in Chiang Mai, frying spring rolls in Ho Chi Minh City, and pan-frying fish in Vientiane.

Thailand

Mee Krob

crisp fried noodles with sweet-sour sauce

Mee krob is typically made for special occasions. Although it is somewhat elaborate, it is served at room temperature, which allows you to do all the preparations in advance. The resulting flavor is rich and sweet, so the noodles are best served as a side dish to accompany curries, rather than as the centerpiece of a meal.

½ lb (250 g) dried rice vermicelli

vegetable oil for deep-frying

¼ lb (125 g) boneless pork loin chop, cut into thin, narrow strips

¼ lb (125 g) shrimp (prawns), peeled and deveined

1 tablespoon chopped garlic

2 tablespoons chopped shallot

1 tablespoon tomato paste

2 tablespoons fish sauce

2 tablespoons palm sugar or brown sugar

3 tablespoons fresh lime juice

½ teaspoon dried red chile flakes

2 green (spring) onions, including 1 inch (2.5 cm) of the tender green tops, cut into 1-inch (2.5-cm) lengths

¼ lb (125 g) deep-fried bean curd (tofu) squares, each about 1½ inch (4 cm) square, cut into thin, narrow strips

1 egg (optional)

1 tablespoon water (optional)

½ lb (250 g) bean sprouts

1 fresh red chile, finely slivered

1 head pickled garlic, finely slivered

❧ Break the mass of noodles into 4–6 portions. Pour the oil to a depth of 2 inches (5 cm) in a wok or deep frying pan and heat to 365°F (185°C) on a deep-frying thermometer. Drop a noodle portion into the hot oil. Let it puff up, which will take only a few seconds, and, using tongs, turn over and fry on the second side until fully puffed, about 2 seconds longer. Using a wire skimmer, transfer the noodles to paper towels to drain. Fry the remaining noodles in the same way. Remove the pan from the heat. Ladle out all but 2 tablespoons of the oil into a heat-resistant measuring pitcher and set aside.

❧ Return the pan to medium-high heat. When the oil is hot, add the pork and stir-fry until the pieces turn opaque and are firm to the touch, about 1 minute. Add the shrimp and stir-fry until they turn bright orange-pink, about 1 minute longer. Using a slotted utensil, transfer the pork and shrimp to a plate and set aside.

❧ Add the garlic and shallot to the oil remaining in the pan and stir-fry until golden brown and aromatic, about 30 seconds. Add the tomato paste, fish sauce, and palm or brown sugar and cook, stirring occasionally, until the sugar dissolves, begins to caramelize, and looks like a thick syrup, 3–5 minutes. Stir in the lime juice, reduce the heat to low, and add half of the fried noodles, the dried chile flakes, green onions, and bean curd strips. Using tongs or 2 spatulas, gently toss to coat the noodles with the sauce, being careful to crush as few noodles as possible. Add half of the remaining noodles and again mix with the sauce. Continue adding noodles, mixing well with each addition, until the noodles are evenly coated with sauce and have a nice, light red tinge. (You may not need to use all of the noodles; save any extra for

another use.) Return the pork-shrimp mixture to the pan and stir to combine. Transfer the noodles to a serving platter and keep warm.

❧ If desired, make a crisp, lacy egg topping: Place a frying pan over medium-high heat, add oil to a depth of ½ inch (12 mm), and heat to 350°F (180°C) on a deep-frying thermometer. In a small bowl, lightly beat the egg with the water. Place the egg bowl near the frying pan. Dip your fingertips into the beaten egg and wave them over the frying pan, allowing the egg to dribble off your fingertips into the hot oil. Repeat this once or twice until you have a lacy nest. Fry until the nest turns golden brown, about 30 seconds. With a wide, flat slotted utensil, transfer the "nest" to paper towels to drain briefly, then break into smaller pieces.

❧ Arrange the bean sprouts around the edge of the platter holding the noodles. Scatter the chile slivers, the pickled garlic slivers, and the crispy egg lace, if using, over the top of the noodles, and serve.

serves 4–6

MAIN DISHES

All of the dishes for a meal are served at the same time and eaten communally.

TO UNDERSTAND the Southeast Asian meal, Westerners must first free themselves from the idea of the main dish. On dinner tables laid along this tropical swath of the globe, there is no culinary centerpiece as in the West. Instead, dishes are viewed as accompaniments to rice, the cornerstone of the daily diet.

Indeed, a meal is traditionally made up of several "main" dishes. A widely accepted formula determines how many to serve: one dish for each diner, plus soup and rice. A typical dinner for four to six persons will include one or two curries, a fish, one or two vegetables, a poultry or meat dish, plus a light soup. In general, a mound of rice is spooned onto each plate, and diners are outfitted with a large spoon and fork. If fingers are preferred—which is the case among traditionalists in many countries and daily in Laos and the Golden Triangle —small finger bowls are sometimes provided.

In Vietnam, another exception, bowls and chopsticks are used. All the dishes, including the soup, are served at the same time, and the meal is shared communally.

The Southeast Asian table also holds *sambals* (spice relishes) and sauces. For the Burmese, *balachuang,* a mix of dried shrimp paste, tamarind, chile, and fried garlic and onion, is essential. The Nonya cook in Malaysia or Singapore puts big dollops of *sambal blacan* into saucers, and *nam prik,* a chile-spiked fish sauce, is a must for Thais. A diner scoops up a small morsel from a bowl of curry or a grilled fish with his or her spoon, pushes a bit of rice onto the spoon with the fork, adds a splash of *sambal* or sauce, and eats the assembled mouthful from the spoon. Throughout the meal, diners dip out spoonfuls of soup from the central bowl to cleanse the palate for the next taste.

Preceding spread: Once used by loggers and for heavy lifting, elephants are now a common sight on Thailand's pristine beaches, where owners hawk rides astride their charges' backs to the tourists. **Left:** In the dry season, Cambodia's Tonle Sap shrinks to one-tenth its size, at which point it yields an extraordinary amount of fish per kilometer, making it one of the richest freshwater fishing grounds in the world. The locals use long wooden rafts with funnel-shaped nets to secure the huge catches of silvery carp and black catfish. **Below top:** Dishes made from fish and shellfish are a typical source of protein in a Southeast Asian meal, such as *ca kho to* (catfish simmered in a clay pot) in Vietnam, *pla numg* (steamed fish with pickled plums) in Thailand, or *udang goreng asam* (shrimp with tamarind) in Malaysia. **Below bottom:** Outside the ancient imperial city of Hue, a Vietnamese cyclist improvises a practical means of transporting some unusual cargo.

The city of Padang, on the island of Sumatra, has given its name to one of Indonesia's most enduring dining traditions, the *nasi padang,* or "Padang rice house," a style of restaurant found throughout the archipelago. A big scoop of hot rice is placed on each diner's plate, and then dishes of food flood every inch of the table, sometimes stacked two—or even three—layers high: *ayam goreng,* curries of every type from *kambing rendang* to *opor ayam,* cold and hot vegetables, salads, shrimp chips, fritters, a half-dozen *sambals.* At the end of the meal, diners are charged only for what they have eaten, with the uneaten dishes promptly returned to the kitchen.

I have been told that in the past the Padang table was typically served by a parade of women dressed in native costumes, a historical footnote that may cause confusion with another Indonesian tradition, the Dutch *rijsttafel,* or "rice table." The latter was originated by the colonial Dutch rulers as a form of entertainment: a cavalcade of several dozen main dishes delivered the ostentatious display of power and money desired by these outsiders. Not surprisingly, the locals found the practice offensive,

Left: These bright red fish were caught in a coral reef off Boracay Island in the central Philippines. Only moments out of the water, they are already on their way to market. **Below top:** A Hmong couple carries home a sack of goods just purchased at the weekly market in Bac Ha, a mountain town in the northern Vietnamese province of Lao Cai, on the border with China. **Below bottom:** Watched over by two seated stone Buddhas, an old Burmese monk finds a doorway in the magnificent Shwedagon Pagoda a good place for meditation.

and the *rijsttafel* went out of fashion with the expulsion of the Dutch. Today, it has been replaced with the *prasmanan,* a buffet at which guests help themselves.

Three other basic culinary elements weave their way through the region. The first is curry, which originated in India and has inspired Southeast Asian cooks to create their own distinctive variations. In Vietnam, curry dishes, eaten primarily in the south, are minor players and rely on a mild premixed curry powder. Burmese curries are generally mild as well and include copious amounts of onion and garlic along with ginger, turmeric, occasionally lemongrass, a few dried spices, and a

Above: Bas-reliefs on the walls of the Bayon temple complex at Angkor Thom depict a variety of scenes from daily life, including fishing with nets, cockfights, and this one of cooks lowering an animal into a cauldron. **Right top:** An Indonesian fish trader carries a few prime specimens of the archipelago's fresh catch, while keeping her hands free. **Right bottom:** According to legend, the craggy outcroppings of Vietnam's Ha Long Bay are the result of a sea creature thrashing its way from the murky depths up to Heaven, leaving over three thousand limestone islands in its wake.

touch of chile. Thai curries, in contrast, are fiery and complex. They marry local ingredients—lemongrass, galangal, shallots, garlic, dried shrimp paste, and kaffir lime rind—with such warm Indian spices as cumin, coriander, fennel, nutmeg, and cardamom. Red or green chiles add heat and color. The resulting mix, simmered with coconut milk and finished with fresh herbs, tends to be soupy and eaten with generous spoonfuls of rice to stretch the protein. Malaysian, Indonesian, and Singaporean curries mirror many of the same spices used in Thai curries, with coconut milk and ground candlenuts added as thickeners and turmeric mixed in for its luscious golden color. Indonesian and Malaysian cooks also prepare *rendang,* or "dry" curry, slowly simmering the meat with curry leaves and ground coriander, turmeric and chiles, cumin and coconut milk until the oil separates from the sauce and the mixture is nearly dry.

The second common element is the spice paste, which is at the heart of much of Thai, Malaysian, Indonesian, and Singaporean cooking. These hand-pounded pastes are the work of culinary artisans. In the past, every Nonya girl in the region was expected to learn how to pound such pastes properly. Indeed, at midmorning, matchmakers would visit homes unannounced, listening for the steady rhythmic pounding that indicated a well-trained prospective bride was at work in the kitchen. Today in Malaysia, a *batu giling,* a thick, rectangular granite slab and a long rolling pin made of stone, is still used by some cooks to crush together galangal, lemongrass, turmeric, candlenuts, shallots, garlic, chiles, and dried shrimp paste, which are then mixed with ground toasted spices. (Alas, modern cooks, with less time and less finesse, resort to blenders and food processors.) The resulting spice paste, or *rempah,* is fried in vegetable oil. A Thai curry paste, or *krung gaeng,* which marries an equally elaborate pantry of ingredients, is traditionally fried in oil-rich coconut cream. In both cases, the frying must be done slowly until the paste is fragrant and beads of oil glisten on the surface.

The third defining element of the Southeast Asian table is fresh- and saltwater fish and

shellfish, which appear in some form at nearly every meal. The mighty Mekong River starts in China and meanders through the rice paddies of Laos, Thailand, and Cambodia until it finally empties into the South China Sea at the southern tip of Vietnam. Everyone who lives along its path depends on the river's bounty for food. With the exception of Laos, each Southeast Asian country has a border on the sea, with the many islands of the Philippines and Indonesia home to particularly fertile fishing grounds. Pomfret, mackerel, snapper, catfish, perch, crab, lobster, shrimp, clams, and cockles are plentiful in the region, and cooks readily toss them into blazing hot woks. Grilled fish is an everyday preparation, too. Pulled from nearby waters, the fish are quickly cleaned, seasoned with aromatic herbs and spices, and then, either naked or wrapped in banana leaves, placed atop wood-fired grills. They are cooked until the flesh is perfectly succulent—and not a moment longer. In some remote rural areas, the process is speeded up,

with the fish going on the grill unscaled and sometimes even ungutted. Also popular is steamed whole fish, a preparation borrowed from the southern Chinese kitchen.

While it is true that Southeast Asians depend mainly on fish for protein, meat and poultry, although generally not as plentiful and usually more costly, also appear on the region's tables. In Indonesia and Malaysia, where Islam is widespread, lamb and beef are popular, primarily in curries. Elsewhere pork is added to the list, turned into such dishes as five-spice pork chops and pork stewed in coconut juice in Vietnam and pork adobo in the Philippines. Chicken, however, is popular throughout the region, simply grilled in Cambodia and Laos, poached and served with rice cooked in stock in Singapore, crisply fried in Indonesia, enclosed in pandanus leaves in Thailand, stir-fried with lemongrass in Vietnam, and simmered in curries in Myanmar and Malaysia.

Yet, as with all meals in Southeast Asia, these curries and grills, braises and stir-fries, from Mandalay to Manila, are served with bountiful scoops of steaming rice.

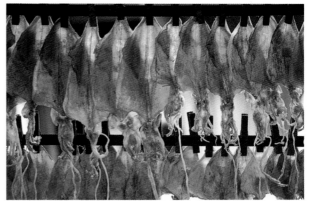

Left bottom: A group of Ma women in Lam Dong Province, in Vietnam's pine-clad central highlands, carry baskets of firewood back to their village. **Above top:** Shoppers who come to buy chicken for dinner at the Binh Tay Market in Cholon, Ho Chi Minh City's sprawling Chinatown, arrive by bicycle to purchase live birds directly from farmers. The area in which poultry is sold is one of only a dozen or so large retail sections in the market, each of which features a different type of produce or livestock. **Above bottom:** Dried squid hang in a Vietnamese marketplace, ready to be purchased by savvy cooks for adding to soups and stews and other dishes, where they will impart a smoky, salty flavor. Locals also enjoy munching on the dried cephalopods for a chewy snack.

Singapore

Kepiting Pedas

chile crab

When I think of Singapore, into my mind flash images of a hawker cook tossing chunks of crab coated in a sizzling-hot oil spiked with red chiles, ginger, and garlic. I see an image of the end of the meal, too; the table "decorated" with neat mounds of crab shells, licked clean, and greasy, red-stained, crumpled napkins.

Chile crab is customarily brought to the table with no plates but lots of small paper napkins. People help themselves to the communal pot of crab, which is accompanied with cucumber chunks and French bread or toast. I unabashedly always ask for steamed rice, however. If you're in a "high-end" hawker center or restaurant, just as you have used up the very last corner of a dozen napkins, a finger bowl arrives.

If you are reluctant to kill a live crab, buy a cooked crab and ask the fishmonger to clean and crack it.

2 live Dungeness or other large crabs, each about 1½ lb (750 g)

6 fresh red chiles

1-inch (2.5-cm) piece fresh ginger, peeled and quartered

3 cloves garlic, quartered

⅓ cup (3 fl oz/80 ml) vegetable oil

1 teaspoon salt

⅓ cup (3½ oz/105 g) tomato ketchup

¼ cup (2 oz/60 g) firmly packed dark brown sugar

1 tablespoon fish sauce

½ cup (4 fl oz/125 ml) chicken stock or water

2 green (spring) onions, including 1 inch (2.5 cm) of the tender green tops, cut into 1½-inch (4-cm) lengths

1 egg

fresh coriander (cilantro) sprigs

1 English (hothouse) cucumber, cut into irregular ¾-inch (2-cm) chunks or wedges

French bread slices or hot steamed long-grain white rice

❦ To prepare the crabs, bring a large stockpot three-fourths full of water to a boil. Using long-handled tongs, drop 1 crab into the boiling water. Quickly add the second crab and boil them both for 2 minutes. Transfer the crabs to a large colander and rinse with cold water until cool. Working with 1 crab at a time, pull off the top shell. If desired, scrub the shell with a brush, rinse it with cold water, pat dry and save it for a garnish. Lift the tip of the triangular apron on the underside of the body and twist it off and discard. Remove the mandibles at the face end. Pull off the feathery gills and the gray intestinal matter from the body and discard. Spoon out the creamy yellow tomalley from the middle of the chest and reserve for another use, if desired. Rinse the body under cold running water and pat dry with paper towels. Using a cleaver or chef's knife, chop the body in half lengthwise, leaving the legs and claws attached. Then cut each half crosswise into thirds to make a total of 6 pieces. Each half will have 1 piece with a claw attached, and the other 2 pieces will each have 2 legs attached. Repeat with the remaining crab. With a mallet, crack the claw and leg shells at the joints and in the middle.

❦ In a mortar or mini food processor, combine the chiles, ginger, and garlic and pound or process until a rough paste forms.

❦ Preheat a wok or large, heavy pan over high heat. When the pan is hot, add the oil, salt, and chile paste and cook, stirring continuously so that the mixture does not brown, until fragrant, about 30 seconds. Toss in the crab and stir-fry with the mixture for 1–2 minutes. Add the ketchup, brown sugar, fish sauce, and stock or water and stir together. Cover, reduce the heat to a gentle boil, and cook, stirring once or twice, until the crab is bright orange and cooked through, 5–6 minutes. (If using precooked crab, cook for 2 minutes only to heat through.)

❦ Uncover the pan, raise the heat to high, and toss in the green onions. Crack the egg into the pan and toss quickly, breaking up the egg to incorporate it into the sauce. When the sauce thickens to a loose glaze, the crab is ready to serve.

❦ Transfer the crab to a large platter and garnish with the fresh coriander sprigs. Serve hot with the cucumber and the French bread or rice.

serves 4

Vietnam

Thit Heo Nuong Vi

grilled five-spice pork chops

Five-spice powder, a highly fragrant Chinese spice blend, is frequently used by Vietnamese cooks.

4 bone-in pork loin chops

½ teaspoon peppercorns

1 whole star anise

1 lemongrass stalk, tender midsection only, finely chopped

4 cloves garlic, halved

1 shallot, quartered

1 tablespoon fish sauce

1½ teaspoons light soy sauce

1 teaspoon Asian sesame oil

1 tablespoon sugar

½ teaspoon five-spice powder

nuoc cham *dipping sauce (page 249)*

☙ Place the pork chops on a flat work surface and, using a meat pounder, pound to ½–¾ inch (12 mm–2 cm) thick.

☙ In a mortar or blender, pound or grind the peppercorns and star anise to a fine powder. Add the lemongrass, garlic, and shallot and pound or blend until a purée forms. Add the fish sauce, soy sauce, sesame oil, sugar, and five-spice powder and mix well.

☙ Put the pork chops in a shallow bowl, add the marinade, and turn to coat. Cover and refrigerate for at least 2 hours or overnight.

☙ Prepare a fire in a charcoal grill. Bring the pork chops to room temperature.

☙ Scrape the marinade off the chops and place on the grill rack about 4 inches (10 cm) above the fire. Grill, turning once, until nicely charred on both sides, about 8 minutes total.

☙ Transfer to a cutting board and cut each chop into several strips, leaving the bone attached. Reassemble the strips on a serving platter to look like whole chops. Serve with the dipping sauce.

serves 6

Malaysia

Ayam Limau Purut

chicken in kaffir lime leaf curry

This Nonya-style curry has the delicate citrus scent and taste of lemongrass, the subtle sweet-sour flavor of tamarind, and the perfumy fragrance of kaffir lime leaf. It is a typical combination that results in a refreshingly light curry sauce ideal for marrying with chicken. In the past, Nonyas (women of Chinese and Malay descent), known for their extraordinary culinary skills, would always hand-pound the spice mixture, a technique they learned by closely watching their mothers and grandmothers. Nowadays, a blender does a decent job of grinding the ingredients. In addition, Nonya girls were taught how to do everything from serving sweets and coffee to distinguished visitors to executing the fine embroidery that decorated their traditional dress.

SPICE PASTE

6 dried red chiles, cracked, seeded, soaked in warm water for 15 minutes, and drained

1 lemongrass stalk, tender midsection only, chopped

2 slices fresh galangal, peeled and coarsely chopped

1 small finger fresh turmeric, 1 inch (2.5 cm) long, peeled and quartered, or 1½ teaspoons ground turmeric

6 cloves garlic, quartered

3 large shallots, about ¼ lb (125 g) total weight, quartered

5 fresh red Fresno or jalapeño chiles, 2–3 oz (60–90 g) total weight, seeded and quartered

⅓ cup (3 fl oz/80 ml) vegetable oil

1 chicken, 3½ lb (1.75 kg), cut into serving pieces

2 cups (16 fl oz/500 ml) coconut milk (page 245)

⅓ cup (3 fl oz/80 ml) tamarind water (see sidebar, page 114)

6–8 kaffir lime leaves, spines removed

½ cup (4 fl oz/125 ml) coconut cream (page 245)

2 teaspoons salt

꙳ To make the spice paste, place the drained dried chiles in a blender with the lemongrass, galangal, turmeric, garlic, shallots, and fresh chiles. Process until a smooth paste forms. If necessary, add a few tablespoons of water to facilitate the blending.

꙳ Preheat a wok or large, heavy pot over medium-high heat. When hot, add the vegetable oil and the spice paste and fry, stirring frequently, until the oil and paste are emulsified, about 3 minutes. Continue gently frying the paste, stirring often, until tiny oil beads appear on the surface, 5–8 minutes.

꙳ Add the chicken pieces and mix to coat with the spice paste. Add the coconut milk, reduce the heat to medium, and cook, stirring occasionally, for 5 minutes. Add the tamarind water, lime leaves, coconut cream, and salt, raise the heat to high, and bring to a boil. Immediately reduce the heat to low, cover, and simmer until the chicken is cooked, about 20 minutes.

꙳ Uncover and raise the heat to medium-high. Cook, stirring, until the sauce thickens slightly, just a few minutes.

꙳ Transfer to a serving dish and serve at once.

serves 4

Singapore

Hai Nan Ji Fan

hainanese chicken rice

Whenever I am in Singapore, one of my first eating stops is for Hainanese chicken rice. The dish, which originated on the island of Hainan, off the coast of southern China, emphasizes the natural sweet flavor of an absolutely fresh chicken. The poached bird is served with rice that is cooked in chicken fat with garlic and then simmered in chicken stock. To eat the chicken, a piece of it is dipped into one or more of the accompanying sauces—sweet chile dip, ginger–green onion dip, a local sweet dark soy sauce, and sometimes oyster sauce—and taken with some of the rice. Chunks of cucumber and a light soup made from the poaching liquid accompany the bird.

The Chinese consider a perfectly cooked chicken to be pale pink at the bone, and they prepare this classic dish by turning off the heat after the second boil is reached and allowing the bird to cook slowly in the cooling liquid for 45–60 minutes. That method has been altered here to suit the Western palate.

2-inch (5-cm) piece fresh ginger, crushed

2 green (spring) onions, including the green tops, bruised

1 tablespoon salt

1 chicken, 3½ lb (1.75 kg)

1 tablespoon Asian sesame oil

about 2 lb (1 kg) chicken necks and backs for stock

RICE

3-inch (7.5-cm) piece chicken fat

2 cups (14 oz/440 g) long-grain white rice

1 tablespoon finely chopped garlic

1 teaspoon salt

2¼ cups (18 fl oz/560 ml) chicken stock from poaching chicken

GINGER–GREEN ONION SAUCE

2-inch (5-cm) piece fresh ginger, peeled

½ teaspoon salt

2 green (spring) onions, including 1 inch (2.5 cm) of the tender green tops, finely chopped

2 tablespoons peanut oil or vegetable oil

SWEET CHILE SAUCE

4 large red jalapeño chiles, seeded

1 teaspoon sugar

pinch of salt

1 teaspoon Asian sesame oil

SOY SAUCE

¼ cup (2 fl oz/60 ml) dark soy sauce

CABBAGE SOUP

4 cups (32 fl oz/1 l) chicken stock from poaching chicken

½ Chinese (napa) cabbage, cored and sliced

salt and ground pepper to taste

1 green (spring) onion, including 1 inch (2.5 cm) of the tender green tops, chopped

1 English (hothouse) cucumber, peeled and sliced

2 tomatoes, sliced

fresh coriander (cilantro) sprigs

❀ Fill a large stockpot with enough water to cover the chicken completely. Put in the ginger, green onions, and salt and bring to a boil over high heat. Add the chicken, breast side down. Continue to cook over high heat until a second boil is reached. Meanwhile, with a fine-mesh skimmer, remove any surface foam and discard, repeating until the liquid is clear, about 5 minutes. When the second boil is reached, reduce the heat to very low, cover, and gently cook the chicken until the meat is just opaque at the bone when the thigh is pierced with the tip of a knife, 35–45 minutes.

❀ When the chicken is ready, prepare a large pan of ice water. To remove the chicken, insert a long-handled wooden spoon into the cavity, lift out the chicken, and plunge it into the ice-water bath to firm up the skin and form a gelatin layer between the skin and meat, about 10 minutes. Remove the chicken and pat dry with paper towels. Rub all over with the sesame oil, then let cool before cutting.

❀ Meanwhile, add the additional necks and backs to the poaching liquid and continue simmering for 1½ hours to make a tasty stock for cooking the rice.

❀ To make the rice, put the chicken fat in a dry saucepan over medium heat and fry until you have about 1½ tablespoons of rendered fat. Discard the fat that has not yet rendered.

❀ Rinse the rice in several changes of cold water until the water runs clear. Drain in a fine-mesh sieve and set aside.

Add the garlic to the rendered fat and sauté over medium heat until soft and lightly golden, about 1 minute. Do not allow to brown. Add the salt and the rice and stir to coat well with the fat. Add the chicken stock, raise the heat to high, and bring to a boil, stirring occasionally to loosen the grains from the bottom of the pan. Continue cooking over high heat until the surface liquid has been totally absorbed and craters appear in the rice. Then cover the pan, reduce the heat to low, and cook for 20 minutes, undisturbed. At this point, all the liquid should be absorbed and the rice grains should be tender. Remove the pan from the heat and let the rice sit, covered, for at least 10 minutes or as long as 40 minutes before serving. When ready to serve, dip a wooden spoon into water and use it to fluff the rice.

To make the ginger–green onion sauce, combine the ginger and salt in a mortar and pound to a paste. Transfer to a heatproof bowl and add the green onions. In a small frying pan, heat the oil until it is almost smoking. Pour the hot oil over the ginger–green onion mixture. It should sizzle. Stir to mix well, then divide the sauce among 4 individual dipping saucers.

To make the sweet chile sauce, combine the chiles, sugar, and salt in a mortar and pound to a paste. Stir in the sesame oil and divide among 4 individual dipping saucers.

Divide the dark soy sauce among 4 individual dipping saucers.

To make the cabbage soup, pour the chicken stock into a saucepan over high heat. Add the cabbage and cook until wilted, about 2 minutes. Season with salt and pepper and scatter the green onions over the top. Keep warm.

To serve, use a cleaver to chop the chicken into bite-sized pieces with or without the bones. The pieces should be about 2½ inches (6 cm) long and 1 inch (2.5 cm) wide. Arrange the pieces on a platter, reassembling them to look like a whole chicken. Garnish with the cucumber and tomato slices and fresh coriander sprigs.

Supply each diner with a saucer of each sauce, a bowl of rice, and a bowl of soup and place the platter of chicken in the center of the table.

serves 4

Sambal Blacan

Sambal blacan, a condiment *sambal* that goes on just about anything and everything placed on the tables of Singaporean, Malaysian, and Nonya cooks, is a highly potent spice paste made from dried shrimp paste, chiles, lime juice or kaffir lime leaves, and salt. It is a mixture that produces a distinctive taste most Westerners must learn to love, but once they begin to appreciate it, the ability of *sambal blacan* to enhance foods becomes almost addictive. The etiquette is simple: place a tiny amount of the *sambal* on the edge of your plate and dip into it with caution, for it is not only pungent but fiery as well.

To make the *sambal*, cut off a thin 1-inch (2.5-cm) square sliver from a block of dried shrimp paste and wrap it in aluminum foil. Switch on the exhaust fan—important—and place the packet directly on a stove-top burner turned on to medium-high. Toast it, turning it once or twice, until fragrant—unmistakable—1 to 2 minutes, then remove and unwrap it. If it is crumbly, it is cooked. Put 5 fresh red chiles, seeded and cut up, into a mortar. Add the toasted shrimp paste and a big pinch of salt and pound to a paste. Stir in 1 to 2 tablespoons fresh lime juice, transfer to a saucer, and serve at room temperature.

Malaysia

Ayam Pongtay

chicken braised with salted soybeans and black mushrooms

Salted soybeans, soft beans floating in light brown liquid, are known by the Hokkien word taucheo *in Malaysia. Along with meaty dried mushrooms, they give this Chinese-inspired dish an earthy flavor.*

8 large dried Chinese black mushrooms, soaked in warm water for 20 minutes

¼ lb (125 g) shallots, peeled and quartered

6 cloves garlic

3 tablespoons salted soybeans

2–3 tablespoons water

3 tablespoons vegetable oil

3 lb (1.5 kg) assorted chicken legs, thighs, and wings

1 tablespoon dark soy sauce

2 teaspoons sugar

sambal blacan *(see sidebar at left)*

❧ Remove the mushrooms from the water, squeezing out any liquid. Strain the soaking liquid through a sieve lined with cheesecloth (muslin) and reserve. Cut off and discard the stems. Set the caps aside.

❧ In a blender, combine the shallots, garlic, salted soybeans, and enough of the water to facilitate the blending. Blend until a smooth paste forms.

❧ Preheat a wok or large, heavy pot over medium-high heat. When the pan is hot, add the vegetable oil and swirl to coat the pan. When the oil is hot, add the shallot-garlic paste and stir-fry until reduced to a dry porridgelike consistency, about 2 minutes. Add the chicken pieces, mushroom caps, the strained liquid, and just enough water to cover the chicken. Bring to a boil, reduce the heat to medium, cover, and boil gently until the chicken is cooked through, about 15 minutes. Uncover the pan, raise the heat to high, and cook rapidly until the sauce reduces and is quite thick. Stir in the dark soy sauce and sugar; mix well.

❧ Transfer the chicken to a serving dish and serve immediately. Pass the *sambal* at the table.

---

serves 4

Thailand

Choo Chee Hoy Phat

scallops in thick red curry sauce

Unlike the more common Thai curry, or gaeng, *which generally has the consistency of soup and is served in a bowl,* choo chee *curry uses less coconut milk, resulting in a thicker sauce that is served on a plate.*

½ cup (4 fl oz/125 ml) coconut cream (page 245)

1 tablespoon red curry paste (page 246)

1 tablespoon palm sugar or brown sugar

1–2 tablespoons fish sauce

1 cup (8 fl oz/250 ml) coconut milk (page 245)

10 kaffir lime leaves, spines removed

1 tablespoon vegetable oil

¾ lb (375 g) sea scallops

handful of fresh Thai basil leaves, plus sprigs for garnish

1 fresh red chile, seeded and finely sliced

🌾 In a wok or saucepan over medium–high heat, bring the coconut cream to a gentle boil. Adjust the heat to maintain a gentle boil and cook, stirring continuously, until tiny beads of oil appear on the surface, 5–8 minutes. Add the curry paste and fry gently, stirring constantly, for about 2 minutes. Add the palm or brown sugar and fish sauce and stir for a few seconds. Add the coconut milk and lime leaves and bring to a boil. Reduce the heat to medium-low and simmer, stirring occasionally, for 5 minutes.

🌾 Meanwhile, in a frying pan over medium–high heat, warm the vegetable oil. While the oil is heating, pat the scallops dry with paper towels. When the oil is hot, add as many of the scallops as will fit in a single layer. Let brown, undisturbed, for about 1 minute. Using tongs, turn the scallops over and brown on the second side, about 1 minute. Transfer to a plate. Repeat with the remaining scallops.

🌾 When the sauce thickens to a creamy consistency, taste and adjust with curry paste, palm or brown sugar, and fish sauce. Add the scallops and basil leaves and stir to heat through. Transfer to a serving platter and garnish with the chile slices and basil sprigs.

serves 4

Vietnam

Ca Hap

steamed fish with lily buds, mushrooms, and glass noodles

The main source of protein in Vietnam is local fish from the sea and from an abundance of freshwater sources. Although the Vietnamese love to fry, grill, or braise the catch, perhaps the most common way to prepare the fish at home is steamed. The ingredients and the cooking technique in this recipe are primarily Chinese. The steaming is done in a shallow plate, so the juices that collect in the bottom of it become an integral part of the sauce. This results in an exceptionally healthful and tasty dish. Serve with steamed rice and, to enjoy the sauce, suggest to diners that they spoon some of the juices from the fish over their rice.

4 dried Chinese black mushrooms

½ cup (1 oz/30 g) dried lily buds (about 30)

2 tablespoons small dried tree ear mushrooms

½ oz (15 g) bean thread noodles

1 whole whitefish such as sea bass, trout, striped bass, or red snapper, 1½–2 lb (750 g–1 kg), cleaned, with head and tail intact

2 cloves garlic, chopped

1½ tablespoons fish sauce

1 tablespoon light soy sauce

1 teaspoon salt

½ teaspoon sugar

¼ teaspoon ground pepper

2 teaspoons peeled and finely shredded fresh ginger

2 green (spring) onions, including 1 inch (2.5 cm) of the tender green tops, cut into 1½-inch (4-cm) lengths and then shredded lengthwise

1 tomato, cut into 8 thin wedges

☸ Place the mushrooms, lily buds, tree ear mushrooms, and bean thread noodles in 4 separate bowls, add warm water to cover, and let stand until soft and pliable, 20–30 minutes.

☸ Meanwhile, rinse the fish with cold water and pat dry with paper towels. Make 3 diagonal slashes almost to the bone on each side of the fish. Place in a shallow bowl. In a small bowl, stir together the garlic, fish sauce, light soy sauce, salt, sugar, and pepper and pour over the fish. Let stand at room temperature while you prepare the remaining ingredients.

☸ Drain the black mushrooms, lily buds, tree ear mushrooms, and noodles and squeeze out the excess water. Cut the stems off at the base of the black mushrooms and discard the stems. Cut the caps into thin strips. Pick off any hard knobs from the center of the tree ear mushrooms and discard. Leave the ears whole if they are small, or cut into fine slivers. Pick off and discard the hard tips of the lily buds. Lay the noodles out straight in a bunch on a cutting board and cut them in half.

☸ In a bowl, mix together both mushrooms, the lily buds, the noodles, the ginger, and the green onions. Arrange one-third of the noodle-vegetable mixture on a heat-resistant shallow plate that will fit comfortably in a bamboo steamer or other steamer rack. Lay the fish on the bed of noodles, pouring in the marinade, and scatter the remaining noodle-vegetable mixture over the fish. Arrange the tomato wedges on top.

☸ Pour water into a wok or other pan and bring to a boil. Place the bamboo steamer or other rack over the water, cover, and steam until the fish is opaque throughout, about 20 minutes. (Plan on 10 minutes per 1 inch/2.5 cm, measured at the thickest section of the fish.) Check the water level toward the end of cooking and replenish with boiling water as needed.

☸ When the fish is ready, carefully remove the plate from the steamer and serve at once.

serves 6

Vietnam

Bo Nhung Dam

beef fondue with vinegar

Table-top cooking is popular in Vietnamese restaurants and homes. For a special occasion, a Chinese clay brazier, fired by glowing charcoal, is set in the middle of the dining table, and one of Vietnam's signature dishes, beef fondue with vinegar, is served. I have long thought that Vietnamese fondue is an echo of both the Chinese and Singaporean steamboat and the French and Swiss fondue. The preparation for this dish—slicing vegetables, cutting beef into paper-thin slices, preparing the broth and sauces—is all completed in advance, while the actual cooking is done at the table. Partially freezing the beef will help in making paper-thin slices. Since this is the first course of the classic beef cooked seven ways (page 58), you may offer it as an appetizer, in which case it will serve twelve.

BEEF PLATTER

1 lb (500 g) boneless lean beef loin, round, or chuck from the top blade, wrapped in plastic wrap and placed in the freezer for 1 hour

ground pepper to taste

1 white onion, thinly sliced

BROTH

1 green coconut, 2 cups (16 fl oz/500 ml) frozen coconut juice, or 1½ cups (12 fl oz/ 375 ml) water

1 tablespoon vegetable oil

1 tablespoon chopped garlic

2 lemongrass stalks, tender midsection only, halved and smashed

1½ cups (12 fl oz/375 ml) distilled white vinegar

4 teaspoons sugar

2 teaspoons salt, or to taste

TABLE SALAD AND ACCOMPANIMENTS

nuoc cham dipping sauce (page 249)

½ lb (250 g) bean sprouts

1 carrot, peeled and finely julienned

1 English (hothouse) cucumber, halved lengthwise and thinly sliced crosswise

1 cup (1 oz/30 g) fresh mint leaves

1 cup (1 oz/30 g) fresh coriander (cilantro) leaves

1 cup (1 oz/30 g) fresh polygonum leaves (page 248)

1 cup (1 oz/30 g) fresh Thai basil leaves

12 dried round rice papers, 12 inches (30 cm) in diameter

⚘ Remove the partially frozen beef from the freezer and cut across the grain into paper-thin slices. Arrange the slices attractively on a serving platter. Sprinkle with the pepper and scatter the onion slices on top. Cover and refrigerate.

⚘ Next, make the broth: If using the coconut, crack it open (see sidebar, page 51) and collect the juice in a bowl. There should be 1½–2 cups (12–16 fl oz/ 375–500 ml); set aside. If using frozen coconut juice, allow it to thaw. If using water, measure it.

⚘ In a saucepan over medium-high heat, warm the vegetable oil. When the oil is hot, add the garlic and lemongrass and sauté until fragrant, about 1 minute. Add the vinegar, coconut juice or water, sugar, and 2 teaspoons salt and bring to a boil. Reduce the heat to medium and simmer for 10 minutes. Transfer the broth to a fondue pot or small Chinese clay pot. Bring to the table and place on a table-top burner.

⚘ To prepare the table salad and accompaniments, pour the dipping sauce into individual saucers. Arrange the bean sprouts, carrot, cucumber, mint, fresh coriander, polygonum, and basil in serving plates surrounding the broth pot. Set a large shallow bowl of warm water on the table for rice-paper dipping, or bring rehydrated rice papers, covered with a damp cloth, to the table. Remove the beef platter from the refrigerator and place it on the table.

⚘ To eat the fondue, take a round of rice paper and, if still dry, dip it into the water, set it on a dinner plate, and allow it to soften for about 30 seconds until it feels like a wet tissue. Place a little of each vegetable and herb in a mound on the paper. With chopsticks, pick up a slice of beef with a few onion slices and submerge it in the hot broth. Cook until medium-rare, about 1 minute. Put the beef on top of the vegetable-covered rice paper. Roll up the rice paper into a log and, holding it in your hand, dip the end into the dipping sauce and eat.

serves 4

Vietnam

Ca Kho To

catfish simmered in a clay pot

This dish calls for caramel syrup, a simple seasoning that Vietnamese cooks adapted from the French and use to enrich the flavors of savory dishes. The recipe, cooked in a small clay pot, serves one as a main course or four as part of a multicourse meal.

3 catfish steaks, each about 1 inch (2.5 cm) thick
(6 oz/185 g total weight)

ground pepper to taste

2 tablespoons fish sauce

2 teaspoons sugar

1 tablespoon vegetable oil

3 cloves garlic, chopped

6 shallots, sliced

2 tablespoons caramel syrup (page 244)

2 green (spring) onions, including the tender green tops, cut into 2-inch (5-cm) lengths

♨ Rinse the fish and pat dry with paper towels. Sprinkle on both sides with pepper. Place in a shallow bowl and add the fish sauce and sugar. Turn to coat, then marinate for about 10 minutes.

♨ Meanwhile, in a 2-cup (16–fl oz/500-ml) clay pot or saucepan over medium heat, warm the vegetable oil. Add the garlic and shallots and cook, stirring, until they start to turn golden, 1–2 minutes. Raise the heat to high, remove the catfish from the marinade, reserving the marinade, and put the fish into the clay pot or pan. Quickly sear on both sides, then add the caramel syrup, the reserved marinade, and the green onions. Reduce the heat to medium-low, cover, and simmer for 8 minutes.

♨ Uncover and check to see if the fish is done. If it is, transfer it to a plate. If not, you can leave it in the cooking vessel while you reduce the sauce. Raise the heat to high and boil to reduce the sauce by half. When the sauce is thick, return the fish to reheat.

♨ Serve the catfish directly from the clay pot, or transfer to a serving plate. Serve immediately.

serves 1

Malaysia

Kambing Rendang

"dry" lamb curry

Traditionally, mutton was used for rendang, *and it required long simmering to make the tough meat tender and tasty. Lamb, however, is as good if not a better choice.* Rendang *has a thick sauce that clings to and blankets the main ingredients. It is a "dry" curry in comparison to the typical "wet," creamy curry sauces.*

SPICE PASTE

1 tablespoon coriander seeds

1 tablespoon cumin seeds

1 teaspoon fennel seeds

½ teaspoon freshly grated nutmeg

6 whole cloves

½ teaspoon ground turmeric

6 dried red chiles, cracked, seeded, soaked in warm water for 15 minutes, and drained

4 large shallots, quartered

4 cloves garlic, quartered

2 lemongrass stalks, tender midsection only, chopped

1-inch (2.5-cm) piece fresh ginger, peeled and quartered

¼ cup (2 fl oz/60 ml) vegetable oil

2 lb (1 kg) lamb stew meat, preferably from the leg, cut into pieces 2 inches (5 cm) square by ½ inch (12 mm) thick

1 cinnamon stick

1½–2 cups (12–16 fl oz/375–500 ml) water

⅓ cup (3 fl oz/80 ml) tamarind water (see sidebar, page 114)

1 cup (8 fl oz/250 ml) coconut cream (page 245)

2 teaspoons sugar

1 teaspoon salt

¼ cup (1 oz/30 g) unsweetened grated dried coconut, lightly toasted

1 small English (hothouse) cucumber, sliced

✤ To make the spice paste, in a small, dry frying pan over medium heat, toast the coriander, cumin, and fennel seeds until fragrant, 1–2 minutes. Transfer to a mortar or spice grinder, add the nutmeg and cloves, and grind to a fine powder. Transfer to a small bowl and stir in the turmeric; set aside.

✤ Place the dried chiles in a blender with the shallots, garlic, lemongrass, ginger, and ground spices. Blend until a smooth paste forms. If necessary, add a few tablespoons of water to facilitate the blending.

✤ In a wok or large, heavy pot over medium heat, warm the oil. When hot, add the spice paste and fry slowly, stirring often, until the oil and paste are emulsified, about 3 minutes. Continue cooking at a gentle boil, stirring often, until tiny oil beads appear on the surface of the mixture, 5–8 minutes.

✤ Add the lamb and stir to coat with the spice paste. Add the cinnamon stick and the water as needed just to cover the lamb. Bring to a boil, then reduce the heat to low, cover, and cook at a gentle boil until the meat is nearly done, about 45 minutes.

✤ Uncover the pan, raise the heat to medium-high, and boil until the liquid is reduced by half, about 15 minutes longer. Add the tamarind water, coconut cream, sugar, and salt and bring to a boil, stirring constantly. Reduce the heat to medium, add the grated coconut and boil gently, stirring occasionally, until the mixture is quite dry and is coated with a thin film of reddish oil, 5–8 minutes.

✤ Transfer to a serving dish and garnish with the cucumber slices. Serve immediately.

serves 4

Pla Nurng

steamed whole fish with pickled plums

*Originally from China, pickled plums are a variety
of green plum preserved in a sour-salty brine and
sold in jars. Despite the name, the tiny fruit, the size
of a kumquat, is actually a type of apricot. It adds
a unique salty-and-tart finish to the sauce.*

*1 whole pomfret, sea bass, or flounder, about
1¼ lb (625 g), cleaned, with head and tail intact*

salt and ground white pepper to taste

*2 green (spring) onions, including 1 inch
(2.5 cm) of green tops, bruised and cut into
1½-inch (4-cm) lengths*

*2 oz (60 g) pork fat, cut into fine, thin strips
(optional)*

*2 pickled plums (see note), pitted and coarsely
chopped*

1 tablespoon fish sauce

¼ teaspoon sugar

*1 tablespoon peeled and finely slivered fresh
ginger*

1 red serrano or jalapeño chile, sliced

fresh coriander (cilantro) sprigs

❀ Rinse the fish and pat dry. Make 3 diagonal
slashes on each side almost to the bone. Sprinkle
with salt and white pepper.

❀ Place half of the green onions on a heat–resistant
shallow plate that will fit comfortably in a bamboo
steamer or other steamer rack. Lay the fish on top of
the green onions. In a small bowl, mix the pork fat
(if using), plums, fish sauce, and sugar and pour over
the fish. Scatter the ginger, the remaining green
onions, and the chile slices over the top.

❀ Pour water into a wok or other pan and bring to
a boil. Place the steamer over the water, cover, and
steam until the fish is opaque throughout, about
15 minutes. (Plan on 10 minutes per 1 inch/2.5 cm,
measured at the thickest section of the fish.)

❀ Carefully remove the plate from the steamer and
garnish the fish with the coriander. Spoon some of
the juices that have accumulated on the bottom
of the plate over the fish. Serve immediately.

serves 4

Thailand

Gaeng Kiow Wan Gai

chicken in green curry with pumpkin and eggplant

Eggplant is a perfect partner for many curries, and there is a marvelous assortment of types showcased in Thai markets. The spectrum of colors ranges from white, lime green, yellow, orange, and purple to the various streaked varieties, and shapes vary from familiar long, stubby bats to golf balls to small apples. A distinctive Thai variety, makhua puang, *is the size of small English peas and grows in clusters. With a slightly bitter taste, they are popular cooked in curries and pounded into fiery dipping sauces.*

Green curry paste tends to be herbaceous, earthy, and mellow when compared with the sharp-edged red pastes. But green curry still has plenty of heat.

2 cans (13½ fl oz/420 ml each) coconut milk (page 245)

4 slices fresh galangal or 2 slices dried galangal

3 tablespoons green curry paste (page 246)

1 lb (500 g) boneless, skinless chicken breasts and thighs, cut into ¾-inch (2-cm) pieces

1-lb (500-g) piece kabocha squash or pumpkin, peeled and cut into ¾-inch (2-cm) chunks

6 golf ball–sized eggplants (aubergines), trimmed and quartered, or 1 Asian (slender) eggplant, trimmed and cut crosswise into 1-inch (2.5-cm) pieces

2 tablespoons fish sauce

1 tablespoon palm sugar or dark brown sugar

8 kaffir lime leaves, spines removed

½ cup (½ oz/15 g) fresh Thai basil leaves

❦ Do not shake the cans of coconut milk. Open the cans and spoon off 1 cup (8 fl oz/250 ml) of cream from the tops. Place the cream in a heavy saucepan and reserve the remaining coconut milk. Place the pan over medium-high heat and bring the cream to a gentle boil. Adjust the heat to maintain a gentle boil and cook, stirring continuously, until tiny beads of oil appear on the surface, 5–8 minutes.

❦ Add the galangal and green curry paste and fry gently, stirring constantly, until the mixture is aromatic and the oil separates from the paste, 8–10 minutes. Add the chicken pieces and fry them in the oily paste until well coated, about 2 minutes. Raise the heat to high and stir in 2 cups (16 fl oz/500 ml) of

the reserved coconut milk (save the remainder for another use), the squash or pumpkin, eggplant pieces, fish sauce, palm or brown sugar, and lime leaves. Adjust the heat to maintain a gentle boil and cook until the squash is tender, about 10 minutes.

❦ Taste and adjust the seasoning with curry paste, fish sauce, or palm sugar. Add the basil leaves and stir just until they begin to wilt.

❦ Transfer to a serving dish and serve at once.

serves 4–6

Thailand

Gai Hor Bai Toey

marinated chicken thighs in pandanus leaves

I refer to pandanus leaves, called bai toey *in Thai, as Asian vanilla with an emerald hue. Also known as screw pine, these thin, pointed leaves are most commonly used to impart a unique vanilla-like flavor and scent and a green color to Southeast Asian cakes. When wrapped around marinated chicken, they deliver a woodsy fragrance and taste to the meat. This dish is perfect picnic or party food.*

½ teaspoon peppercorns

2 cloves garlic

2 tablespoons fresh coriander (cilantro) roots or stems

2 lemongrass stalks, tender midsection only, finely minced

2 tablespoons oyster sauce

2 tablespoons light soy sauce

2 teaspoons sugar

1½ teaspoons Asian sesame oil

1½ lb (750 g) boneless, skinless chicken thighs, cut into 1½-inch (4-cm) pieces

36 pandanus leaves, each about 12 inches (30 cm) long by 2 inches (5 cm) wide (see note)

peanut oil or corn oil for deep-frying

Sweet-Sour Cucumber Relish (page 103)

Sriracha sauce (page 251)

In a mortar, pound the peppercorns to a coarse powder. Add the garlic, coriander roots or stems, and lemongrass and pound together to form a coarse paste. Scrape into a bowl and add the oyster sauce, light soy sauce, sugar, and sesame oil. Mix together and add the chicken. Mix well, cover, and refrigerate for 2 hours.

Remove the chicken from the refrigerator. To make the chicken bundles, lay a pandanus leaf on a work surface. Make a mound of chicken about 1½ inches (4 cm) high (using 1 or 2 pieces of chicken) about 4 inches (10 cm) from the stem end of the leaf. The idea is to tie the leaf into a knot that encloses the chicken. Bring up the ends, then pull the long end over and around to cover the front of the chicken pieces. Tuck the end under and up to meet at the top with the stem end. Tug a bit to enclose the chicken securely in the tiny bundle.

Pour the peanut oil or corn oil to a depth of 2 inches (5 cm) in a deep, heavy frying pan and heat to 350°F (180°C) on a deep-frying thermometer. Working in batches, add the chicken bundles and fry until the meat is firm and cooked through, about 4 minutes. Using a slotted spoon or tongs, transfer the bundles to paper towels to drain.

Arrange the chicken bundles on a platter. Serve immediately with the cucumber relish and Sriracha sauce for dipping. To eat, unwrap the leaves and discard them.

makes about 3 dozen pieces; serves 6–8

Spice Pastes

Shoppers at Thailand's many markets are greeted by displays of premade curry pastes. These mountains of intense flavor look rich, colorful, and luscious. Some of the best Malaysian and Indonesian sauces share a similar combination of spices, herbs, and rhizomes. Called *rempahs*, they are equally appealing, especially to anyone who is lucky enough to watch them being expertly made. In the past, the ability of a young woman to prepare a perfectly smooth *rempah*, grinding and pounding the dry and wet ingredients in a mortar and pestle and with a *batu giling* (granite slab and roller), made a matchmaker's job easy.

I long wondered what the secret was to drawing out the best flavor from these spice mixtures. Singporean chef Chris Yeo explained that in the case of *rempah*, the spice paste must be fried slowly in plenty of oil to develop the full character of the ingredients. The frying marries and mellows the elements and keeps the mixture lubricated as it cooks. Chai Aksomboon, an accomplished Thai chef, fries and simmers his curry paste in coconut cream and coconut milk for the same reasons. Without this step, he explained, the pastes would have a harsh, raw taste and the spices would be unpleasantly sharp.

Malaysia

Sambal Udang

shrimp in a sweet, spicy sambal

These shrimp are often served as an accompaniment to nasi lemak, rice cooked in coconut milk, a popular breakfast from Kuala Lumpur to Jakarta.

SPICE PASTE

¼-inch (6-mm) piece fresh galangal, peeled and minced

1 lemongrass stalk, tender midsection only, chopped

2 candlenuts or blanched almonds, soaked in warm water for 10 minutes and drained

3 large red Fresno chiles, seeded and quartered

¼ lb (125 g) shallots (about 3 large), quartered

3 cloves garlic, quartered

1 slice dried shrimp paste, ⅛ inch (3 mm) thick

¼ cup (2 fl oz/60 ml) vegetable oil

1 yellow onion, sliced

¾ lb (375 g) large shrimp (prawns), peeled and deveined

1 teaspoon salt

1 tomato, cut into wedges

2 tablespoons sugar

2 tablespoons fresh lime juice, or to taste

❧ To make the spice paste, in a mortar or blender, pound or process the galangal and lemongrass to a pulp. Add the candlenuts or almonds and pound or blend to a coarse paste. Add the chiles, shallots, garlic, and shrimp paste and pound or blend to as smooth a paste as possible. If necessary, add a few spoonfuls of water to facilitate the blending.

❧ To cook the spice paste, preheat a wok or frying pan over medium heat and add the oil. When hot, add the spice paste and fry slowly, stirring often, until emulsified, about 3 minutes. Boil gently, stirring often, until tiny beads of oil appear, 5–8 minutes.

❧ Raise the heat to high, add the onion, and stir-fry until the onion layers begin to separate, about 1 minute. Add the shrimp and stir-fry until they turn bright orange-pink, about 2 minutes. Sprinkle with the salt, stir in the tomato, sugar, and lime juice, and heat through, about 1 minute. Serve immediately.

serves 4

Thailand

Gaeng Ped Supparot

duck in red curry

This recipe was inspired by my first Thai cooking teachers, Chai and Kwan Aksomboon. They probably didn't realize that those early lessons would lead me to Thailand and then to change the course of my career: I have since opened a Thai cooking school at the Oriental Hotel in Bangkok and now design and lead culinary tours to Southeast Asia. On my first trip, I found that the juxtaposition of Chinese and Thai ingredients and cooking techniques was commonplace. The traditional Chinese roast duck cooked in a typical Thai red curry paste characterizes the melding of two great cuisines. The duck can be purchased at a Chinese shop selling prepared foods. Ask the counterperson to chop it for you Chinese style—that is, in small pieces.

½ cup (4 fl oz / 125 ml) coconut cream
(page 245)

3 tablespoons red curry paste (page 246)

1–2 tablespoons palm sugar or brown sugar

1–2 tablespoons fish sauce

½ Chinese roast duck, chopped into small pieces

2½ cups (20 fl oz / 625 ml) coconut milk
(page 245)

8 kaffir lime leaves, spines removed

1 cup (6 oz / 185 g) cubed pineapple
(1-inch / 2.5-cm cubes)

8 cherry tomatoes, halved

1 cup (1 oz / 30 g) fresh Thai basil leaves

🦐 In a wok or deep saucepan over medium heat, combine the coconut cream and curry paste and cook, stirring, until tiny beads of oil appear on the surface, 5–8 minutes. Add the palm or brown sugar, fish sauce, and duck and stir to mix. Add the coconut milk and lime leaves, bring to a boil, and immediately reduce the heat to medium-low. Simmer gently for about 5 minutes to heat the duck pieces.

🦐 Add the pineapple, tomatoes, and basil leaves and stir just until the basil leaves are wilted. Transfer to a serving dish. Serve hot or at room temperature.

serves 4

Philippines

Kari-Kari

braised oxtails in peanut sauce

The cuisine of the Philippines is a mixture of influences—Chinese, Spanish, American, Malay—which gives it an exoticism that is difficult to describe. Many Filipinos regard kari-kari, *with its echo of each of these kitchens, as the quintessential Philippine dish. The slow-cooked oxtails, like most other braised dishes, taste even better the next day.*

3½–4 lb (1.75–2 kg) oxtails, cut into 2-inch (5-cm) pieces

1 tablespoon salt

1 teaspoon ground pepper

4 tablespoons (2 fl oz / 60 ml) vegetable oil

1 tablespoon annatto seeds

2 yellow onions, chopped

6 cloves garlic, quartered

6–8 cups (48–64 fl oz / 1.5–2 l) water

⅓ cup (3 oz / 90 g) long-grain white rice

½ cup (3 oz / 90 g) unsalted roasted peanuts

¾ lb (375 g) green beans, trimmed and cut into 2-inch (5-cm) lengths

1 large Asian (slender) eggplant (aubergine), cut crosswise into 1-inch (2.5-cm) pieces

fish sauce to taste

꙰ Sprinkle the oxtails with the salt and pepper. In a large Dutch oven or other large, heavy pot over medium-high heat, warm 2 tablespoons of the vegetable oil. When the oil is hot, add a few oxtail pieces and brown well on all sides, turning frequently. Transfer the oxtails to a plate and repeat with the remaining oxtails. Pour off the oil from the pot and discard. Set the pot aside.

꙰ Meanwhile, in a small frying pan over medium-low heat, warm the remaining 2 tablespoons oil with the annatto seeds. Fry the seeds until the oil takes on a red stain, just a few minutes. Remove from the heat and let the oil cool. With the back of a spoon, press the seeds and allow the mixture to stand for 5 minutes. Strain through a fine-mesh sieve held over the reserved pot. Discard the contents of the sieve.

꙰ Place the pot with the oil over medium heat, add the onions and garlic, and cook slowly, stirring occasionally, until they are soft and lightly golden, about 8 minutes. Return the oxtails to the pot and add the water just to cover the meat. Bring to a boil over high heat, reduce the heat to medium, cover partially, and cook at a gentle boil until the oxtails are nearly tender, about 2 hours.

꙰ In small, dry frying pan over medium heat, toast the rice, shaking the pan and stirring often, until the rice turns golden brown, about 15 minutes. Remove from the heat and let cool. Pour the rice into a blender, process to a fine powder, and transfer to a bowl; set aside. Add the peanuts to the blender and process to finely mince.

꙰ When the oxtails are nearly done, uncover and add the ground rice and peanuts, the green beans, and the eggplant. Raise the heat to high and bring to a boil. Cook, stirring occasionally, until the meat is tender, the vegetables are fully cooked, and the sauce has thickened, about 10 minutes. The meat is done when it pulls away from the bone easily.

꙰ Transfer the oxtails and vegetables to a serving dish and serve. Pass the fish sauce at the table.

serves 6

Vietnam

Banh Xeo

crepes with shrimp, chicken, and vegetables

I once paused to watch a street-side banh xeo *cook at work, as she deftly prepared one crepe after another in rapid succession on a small burner. She poured the batter into a wide, shallow pan, placed it over the fire, and swirled the pan to coat the bottom. Alongside her were mix-and-match bowls filled with ingredients. She scooped out several different items and tossed them onto the sizzling crepe. It was done in no time, and she neatly folded it over for a waiting customer.*

Yellow mung beans are peeled and split dried green mung beans. They are sold in bags in Asian markets.

BATTER

1 cup (4 oz/125 g) rice flour

½ teaspoon salt

½ teaspoon sugar

¼ teaspoon ground turmeric

1 cup (8 fl oz/250 ml) coconut milk (page 245)

about 1¼ cups (10 fl oz/310 ml) cold water

2 green (spring) onions, including 1 inch (2.5 cm) of the tender green tops, thinly sliced

FILLING

½ cup (3½ oz/105 g) dried yellow mung beans, rinsed (see note)

1½ lb (750 g) bean sprouts

12 fresh white mushrooms, brushed clean and thinly sliced

½ lb (250 g) boneless, skinless chicken meat, cut into ⅓-inch (9-mm) pieces

½ lb (250 g) shrimp (prawns), peeled, deveined, and cut into ⅓-inch (9-mm) pieces

6 tablespoons (3 fl oz/90 ml) vegetable oil

TABLE SALAD AND SAUCE

1 head looseleaf lettuce, separated into leaves

1 cup (4 oz/125 g) finely julienned carrots

leaves from 1 bunch fresh mint

1 cup (1 oz/30 g) fresh coriander (cilantro) leaves

1 English (hothouse) cucumber, peeled, seeded, and julienned

12 Thai or Chinese pickled shallots

nuoc cham dipping sauce (page 249)

☙ To make the batter, in a bowl, stir together the rice flour, salt, sugar, and tumeric. Whisk in the coconut milk and just enough water needed to make a thin batter. Mix in the green onions and set aside.

☙ To make the filling, place the mung beans in a small saucepan, add water to cover by 1 inch (2.5 cm), and bring to a boil over high heat. Reduce the heat to medium and simmer, uncovered, until tender, about 15 minutes. Drain and set aside.

☙ Bring a saucepan three-fourths full of water to a boil, add the bean sprouts, and blanch for 15 seconds. Drain well and set aside.

☙ Divide the mushrooms, chicken, shrimp, and bean sprouts into 6 equal piles. Place a nonstick 9-inch (23-cm) shallow wok or omelet pan over medium-high heat. When hot, add 1 tablespoon of the vegetable oil and tilt the pan to spread the oil over the bottom. Pour off any excess oil into a bowl and reserve. Add one-sixth each of the mushrooms, chicken, and shrimp to the pan and stir-fry until the chicken and shrimp are cooked, about 30 seconds. Transfer the filling mixture to a plate.

☙ Ladle ½ cup (4 fl oz/125 ml) of the batter into the pan and immediately tilt it to spread a thin film up the sides of the pan. Sprinkle 2 tablespoons of the mung beans evenly over the batter. Cover, reduce the heat to medium, and cook until steam seeps out from under the cover, 2–3 minutes. Uncover, spread the reserved cooked filling mixture over the crepe, raise the heat to medium-high, and fry until the crepe shrinks away from the sides of the pan and looks dry and light brown, 1–2 minutes. Scatter one-sixth of the blanched bean sprouts over the crepe. For added crispness, dribble the reserved oil along the sides of the pan. Dip the tip of a spatula in a little oil and use it to lift the crepe and fold it in half. Fry for 30 seconds longer to brown the bottom. Transfer to a plate, browned side up, tent loosely with aluminum foil, and keep warm in a low oven. Repeat with the remaining ingredients to make 6 crepes total.

☙ To serve, prepare the table salad and sauce: Arrange the lettuce, carrots, mint, coriander, cucumber, and shallots in separate piles on a large platter. Pour the sauce into 6 small saucers. Divide the crepes among individual plates. Each diner tears off a small section of crepe, places it in the middle of a lettuce leaf, and tops it with the other ingredients on the salad platter. Then he or she rolls up the leaf, dips it into the sauce, and eats it out of hand.

makes 6 crepes

Thailand

Hoi Ma Laeng Poo

mussels with garlic and basil

When you visit one of Bangkok's enormous seafood garden restaurants, be careful you are not bumped by one of the waiters whizzing by on roller skates. The skates give them a fast start out of the kitchen as they deliver hot dishes to the tables. I remember catching the full bouquet of aromas from a passing plate of just-cooked mussels. It was loaded with the scent of toasted garlic laced with chiles and anise-flavored Thai basil.

½ teaspoon peppercorns

2 red jalapeño or serrano chiles, seeded and coarsely chopped

2 cloves garlic, quartered

1 tablespoon chopped fresh coriander (cilantro) roots or stems

3 tablespoons vegetable oil

1½ tablespoons oyster sauce

1 tablespoon fish sauce

2 lb (1 kg) mussels, scrubbed and debearded

¼ cup (2 fl oz/60 ml) chicken stock

½ teaspoon sugar

½ cup (½ oz/15 g) fresh Thai basil leaves

fresh coriander (cilantro) leaves

☙ In a mortar, pound the peppercorns until crushed, then add the chiles, garlic, and coriander roots or stems and pound or grind until a rough paste forms.

☙ Preheat a wok or frying pan over medium-high heat. When hot, add the oil and swirl to coat the pan. When the oil is hot, add the chile paste and fry until fragrant, about 30 seconds. Stir in the oyster sauce and fish sauce. Add the mussels, discarding any that fail to close to the touch, and stir and toss with the sauce to mix. Add the stock and sugar, then cover and cook until the mussels open, about 2 minutes. Taste and adjust the seasoning with fish sauce.

☙ Toss in the basil leaves and cook only until they begin to wilt. Transfer the mussels to a platter, discarding any that failed to open, and garnish with the coriander leaves.

serves 4–6

Indonesia

Ikan Goreng Sambal Bawang

balinese fried fish with shallot, lemongrass, and lime

My memories of Bali are filled with images of Balinese women walking barefoot along country roads in early morning, baskets stacked with fruits, vegetables, and spices balanced on their heads. They are on their way home to their kampongs, or villages, where they will begin to prepare the dishes that will make up the day's meals.

Bali is an island of fishing villages: the local diet is rich in catches pulled from the sea and from the interior lakes. Whole or cut-up fish is typically grilled, deep-fried, steamed, or curried and served with a sambal. This particular dish is so exceptional that it deserves to be accompanied with nasi kunyit (page 138), a rice preparation reserved for festive occasions. The sambal that is served spooned over the fish is nicely tart and wonderfully refreshing.

4 whole small rock cod, pomfret, red snapper, bream, striped bass, or perch, each about 1 lb (500 g), cleaned, with head and tail intact

juice of 1 lime

1 teaspoon ground turmeric

salt and freshly ground pepper to taste

SAMBAL

1 slice dried shrimp paste, ⅛ inch (3 mm) thick

2 lemongrass stalks, tender midsection only, finely slivered (about 2 tablespoons)

3 small shallots, halved lengthwise, then finely slivered crosswise

4 red Thai, jalapeño, or serrano chiles, seeded and finely slivered

2 cloves garlic, finely slivered

2 kaffir lime leaves, spines removed and leaves finely slivered

½ teaspoon salt

juice of 1 lime

2 tablespoons vegetable oil

vegetable oil for deep-frying

❀ Rinse the fish and pat dry with paper towels. With kitchen shears, cut off the top dorsal fin, bottom ventral fins, and the side fins. Working with 1 fish at a time, make 3 diagonal cuts almost to the bone in the thickest part on each side of the body. Rub the entire fish with some of the lime juice and turmeric. Season both sides with salt and pepper. Cover and refrigerate for a few hours.

❀ To make the *sambal*, wrap the dried shrimp paste in a piece of aluminum foil and place the packet directly on a stove-top burner turned on to medium-high heat. Toast it, turning it once or twice, until fragrant, 1–2 minutes. Remove the packet and open it; if the shrimp paste crumbles, it is ready. Let cool. Put the cooled shrimp paste into a bowl and add the lemongrass, shallots, chiles, garlic, lime leaves, salt, lime juice, and oil. Stir well and set aside.

❀ Pour vegetable oil to a depth of 1 inch (2.5 cm) in a large frying pan and heat to 365°F (185°C) on a deep-frying thermometer. Sprinkle the fish on both sides with salt.

❀ When the oil is ready, slip the fish into the oil in a single layer without touching (you may need to fry them in 2 batches) and deep-fry, undisturbed, until browned and crusty, about 3 minutes. Turn the fish over and fry on the second side until browned, crusty, and cooked through, about 3 minutes longer, depending upon the thickness of the fish. (Calculate 10 minutes cooking time per 1 inch/2.5 cm, measured at the thickest section of the fish.)

❀ Using a slotted utensil, carefully transfer the fish to paper towels to drain. Arrange on a platter, spoon the *sambal* over the fish, and serve immediately.

serves 4

Malaysia

Ikan Panggang

grilled fish in banana leaf

In Asia, plant leaves such as those of the banana and lotus are commonly used to wrap foods for grilling. The foods turn out moist, and all their natural juices are collected in the leaf. The leaf, in turn, permeates the food with an appealing herbaceous fragrance. Fresh whole fish are usually wrapped for grilling, but fish steaks or fillets can be cooked this way as well. If you are a novice at this technique, you have the option of wrapping the banana-leaf packet in a sheet of heavy-duty aluminum foil as a safety net.

1 whole sea bass, red snapper, tilapia, or salmon trout, about 1½ lb (750 g), cleaned, with head and tail intact

salt and ground pepper to taste

SPICE PASTE

1 slice dried shrimp paste, ⅛ inch (3 mm) thick

1 lemongrass stalk, tender midsection only, chopped

4 shallots, quartered

3 cloves garlic, quartered

3 red Fresno or jalapeño chiles, cut up

3 kaffir lime leaves, spines removed and leaves cut into fine slivers

1 tablespoon fresh lime juice

1½ teaspoons sugar

1½ teaspoons salt

1 piece banana leaf, 4 inches (10 cm) longer than the fish and twice as wide

vegetable oil for brushing

2 limes, cut into wedges

1 English (hothouse) cucumber, cut into irregular ½-inch (12-mm) chunks

❀ Rinse the fish and pat dry with paper towels. Make 3 diagonal cuts almost to the bone in the thickest part on each side of the body. Season both sides with salt and pepper.

❀ To make the spice paste, wrap the dried shrimp paste in a piece of foil and place the packet directly on a stove-top burner turned on to medium–high heat. Toast it, turning it once or twice, until fragrant, 1–2 minutes. Remove the packet and open it; if the shrimp paste crumbles, it is ready. Let cool. Put the cooled shrimp paste into a mortar or blender and add the lemongrass, shallots, garlic, and chiles. Pound or blend until a smooth paste forms. Add a few tablespoons of water if needed to facilitate the blending. Transfer to a bowl and stir in the kaffir lime leaves, lime juice, sugar, and salt. Set aside.

❀ Prepare a fire in a charcoal grill. Brush the grill rack with vegetable oil.

❀ Bring a large saucepan three-fourths full of water to a boil. Dip the banana leaf into the water for a few seconds. Remove and pat dry with a kitchen towel. Lay the leaf, shiny side down, on a work surface. Brush the middle section with vegetable oil. Rub the fish inside and out with the spice paste and set it on the oiled section of the banana leaf. Bring the sides of the leaf up to meet and overlap in the center, then fold over both ends to enclose the fish. Secure with bamboo skewers or large toothpicks. Wrap the entire package in a sheet of heavy-duty aluminum foil large enough to enclose it completely.

❀ Place the foil-wrapped fish, fold side down, on the oiled grill rack over a hot fire and grill, turning once. To calculate the timing, measure the fish at its thickest point and figure on 10 minutes per inch (2.5 cm). Split the time evenly between the 2 sides. When the fish is ready, it should be fold side up. Carefully open the foil and then the leaf. The flesh should be opaque throughout when tested with the tip of a knife. Allow the fish to cook for a minute longer to evaporate some of the accumulated moisture. Remove from the heat, then remove the foil and discard.

❀ Transfer the banana leaf–wrapped fish to a serving platter. Open the leaf and tuck the long sides and ends under the fish. Garnish with the lime wedges and cucumber. Serve immediately.

serves 2–4

The everyday Malaysian meal consists of a pot of white rice, some fish, vegetables, perhaps a little meat, and the inevitable sambals.

Cambodia

Mouan Ang

grilled chicken with pepper-lime dip

As with many Southeast Asian dishes, the condiments and dips used here embellish an already delectable dish. The Cambodian pepper-lime dip known as tik marij is a typical table condiment, and it sets off the flavors of this classic chicken dish deliciously.

1 teaspoon each peppercorns and coarse salt

6 cloves garlic, quartered

¼ cup (2 fl oz/60 ml) mushroom soy sauce

2 tablespoons sugar

1 tablespoon vegetable oil

2 small chickens, 2½ lb (1.25 kg) each, halved

fresh coriander (cilantro) sprigs

PEPPER-LIME DIP

1 tablespoon ground peppercorns

1½ teaspoons coarse salt or sea salt

2 limes, halved

In a mortar, coarsely grind the peppercorns. Add the garlic and crush to a coarse paste. Transfer the mixture to a bowl and stir in the mushroom soy sauce, sugar, vegetable oil, and coarse salt. Place the chicken halves in a large, shallow baking dish and add the soy sauce mixture. Turn to coat the chicken evenly. Cover and refrigerate for at least 1 hour or up to as long as overnight.

Prepare a fire in a charcoal grill. Place the chicken halves, skin side down, on the grill rack about 4 inches (10 cm) from the fire and grill until the skin is nicely charred, about 15 minutes. Turn and grill until nicely charred on the second side and the juices run clear when a thigh is pierced, 10–15 minutes longer. Transfer to a cutting board and cut into serving pieces. Arrange on a platter. Garnish with fresh coriander sprigs.

To make the dip, equally distribute the pepper and salt among 4 dipping saucers. Have each diner squeeze ½ lime into his or her saucer and stir until the salt dissolves. One can either dip the chicken pieces into the dip or slather them with the dip.

serves 4

The Spice Pantry

Southeast Asian cooks rely on dried whole spices—coriander, cumin, fennel, cinnamon, clove, cardamom—purchased from spice merchants in the many open-air markets and picturesque shops throughout the region. Walk into the sprawling Thein Gyi Zei, the so-called Indian market in central Yangon (Rangoon), and the aroma of exotic spices, mingled with those of dried fish, tropical fruits, and countless other foodstuffs, washes over you. Vendors surrounded by sacks of cinnamon bark and cardamom pods, cumin seeds and nutmeg kernels, weigh out small amounts for their customers, deftly handling simple scales dulled with the patina of age.

On Sabah, which covers the northwest tip of Borneo, the outdoor Sunday markets, or *tamus*, are seas of cattle dealers, betel-nut sellers, cloth merchants, vegetable brokers, and, of course, spice vendors, all shading themselves from a relentless tropical sun.

In the ancient heart of Hanoi, where trades and goods traditionally were confined to streets that bore their names, spice dealers share space with other merchants, thousand-year-old temples, grilled fish restaurants, and small parks. In Singapore on Serangoon Road, called Little India by the locals, spice sellers, tucked into storefronts and booths among sari shops, pot-and-pan emporiums, and jewelry stores, sell the spices for a Malaysian *rempah* or an Indian *masala*.

Southeast Asian cooks who buy whole spices nearly always toast them before use to bring out their flavor and eliminate any raw aftertaste. The flavor is further heightened when the seeds are pounded in a mortar to draw out the aromatic oils. A spice grinder does a respectable job as well.

To toast whole spices, use a dry (ungreased) cast-iron frying pan over medium-low heat. Add the spice and toast it, stirring frequently, until it exudes a heady bouquet and turns a shade or two darker. Depending upon the spice, this may take anywhere from a minute to five minutes. While the spice is still warm, transfer it to a mortar or spice grinder and pound or grind to a fine powder.

Vietnam

Thit Heo Kho Nuoc Dua

pork stewed with coconut juice

I was introduced to this pork stew at the home of friend and Vietnamese food mentor Paul Kwan. Fresh ham with the rind intact is traditionally used for this typical family-style dish from southern Vietnam, but Paul prefers to use pork butt.

The coconut juice is the liquid trapped inside a coconut and should not be confused with coconut milk, which is made from the meat of a mature coconut. Paul prefers the sweet juice of young green coconuts, and one of his secrets is to scrape some of the young coconut meat from the shell, chop it up, and squeeze it to extract some additional juice, which he then adds to the pork. Because you cannot always count on imported fresh coconuts—they are often bland, not sweet, and lack a good coconut taste—he opts for the convenience of reliably sweet and flavorful frozen coconut juice, which can be found in most Asian markets.

In Vietnam, hard-boiled eggs are added to the simmering sauce near the end of cooking. Serve with pickled sour mustard greens (page 113).

1 green coconut or 2 cups (16 fl oz/500 ml) frozen coconut juice (see note)

2 tablespoons vegetable oil

3 cloves garlic, chopped

2 shallots, chopped

2 lemongrass stalks, tender midsection only, finely minced

2 lb (1 kg) boneless pork butt, cut into 1-inch (2.5-cm) cubes

2 tablespoons caramel syrup (page 244)

⅓ cup (3 fl oz/80 ml) fish sauce, or to taste

2 tablespoons sugar, or to taste

1 teaspoon five-spice powder

½ teaspoon ground black pepper

½ teaspoon ground white pepper

1–2 cups (8–16 fl oz/250–500 ml) chicken stock or water

3 hard-boiled eggs, peeled

❧ If using the coconut, crack it open (see sidebar, page 51) and collect the juice in a bowl. You will need 2 cups (16 fl oz/500 ml). If you have less, use water to make up the difference. Set aside. If using frozen coconut juice, allow it to thaw.

❧ Preheat a saucepan over medium-high heat. When the pan is hot, add the vegetable oil and swirl to coat the bottom of the pan. When the oil is hot, add the garlic, shallots, and lemongrass and stir-fry until golden brown, about 30 seconds. Raise the heat to high and add a small batch of the pork. Brown evenly on all sides and transfer to a dish. Repeat until all the pork is browned.

❧ Return all the pork to the pan and add the caramel syrup, fish sauce, sugar, five-spice powder, black pepper, and white pepper. Stir well and cook over medium heat, stirring occasionally, until bubbly and fragrant, about 2 minutes. Add the coconut juice and enough chicken stock or water just to cover the pork. Bring to a boil and skim off any foam or other impurities that rise to the surface. Reduce the heat to medium-low, cover, and simmer until tender, about 1½ hours.

❧ Starting 1 inch (2.5 cm) from the end of a hard-boiled egg and stopping within 1 inch (2.5 cm) of the opposite end, make 4 evenly spaced lengthwise scores around the egg. Repeat with the remaining eggs. Add the eggs to the stew and simmer until the meat is tender, about 15 minutes longer.

❧ Transfer the contents of the saucepan to a serving dish and serve immediately.

serves 6

Malaysia

Sambal Goreng Sotong

squid with tamarind

Here, squid, popular throughout the monsoon-swept lands of Southeast Asia, is prepared with chiles and tamarind in a sambal goreng *typical of Malaysia.*

1 lb (500 g) squid

SPICE PASTE

6 candlenuts or blanched almonds, soaked in warm water for 10 minutes and drained

2 lemongrass stalks, tender midsection only, coarsely chopped

4 large shallots, quartered

5 large fresh red chiles

3 cloves garlic

1 slice dried shrimp paste, ⅛ inch (3 mm) thick

¼ cup (2 fl oz/60 ml) vegetable oil

¼ cup (2 fl oz/60 ml) tamarind water (see sidebar, page 114)

1 tablespoon dark brown sugar

salt to taste

☙ Clean the squid (page 251), leaving the tentacles whole. Slit each body lengthwise. Score with a cross-hatch pattern and then cut lengthwise into strips 1 inch (2.5 cm) wide. Set aside.

☙ To make the spice paste, in a mortar or blender, combine the candlenuts or almonds, lemongrass, shallots, chiles, garlic, and shrimp paste. Pound or blend with a little water into a smooth paste.

☙ In a wok or large frying pan over medium heat warm the vegetable oil. When hot, add the spice paste and fry slowly, stirring often, until the oil and paste are emulsified, about 3 minutes. Cook at a gentle simmer until tiny oil beads appear on the surface, 5–8 minutes. Stir in the tamarind water and brown sugar, reduce the heat to low, and simmer until the mixture thickens slightly, 1–2 minutes.

☙ Raise the heat to high and add the squid. Cook, stirring, for 1 minute. Season with salt and remove from the heat. Transfer to a serving dish and serve.

serves 4

Bo Luc Lac

shaking beef with garlic sauce

Although the sound of the sizzling oil coupled with the rapid shaking of the pan gave birth to the name of this dish, it may be more appropriate to call it sautéed beef with lots of sweet garlic sauce.

¾ lb (375 g) beef sirloin, cut into 1-inch (2.5-cm) cubes

6 cloves garlic, chopped (about 2 tablespoons)

1 tablespoon fish sauce

1 tablespoon sugar

¼ teaspoon salt

3 tablespoons vegetable oil

SALAD

1 small red (Spanish) onion, thinly sliced

1½ teaspoons distilled white vinegar

1½ teaspoons Japanese-style soy sauce

1½ teaspoons olive oil

½ teaspoon sugar

¼ teaspoon each salt and ground pepper

1 bunch watercress, tough stems removed

In a bowl, combine the beef with half of the garlic, the fish sauce, sugar, salt, and 1 tablespoon of the vegetable oil. Turn the beef to coat well, cover, and let stand for at least 30 minutes at room temperature or refrigerate for as long as 2 hours.

To make the salad, in a bowl, toss together the onion and vinegar and set aside for 5 minutes. In a small bowl, stir together the soy sauce, olive oil, sugar, salt, and pepper. Add to the onion and mix well. Add the watercress, toss, and arrange on a platter.

Preheat a wok or frying pan over high heat. When hot, add the remaining 2 tablespoons oil and swirl to coat the pan. When the oil is hot, add the remaining garlic and stir-fry until lightly browned, about 1 minute. Add the beef in a single layer and let sit, undisturbed, until seared, about 1 minute. Give the pan handle a quick shake to flip the meat over to brown and sear on the second side, about 1 minute, then cook for about 3 minutes longer. The meat should be medium-rare.

Arrange the beef on top of the watercress salad and serve immediately.

serves 4–6

Vietnam

Ga Xa Ot

lemongrass chicken

It is almost impossible to think of Vietnamese food without lemongrass chicken coming to mind. Indeed, every restaurant menu includes this aromatic mix of cubed chicken, hot chiles, and citrusy lemongrass. The secret ingredient, however, is caramel syrup, which is added near the end of cooking to give the chicken a beautiful sheen and slightly sweet flavor.

Southern Vietnamese cooks also prepare a lemongrass chicken curry, which calls for many of the same ingredients, although not the caramel syrup, and adds curry powder and coconut milk to create a rich, saffron-colored sauce.

MARINADE

2 cloves garlic, chopped

1 tablespoon fish sauce

2 teaspoons sugar

1 teaspoon cornstarch (cornflour)

½ teaspoon ground pepper

1 tablespoon vegetable oil

¾ lb (375 g) boneless, skinless chicken thighs, cut into ¾-inch (2-cm) cubes

2 tablespoons vegetable oil

2 cloves garlic

2 large shallots, thinly sliced

3 lemongrass stalks, tender midsection only, finely chopped

1 green jalapeño or serrano chile, seeded and chopped

½ red bell pepper (capsicum), seeded and thinly sliced

¼ cup (1 oz/30 g) julienned carrot (1½ inches/ 4 cm long)

1 tablespoon fish sauce

1 tablespoon caramel syrup (page 244)

¼ cup (2 fl oz/60 ml) chicken stock or water

꽃 To make the marinade, in a large bowl, stir together the garlic, fish sauce, sugar, cornstarch, ground pepper, and vegetable oil. Mix well. Add the chicken, toss to coat evenly, and let stand at room temperature for 30 minutes.

꽃 Preheat a wok or large frying pan over medium heat. When the pan is hot, add the vegetable oil and swirl to coat the pan. When the oil is hot, add the garlic, shallots, and lemongrass and stir-fry slowly until they turn a light gold and the shallots smell sweet, 3–5 minutes.

꽃 Add the chicken with its marinade, the chile, bell pepper, and carrot and stir-fry until the chicken turns opaque and feels firm to the touch, 3–4 minutes. Add the fish sauce and caramel syrup and stir-fry until the chicken is fully cooked, about 1 minute longer. The sauce will be sticky, so add the chicken stock or water to dilute it, mixing well. There should be only a little gravy left at the bottom of the pan.

꽃 Transfer the chicken to a serving platter and serve immediately.

serves 6

Malaysia

Udang Goreng Asam

fried shrimp in the shell with tamarind

The intense flavor of shrimp fried in the shell is popular in Asian cooking, and the crispy shells are usually edible. If you can find them, whole shrimp with the heads attached are preferred, but headless shrimp are delicious as well. Udang goreng asam *is delicious as a snack with* chin chow, *an iced black jelly beverage that is especially good with rich, spicy foods.*

¾ lb (375 g) shrimp (prawns) in the shell

½ cup (4 fl oz / 125 ml) tamarind water (see sidebar, page 114)

3 tablespoons peanut oil or vegetable oil, or as needed

½ teaspoon salt

1 teaspoon sugar

3 green (spring) onions, including tender green tops, cut into 1½-inch (4-cm) lengths

♛ To prepare the shrimp, rinse well and pat dry with paper towels. Cut into the shell with a sharp knife to devein. Put the shrimp into a bowl and add the tamarind water. Let stand for 30 minutes at room temperature, turning occasionally.

♛ Preheat a wok or large frying pan over medium-high heat. Add the oil and salt and swirl to coat the pan. When the oil starts to smoke, remove the shrimp from the tamarind water, reserving the liquid, and place as many as will fit in a single layer in the pan. Fry in the hot oil, undisturbed, until the bottoms are browned and crusty, about 1 minute. Turn the shrimp over and fry on the second side until browned and a bright orange-pink, about 1 minute longer. Using a slotted utensil, transfer to paper towels to drain. Keep warm. Fry the remaining shrimp in the same manner, using more oil if needed.

♛ Pour the reserved tamarind water into the hot pan and add the sugar. Boil briskly until it forms a glaze, about 1 minute. Return the shrimp to the pan along with the green onions and cook, stirring constantly, until the shrimp are coated with the glaze. Transfer to a serving dish and serve immediately.

serves 6

Thailand

Gaeng Mussaman Nuea

mussaman beef, potatoes, and peanut curry

Thai mussaman curry paste is a red curry mixture fused with the aromatic Indian spices of cardamom, nutmeg, and cloves. The name comes from "Muslim-style," as the curry originated in southern Thailand where many Muslims from Malaysia settled and Muslim traders from India came to sell their wares. The inclusion of peanuts, potatoes, and cardamom distinguishes it from other Thai curries. The sauce tastes even better the next day, so make plenty for leftovers.

2 cans (13½ fl oz/420 ml each) coconut milk (page 245)

2 lb (1 kg) beef chuck, cut into 1¾-inch (4.5-cm) pieces

3 tablespoons mussaman *curry paste (page 247)*

1 large potato, peeled and cut into 1½-inch (4-cm) cubes

1 yellow onion, cut into 6 wedges

¼ cup (1½ oz/45 g) unsalted roasted peanuts

2 tablespoons fish sauce, or as needed

2 tablespoons palm sugar or dark brown sugar

⅓ cup (3 fl oz/80 ml) tamarind water (see sidebar, page 114)

2 cinnamon sticks

6 cardamom pods, toasted (page 244)

3 bay leaves

½ cup (2½ oz/75 g) English peas

2 tablespoons fresh lemon juice

❦ Do not shake the cans of coconut milk. Open the cans and spoon off a total of 1 cup (8 fl oz/250 ml) of cream from the tops. Place the cream in a heavy frying pan and set aside.

❦ Pour the remaining coconut milk into a large saucepan and place over medium-high heat. Add the beef and bring to a boil. Reduce the heat to medium to maintain a gentle boil. Cook uncovered, stirring occasionally, for 1 hour.

❦ Meanwhile, place the coconut cream over medium-high heat and bring to a boil. Adjust the heat to maintain a gentle boil and cook, stirring continuously, until tiny beads of oil appear on the surface, 5–8 minutes. Add the *mussaman* curry paste

and cook, stirring frequently, until the mixture is aromatic and the oil separates from the paste, 5–8 minutes. Add the paste mixture to the saucepan holding the beef along with the potato, onion, peanuts, 2 tablespoons fish sauce, palm or brown sugar, tamarind water, cinnamon sticks, cardamom pods, and bay leaves. Cook, uncovered, until the vegetables are tender, 10–15 minutes.

❦ Add the peas and simmer for 2 minutes longer. Taste and adjust the seasonings with curry paste, fish sauce, or palm or brown sugar. Stir in the lemon juice and transfer to a serving dish. Serve immediately.

serves 6–8

Laos

Sousi Pla

fish braised in spicy coconut sauce with basil

This spicy Laotian coconut sauce has the basic elements of a Thai curry without the dry seed spices of cumin, coriander, and cardamom. The difficulty Arab traders faced bringing these seed spices to the inland regions is one factor that differentiates the two cuisines. Thus, the cooks of landlocked Laos are more reliant on fresh herbs—basil, dill, coriander, mint.

2 dried red chiles, cracked, seeded, soaked in warm water for 15 minutes, and drained

4 shallots, about 2 oz (60 g) total weight, quartered

4 large cloves garlic

2 lemongrass stalks, tender midsection only, chopped

1 slice fresh galangal, peeled and chopped

6 kaffir lime leaves, spines removed

½ cup (4 fl oz/125 ml) coconut cream (page 245)

1 cup (8 fl oz/250 ml) thin coconut milk (page 245)

1 tablespoon fish sauce, or to taste

1 lb (500 g) fish fillets or steaks (about 1½ inches/4 cm thick) such as catfish or snapper

salt and ground pepper to taste

vegetable oil for frying

handful of fresh Thai basil leaves

In a mortar, combine the chiles, shallots, garlic, lemongrass, galangal and 3 of the lime leaves. Pound to a smooth paste. Alternatively, use a blender, adding 2–3 tablespoons of the coconut cream to the spice mixture to facilitate the blending.

In a saucepan over medium-high heat, bring the coconut cream almost to a boil, stirring continuously. Cook, continuing to stir, until tiny beads of oil appear on the surface, 5–8 minutes. Add the spice paste and coconut milk and cook at a gentle boil, stirring frequently, until small pools of oil appear on the surface and the sauce mixture is creamy and a khaki color, 8–10 minutes. When the mixture is ready, stir in the remaining 3 lime leaves and fish sauce. Remove from the heat and keep warm.

Cut the fish fillets into pieces 2 inches (5 cm) wide or cut the steaks into slices 1½ inches (4 cm) thick. Pat the pieces dry with paper towels. Sprinkle the fish pieces on both sides with salt and pepper.

Pour the vegetable oil to a depth of ½ inch (12 mm) into a frying pan and place over medium-high heat. When the oil is hot but not smoking, add the fish pieces in a single layer. Fry the fish until brown and crusty on the first side, about 2 minutes. Turn the fish over and fry until brown and crusty on the second side, about 2 minutes longer.

Using a slotted utensil, transfer the fish to the spicy coconut sauce and cook together over low heat only long enough for the fish to absorb some of the sauce, about 30 seconds. Stir in the basil leaves until just beginning to wilt.

Transfer the fish and sauce to a serving dish and serve immediately.

serves 4–6

Thailand

Goong Ob Woon Sen

shrimp with glass noodles in a clay pot

Seafood in Thailand seems fresher and larger than anywhere else. I've seen shrimp the size of lobsters, with long, twisting antennae and big, broad tails. Indeed, the different kinds of seafood available in Thai markets outnumber what is found at the best fish-mongers in the West. For this recipe, you will need to seek out the largest shrimp you can find. You will also need whisky, which, although highly coveted by the Thais—a gift of a bottle of Scotch symbolizes both status and goodwill—is little known in the kitchen.

1 teaspoon peppercorns

8 cloves garlic

2 tablespoons chopped fresh coriander (cilantro) roots or stems

½ teaspoon salt

3 tablespoons vegetable oil

1 lb (500 g) shrimp (prawns) (about 16), peeled, with the tail segment left intact, and deveined

SAUCE

2 cups (16 fl oz/500 ml) chicken stock or water, or as needed

1 tablespoon oyster sauce

1 tablespoon light soy sauce

1 tablespoon dark soy sauce

1 tablespoon whisky

1 teaspoon Asian sesame oil

1 teaspoon sugar

1 teaspoon peeled and minced fresh ginger

3 green (spring) onions, including 1 inch (2.5 cm) of the tender green tops, cut into 1½-inch (4-cm) lengths

½ lb (250 g) bean thread noodles, soaked in warm water for 20 minutes and drained

½ lb (250 g) asparagus, tough ends removed, cut on the diagonal into 1½-inch (4-cm) lengths, blanched for 15 seconds in boiling water, and drained

fresh coriander (cilantro) sprigs

In a mortar, pound the peppercorns until crushed, then add the garlic, coriander roots or stems, and salt and pound to form a paste. Mix 1 tablespoon of the vegetable oil into the paste. Place the shrimp in a bowl, add the paste, and toss to coat the shrimp evenly. Set aside for 10 minutes.

To make the sauce, in a bowl, stir together the stock or water, oyster sauce, light soy sauce, dark soy sauce, whisky, sesame oil, and sugar. Set aside.

Preheat a 2-qt (2-l) clay pot or a saucepan over medium heat. When it is hot, add the remaining 2 tablespoons vegetable oil and swirl to coat the pan. Add the shrimp, a few at a time, and brown without stirring for about 1 minute. Turn the shrimp over and brown on the second side, again for about 1 minute. Transfer the shrimp to a bowl and repeat with the remaining shrimp.

Raise the heat to high and add the ginger, green onions, and the sauce. Bring to a boil, add the noodles, and stir to mix with the sauce. Scatter the asparagus evenly over the noodles and then top with the shrimp. Cover, reduce the heat to medium, and boil gently, stirring once or twice, until all the liquid has been absorbed, about 10 minutes.

Remove from the heat and garnish with the fresh coriander sprigs. Serve directly from the clay pot or transfer to a warmed serving dish.

serves 4

Fishermen at work in the clear waters of the Gulf of Thailand haul in nets heavy with fish of every shape, size, and color.

Singapore

Fish Head Curry

Race Course Road in Singapore, nicknamed Curry Street, is where the locals go for "banana leaf," which is shorthand for an incredible curry feast served on a banana-leaf placemat. When you sit down, a banana leaf the size of an extra-large placemat is laid in front of you. Then a waiter ladles out curried vegetables, grilled and fried meats, and spicy relishes, all in clumsy little piles scattered on top of the leaf. The fish head curry, dripping with sauce, tomatoes, okra, and eggplant, is the centerpiece. Forks and spoons are available, but to appreciate the experience, fingers are the best utensils.

Kari ikan *is a ready-mixed curry powder specifically formulated for fish. If it is not available, use your favorite curry powder. A glass of iced sweetened limeade is perfect to temper the spiciness.*

1 fish head from a red snapper, rock cod, sea bass, or striped bass, about 1½ lb (750 g)

SPICE PASTE

2 tablespoons coriander seeds

1 tablespoon cumin seeds

1 tablespoon fennel seeds

1 teaspoon fenugreek seeds

6 dried red chiles, cracked, seeded, soaked in warm water for 15 minutes, and drained

1-inch (2.5-cm) piece fresh ginger, peeled and quartered

½-inch (12-mm) piece fresh turmeric, peeled and halved, or 1 teaspoon ground turmeric

½ lb (250 g) shallots (about 7 large), quartered

6 cloves garlic

¼ cup (2 fl oz/60 ml) vegetable oil

2 small yellow onions, quartered

½ cup (4 fl oz/125 ml) tamarind water (see sidebar, page 114)

1 cup (8 fl oz/250 ml) coconut milk (page 245)

2 tablespoons fish curry powder (kari ikan)
(see note)

3½ cups (28 fl oz/875 ml) water

1½ tablespoons sugar

1 tablespoon salt

3 fresh or dried curry leaf sprigs

½ lb (250 g) okra, pods halved crosswise

2 Asian (slender) eggplants (aubergines), each cut crosswise into 6 pieces

2 small, firm tomatoes, quartered

4 banana leaves, cut into extra-large placemats

hot steamed long-grain white rice

☙ Bring a large saucepan three-fourths full of water to a boil. Add the fish head and blanch for 1 minute. Lift out of the water and let cool.

☙ To make the spice paste, in a small, dry frying pan over medium heat, toast the coriander, cumin, fennel, and fenugreek seeds until fragrant, 1–2 minutes. Transfer to a mortar or spice grinder and grind to a fine powder. In a blender, combine the chiles, ginger, turmeric, shallots, garlic, and the ground spices. Blend until a smooth paste forms, adding a few tablespoons of water if needed to facilitate the blending.

☙ In a large saucepan over medium heat, warm the vegetable oil. Add the spice paste and fry slowly, stirring often, until the oil and paste are emulsified, about 3 minutes. Continue cooking at a gentle boil, stirring often, until tiny beads of oil appear on the surface, 5–8 minutes. Add the onions and fry with the paste until soft and translucent, about 2 minutes.

☙ Raise the heat to high, add the tamarind water, and cook, stirring, for a few seconds. Stir in the coconut milk. In a small bowl, stir the curry powder into ¼ cup (2 fl oz/60 ml) of the water, then add to the pan along with the remaining water, the sugar, salt, and curry sprigs. Bring to a boil, reduce the heat to medium-low, and simmer, uncovered, for 10 minutes. Taste and adjust the seasoning with salt and sugar. Add the fish head, the okra, the eggplants, and the tomatoes and simmer until the fish is cooked and the vegetables are tender, about 15 minutes.

☙ To serve in the traditional manner, lay a banana-leaf placemat at each setting. Transfer the fish head curry to a large bowl and set it in the center of the table. Scoop steamed rice onto the middle of the "mat." Ladle the sauce and some of the fish head and vegetables over the rice. Eat with your fingers.

serves 4

Table Etiquette

Until the Europeans' arrival in the sixteenth century, most Southeast Asians ate with their fingers, a custom infrequently seen in urban centers today and one that I have never mastered.

On a trip to Kuala Lumpur, I met Chef Wan, the country's leading television cooking personality, who took me to an Indian café for a lunch of fish head curry. When the food arrived, he politely asked if it would offend me if he ate with his fingers. "No," I said immediately. I understood that fish head curry was an ideal dish for eating this way, plus I saw our lunch as an opportunity to learn the intricacies of traditional dining. I watched Chef Wan form a small ball of rice, dip it into a sauce, deftly grab a piece of fish, and pop the whole thing into his mouth—all with the fingers of just one hand. Then I tried but failed miserably, with rice grains everywhere but in my mouth.

I turned to the fork and soup spoon, common eating tools in this part of the world, although handled quite differently than in the West. In Southeast Asia, the fork is used to push food into the bowl of the spoon or to hold down food while it is torn with the spoon. The spoon then carries the food to the mouth.

Vietnam

Cha Ca Hanoi

hanoi-style fried fish

This dish is virtually the only one served at Cha Ca La Vong, a famous rustic eatery in the oldest commercial neighborhood in Hanoi. On my visit, a waiter brought a table-top charcoal brazier topped with a small sauté pan. Inside the pan were a few crisp cubes of fish sizzling in golden oil, looking something like fondue. As I took pieces of fish and various fresh greens—basil, coriander, green onions, dill—from the pan and dunked them into a bowl of rice noodles, the waiter promptly replenished the pan with more cubes of the light, sweet fish. He didn't stop until I insisted I had had enough. This recipe approximates that remarkable meal. Frying the fish is best done at the table with the dinner guests helping as they would for fondue.

1½ lb (750 g) rock cod, bass, catfish, or other firm whitefish fillets, cut into ¾-inch (2-cm) cubes

2 tablespoons fish sauce

1½ teaspoons salt

½ teaspoon ground pepper

1 lb (500 g) dried rice vermicelli, soaked in warm water for 15 minutes and drained

½ cup (4 fl oz/125 ml) vegetable oil

¼ teaspoon ground turmeric

6 thin slices fresh ginger

9 green (spring) onions, including 1 inch (2.5 cm) of the tender green tops, halved lengthwise and cut crosswise into 1½-inch (4-cm) lengths

leaves from 1 bunch fresh Thai basil

leaves from 1 bunch fresh coriander (cilantro)

12 fresh dill sprigs, long stems removed

leaves from 1 bunch fresh mint

1 cup (6 oz/185 g) crushed unsalted roasted peanuts

nuoc cham *dipping sauce (page 249)*

2 limes, cut into wedges

⚜ In a bowl, toss the fish cubes with the fish sauce, salt, and pepper and set aside.

⚜ Bring a large saucepan three-fourths full of water to a boil. Add the drained noodles and cook for 1 minute. Pour into a colander, rinse with cold water, and drain well. Divide the noodles among 6 bowls.

⚜ In a small saucepan over medium-high heat, warm the vegetable oil. Add the turmeric and ginger and heat until the oil turns yellow and is fragrant, about 1 minute. Remove from the heat.

⚜ Arrange the green onions, basil, coriander, dill, mint, and peanuts on a serving platter. Divide the dipping sauce among 6 small saucers and place on the table along with the lime wedges.

⚜ Place a table-top burner on the dining table. Preheat an 8-inch (20-cm) frying pan on a stove top over medium-high heat. Pour the turmeric-flavored oil to a depth of ¼ inch (6 mm) into the pan and heat to 325°F (165°C) on a deep-frying thermometer. Add a small batch of the fish (about one-third) to the oil and, using chopsticks, turn the fish pieces as necessary to brown them lightly and cook them through, 2–3 minutes. Add a handful of the green onions, basil, coriander, dill, mint, and peanuts (about one-third of each) to the pan and stir with the chopsticks for a few seconds. When the herbs have wilted, spoon some of the fish mixture and some seasoned oil into each bowl of rice noodles. Start the next batch of fish frying and repeat until all the fish, green onions, herbs, and peanuts are used up.

⚜ Each diner squeezes a little lime juice or drizzles a little of the dipping sauce on the fish and vegetables, mixing them with the noodles.

serves 6

Philippines

Adobong Manok

chicken adobo

Adobo, *meats simmered in vinegar and garlic, was adapted from the Spanish colonial kitchen and was originally intended as a preserving method. Filipino cooks prepare it in many ways, with chicken or pork* adobo *the most popular. Serve with steamed rice.*

1 cup (8 fl oz/250 ml) distilled white vinegar

¼ cup (2 fl oz/60 ml) light soy sauce

6 cloves garlic

3 shallots, quartered

1 bay leaf

1 teaspoon sugar

½ teaspoon each salt and coarsely ground pepper

3 lb (1.5 kg) assorted chicken legs, thighs, and wings

1 cup (8 fl oz/250 ml) water, or as needed

1 tablespoon vegetable oil

In a Dutch oven or other heavy nonaluminum pot, combine the vinegar, soy sauce, garlic, shallots, bay leaf, sugar, salt, and pepper. Add the chicken pieces, mix well, and let marinate for 1 hour, turning occasionally.

Add the water to the chicken just to cover and place over high heat. Bring to a boil, reduce the heat to low, cover, and simmer gently, stirring occasionally, until tender and cooked through, about 45 minutes. Using a slotted utensil, transfer the chicken to a plate. Scoop off and discard the fat from the surface of the liquid with a large spoon, then return the pot to high heat. Boil vigorously until the sauce has reduced to about ¾ cup (6 fl oz/180 ml) and is the consistency of a thin syrup, about 10 minutes.

Meanwhile, place a wok over medium-high heat. When the pan is hot, add the oil and swirl to coat the pan. When the oil is hot, add the chicken pieces in a single layer. Brown well on both sides, turning once, about 5 minutes total. Return the chicken to the reduced sauce and mix to coat evenly.

Transfer the chicken and sauce to a shallow serving bowl and serve immediately.

serves 4

Indonesia

Opor Ayam

mild chicken curry

In Indonesia, selamatans, or ritual feasts, are always served in an elaborate display that includes ornate bowls of scented flowers as decoration. Blessings are invariably offered at these celebratory affairs, and this mild curry traditionally appears on the menu. Also enjoyed by the neighboring Malaysians, the original version has become obscured through the cross-cultural sharing of recipes. Serve with rice and sambals.

1 small chicken, about 2½ lb (1.25 kg), cut into serving pieces

juice of 1 lemon

SPICE PASTE

1 tablespoon coriander seeds

1½ teaspoons cumin seeds

½ teaspoon fennel seeds

½ teaspoon white peppercorns

6 candlenuts or blanched almonds, soaked in water for 10 minutes and drained

6 large shallots, quartered

4 cloves garlic, quartered

1-inch (2.5-cm) piece fresh ginger, peeled and coarsely chopped

4 slices fresh galangal, peeled and chopped, or 2 slices dried galangal

2–3 tablespoons vegetable oil

2 lemongrass stalks, tender midsection only, smashed and cut in half

2 salam leaves (page 250)

2 kaffir lime leaves, spines removed

2 cups (16 fl oz/500 ml) thin coconut milk (page 245)

2 teaspoons palm sugar or dark brown sugar

¼ cup (2 fl oz/60 ml) tamarind water (see sidebar, page 114)

1–2 teaspoons salt, or to taste

2 tablespoons fresh lemon juice

fried shallots (see sidebar, page 79)

☙ Put the chicken pieces in a large bowl and rub with the lemon juice. Set aside while you prepare the spice paste.

☙ To make the spice paste, in a small, dry frying pan over medium heat, toast the coriander, cumin, and fennel seeds and the white peppercorns until fragrant, 1–2 minutes. Transfer to a mortar or spice grinder and pound or grind to a fine powder.

☙ In a blender, combine the candlenuts or almonds, shallots, garlic, ginger, galangal, and ground spices. Blend to form a smooth paste. If necessary, add 2–3 tablespoons of water to facilitate the blending.

☙ Preheat a wok or Dutch oven over medium-high heat. When the pan is hot, add 2 tablespoons of the vegetable oil and swirl to coat the pan. When the oil is hot but not smoking, add the spice paste and cook, stirring, until the oil and paste are emulsified, about 3 minutes. Reduce the heat to medium-low and simmer gently, stirring frequently, until fragrant and the paste looks dry and is a light khaki color, 5–7 minutes. Do not allow the paste to brown.

☙ Add the chicken pieces and lemongrass and fry together, stirring often, until the chicken pieces are nicely coated with the spice paste, about 5 minutes. Add the *salam* leaves, lime leaves, coconut milk, palm sugar or brown sugar, and tamarind water. Raise the heat to high and bring the mixture to a boil. Reduce the heat to medium and boil gently uncovered, stirring occasionally, until the chicken is cooked through and the sauce has thickened and has an oily surface, about 20 minutes. The sauce should be a light khaki color. Spoon off the excess surface oil. Add salt to taste and the lemon juice.

☙ Transfer the chicken to a serving dish and garnish with the fried shallots. Serve immediately.

serves 4

Arab and Indian traders, Portuguese and Dutch colonialists, and Chinese immigrants have all left their imprint on the Indonesian kitchen.

Myanmar (Burma)

Wetha See Byan

dry pork curry

The success of this Burmese curry depends on the slow cooking of the purée of onions, garlic, and ginger.

2 yellow onions, roughly chopped

4 large cloves garlic, quartered

1-inch (2.5-cm) piece fresh ginger, peeled and coarsely chopped

1 teaspoon ground turmeric

½ teaspoon dried red chile flakes

⅓ cup (3 fl oz/80 ml) vegetable oil

2 lemongrass stalks, tender midsection only, finely chopped

2 lb (1 kg) boneless pork shoulder, cut into 1½-inch (4-cm) cubes

⅓ cup (3 fl oz/80 ml) tamarind water (see sidebar, page 114)

1½ tablespoons fish sauce

½ cup (½ oz/15 g) fresh coriander (cilantro) leaves

In a blender, combine the onions, garlic, ginger, turmeric, and chile flakes. Blend until a smooth purée forms. In a large saucepan over medium-high heat, warm the vegetable oil until it is almost smoking. Add the purée and stir immediately to incorporate it with the oil. Reduce the heat to low, cover, and simmer gently, stirring every 5 minutes, for 15 minutes. If the purée appears dry (without being oily), stir in a little water, re-cover, and continue to simmer until the oil appears around the edge of the purée, 8–10 minutes. Raise the heat to medium-high, add the lemongrass and pork, stir well, cover, reduce the heat to low, and simmer gently, stirring every 10 minutes to avoid scorching. When the mixture becomes oily, after about 30 minutes, stir in the tamarind water and fish sauce. Cover and simmer over low heat until the oil returns again, about 5 minutes. Adjust the seasoning with fish sauce.

Remove from the heat. Fold in the coriander, transfer to a warmed platter, and serve.

serves 6

Indonesia

Ayam Goreng Kalasan

fried chicken simmered in coconut juice and lime

Kalasan is an ancient Buddhist temple in central Java, located in the same area as the more famous sites of Borobudur and Prambanan. It is a mystery as to why this chicken dish is named after the temple, but it is commonly served during festive occasions. The chicken is first braised in coconut juice and a few spices, and then it is deep-fried until the skin is crisp and flavorful. I sometimes break with tradition, however, and grill rather than deep-fry the chicken, placing it over hot coals for about five minutes on each side. I also cannot resist the tasty braising liquid, and I often skim off the fat, reduce the liquid to a light sauce consistency, and pour a little over the chicken at the table.

1 chicken, 3½ lb (1.75 kg), quartered or cut into serving pieces

juice of 2 limes

SPICE PASTE

6 peppercorns

4 red Fresno or jalapeño chiles, seeded and quartered

2 large shallots, quartered

3 cloves garlic, quartered

1 green coconut or 2 cups (16 fl oz/500 ml) frozen coconut juice

1 lemongrass stalk, tender midsection only, smashed

5 kaffir lime leaves, spines removed

1 salam *leaf (page 250)*

2 teaspoons salt

ground pepper to taste

vegetable oil for deep-frying

☙ Rub the chicken pieces with the lime juice and set aside while preparing the spice paste.

☙ To make the spice paste, in a mortar, pound the peppercorns. Add the chiles, shallots, and garlic and pound to form a smooth paste. Alternatively, make it in a blender, adding a few tablespoons of water to facilitate the blending.

☙ If using the coconut, crack it open (see sidebar, page 51) and collect the juice in a bowl. You will need 2 cups (16 fl oz/500 ml). If you have less, use water to make up the difference. If using frozen coconut juice, allow it to thaw.

☙ Put the spice paste into a wok or large, heavy pot. Add the chicken pieces, coconut juice, lemongrass, lime leaves, *salam* leaf, 1 teaspoon of the salt, and several grinds of pepper. Bring to a boil over high heat, reduce the heat to medium, cover, and boil gently for 20 minutes. Using a slotted utensil, transfer the chicken to a plate, draining it well. If you would like to serve a little sauce with the chicken, strain the cooking liquid and spoon off any fat from the surface. Return it to a clean saucepan and boil over medium-high heat until it is reduced to a light sauce consistency. Keep warm over very low heat.

☙ Pour the oil to a depth of about 2 inches (5 cm) in a wok or heavy, deep frying pan and heat to 350°F (180°C) on a deep-frying thermometer. Blot the chicken pieces dry with paper towels and sprinkle them with the remaining 1 teaspoon salt. When the oil is ready, add half of the chicken pieces and deep-fry, turning as needed, until golden brown on all sides, about 5 minutes total.

☙ Using tongs or a wire skimmer, transfer the chicken pieces to paper towels to drain. Repeat with the remaining chicken pieces.

☙ Arrange the chicken pieces on a serving platter and serve immediately. If using the sauce, pour it into a small bowl and pass it at the table.

serves 4

SWEETS

Sweets—rice cakes, banana fritters, dessert soups—are typically eaten as afternoon snacks.

THE TRADITIONAL SWEET ENDING for a Southeast Asian meal at home is seasonal fruits. They contribute a light and refreshing finale to the array of flavor-packed dishes that are the mainstays of local dinner tables. Watermelon and honeydew are popular with everyone, while juicy orange sections are particularly favored by the many ethnic Chinese who live in the region.

I have led a number of culinary tours to Southeast Asia, and on every one of them I have been asked about durian, a spiky, battleship green fruit that has been declared the king of fruits by those who love it. Although it is often described as smelling like a sewer but tasting like heaven, no matter how hard I try to find a positive thing to say about this ugly fruit, I cannot come up with a single redeeming feature to cite. It has a soft, almost slimy texture and, to my mind, tastes like a combination of overripe Limburger cheese and rotting spring onions. Strict rules prohibiting the bringing of durian into hotel rooms or onto trains or planes is proof of its truly powerful odor. Yet its devotees swear to its virtues. Watch a group of durian aficionados consume their cherished fruit, and you will see men and women elevated to an almost euphoric state.

I have made several efforts to join the durian partisans. In Malaysia I was driven to a roadside stand known for carrying particularly good specimens. The farmer pointed out a perfectly ripe fruit still hanging on the tree, indicating that he had selected it for me. With a swift swing of his cleaver, it was separated from the branch. With a firm whack across the body of the fruit, it opened to reveal golden yellow, slippery flesh clinging to a flat stone, much like a mango seed.

Durian is never eaten in a hurry but instead enjoyed in a deliberately slow, methodical fashion. In other words, dedicated consumers take this expensive experience—the fruit is pricey unless the year produces a bumper crop—very seriously. They allot plenty of time to savor the fruit properly, in part because it is considered an aphrodisiac. I gave this just-harvested durian a fair trial, but I still came away from the experience not understanding

Preceding spread: In Hanoi's old quarter—teeming with vendors selling everything from fruits, vegetables, and meats to jewelry, cookware, and herbal medicines—a lime seller expertly bags her emerald wares. **Left:** A lucky group of Hmong girls enjoy a special treat of ice-cold popsicles at the weekly market in Bac Ha, in northern Vietnam. Many villages in the area are without electricity, making such frozen treats available only in the larger towns where refrigeration exists. **Above top:** Singapore's grand colonial hotel, the Raffles, with Raffles City—a separate hotel, office building, and shopping complex—rising above it. **Above bottom:** In the past, Indonesia's Moluccas—the Spice Islands of Dutch colonial rule—were the source of highly valuable nutmeg, cloves, cinnamon, and the rich red mace pictured here.

its appeal. Later that evening when I returned to a friend's home, his wife proudly presented me with a durian cut and ready to eat. She had gone to a shop that specializes in the pre-trimmed and carefully packed fruit, prepared at a price comparable to a good bottle of Champagne. I tried again but to no avail, although I was careful to hide my dislike from my kind hosts.

I have found countless other fruits in Southeast Asia to be spectacular, however, and I am discovering new ones all the time, including, most recently, the creamy, white-fleshed dragon fruit that flourishes in Vietnam. After a couple of hours of touring temples in Thailand, for example, I am ready to find a fruit stand and sit down to a plate of lichee, rambutan, star fruit, and mangosteen. Peeling off the leatherlike skin of the last and finding a juicy, sweet podlike fruit inside is the perfect antidote to the hot afternoon. Chased with a glass of iced tea, the fruits rejuvenate me for more touring.

As pointed out, a home-cooked meal, with the exception of a celebration or the

Below: Much of daily life in Ho Chi Minh City is lived outdoors, in its winding back streets, open-air markets, and modest food stalls, and at times a respite from the constant clouds of traffic—taxis, cyclos, motorbikes, bicycles—is in order. **Right top:** The summit of Mount Kinabalu, which rises in Sabah, the eastern Malaysian state that covers the northern tip of Borneo, offers breath-taking views of low clouds cradled by the mountain's sharp granite peaks. **Right bottom:** A tempting assortment of colorful drinks chills in an outdoor market in Jakarta, waiting to quench the thirst of afternoon shoppers.

appearance of a special dinner guest, con-
cludes with fruit. Southeast Asians do have
a sweet tooth, of course, but they prefer to
satisfy it with snacks eaten between meals.
Wonderful small cakes are enjoyed with afternoon tea or coffee, for example. Although a
number of different kinds exist, they are not
generally what Westerners might imagine.
For instance, few traditional cakes are made
with wheat flour. Instead, regular rice flour
or glutinous rice flour is used, typically combined with coconut milk to create a rather
dense gelatin-like product with a slightly
sticky texture. These are unexpected tastes and
consistencies for most Westerners—even for
me, although I arrived in Asia somewhat
accustomed to them because of the rustic and
humble cakes that my Cantonese grand-
mother and aunties made when I was a child.

In my last two decades of travel in
Southeast Asia, however, I have noticed
changes in these sticky, dense cakes, especially
in those known in Singapore as *kueh*. Today
they have a texture more like a thick pudding, making them easier to cut and more
appealing. Some, like *kueh lapis,* have nine or
more very thin layers, with every other layer
a different color. Also, gone is the tired, old
gaudy red used by generations of cooks to
color the batter. Nowadays, the cakes are
turned out in more contemporary and pleas-
ing shades. In another change from the past,
nearly everyone buys the cakes at pastry shops
rather than making them at home, with the
result that these traditional sweets have a
more professional and attractive appearance.

Thais buy similar dense, sticky cakes, which
they call *kanom*. They are fashioned from rice
and tapioca flours, palm sugar, coconut milk,
egg yolks, and other ingredients and are often
perfumed with jasmine or another flower
essence. Market vendors arrange them in eye-
catching displays to snare passing shoppers,
who love a sweet bite at midafternoon or late
in the evening. These sweets vendors also typically carry *loog chooh,* the Thai equivalent
of marzipan, in which mung bean paste is artfully shaped into miniature fruits and then
dipped into boldly colored gelatin. On special
occasions, home cooks prepare a sweet ending

for a meal, such as sticky rice with mangoes; a steamed custard of coconut milk, palm sugar, and duck eggs; or bananas simmered in coconut milk, a snowy white preparation sometimes punctuated with a dash of color in the form of mung beans. This last dish is known as *kluay buat chee,* literally "nun bananas," because of the white robes traditionally worn by the country's Buddhist nuns.

Unlike the Thais, who were never colonized, the Filipinos, especially those of the elite class, draw heavily from the dessert tradition of Europe, serving such classics of their one-time Spanish rulers as flan, meringues, *buñuelos* (sweet fritters), and *bizcocho de fraile* (friar's cake). But many native sweets exist as well, including *suman,* glutinous rice, coconut milk, and palm sugar mixed together and then steamed in banana leaves, and *bibingka,* any of a number of moist rice flour cakes.

A sweet soup called *halo-halo,* served in a wide glass and eaten with a spoon, is also popular in the Philippines. It is a combination of shaved ice, coconut milk, palm sugar, and a varying list of other ingredients, from mung beans and corn kernels to fried rice grains and palm seeds. The finished dish has the look of an exotic snow cone. Similar sweet soups, both hot and cold, are eaten throughout the region. Some use coconut milk as the base, while others call for sugar syrup, and all of them are loaded with an intriguing array of additions, from red beans, fresh water chestnuts, and sweet potato to taro root, pumpkin, tapioca, and black seaweed jelly.

These soups are unusual sweets for anyone who has not been raised in Southeast Asia. In fact, my love for Western desserts at first left me unappreciative of these cakes and soups, and it took time to develop a taste for them. But then I discovered how refreshing many of them are, how they quench my thirst in the hot sun and humidity. I also learned that they can balance the customary rich flavors of the dishes sold by cooks in hawker centers, which are among my favorite places to eat. Fortunately, at work in the stalls just next door to the folks who fry noodles and ladle out soups and curries are vendors of the region's distinctive sweets and tropical fruits.

Above top: Fresh fruit is an integral part of the Thai diet, crushed into cooling drinks, carved into elaborate garnishes, or simply eaten out of hand as a refreshing snack. **Above bottom:** The spire of Thatbyinnyu temple in Bagan (Pagan), the capital of Myanmar (Burma) during its architectural golden age, is bathed in the reddish glow of the setting sun. **Right:** A seaside rope swing gives children—and adventurous souls of all ages—a breathtaking perspective on the azure waters that surround Boracay Island, in the Philippines.

Vietnam

Banh Dua Ra Men

coconut caramel flan

This is the Vietnamese version of French crème caramel, with coconut milk the tropical addition.

CARAMEL

¾ cup (6 oz/185 g) sugar

½ cup (4 fl oz/125 ml) water

CUSTARD

1½ cups (12 fl oz/375 ml) milk

1½ cups (12 fl oz/375 ml) coconut milk (page 245)

⅓ cup (3 oz/90 g) sugar

4 eggs

1 teaspoon vanilla extract (essence)

¼ cup (1 oz/30 g) unsweetened grated dried coconut

☙ Preheat an oven to 325°F (165°C). To make the caramel, put the sugar and water in a heavy saucepan over medium–high heat and heat, stirring, until the sugar dissolves. Cook without stirring until the mixture turns a rich caramel color, 8–12 minutes. Remove from the heat and immediately pour into eight ½-cup (4–fl oz/125-ml) custard cups. Tilt the dishes to coat the bottoms evenly. Set aside.

☙ To make the custard, in a saucepan, combine the milk, coconut milk, and sugar. Place over medium heat and heat only until hot. Remove from the heat.

☙ In a bowl, beat the eggs until blended. Slowly stir in the hot milk mixture, then mix in the vanilla. Pour the mixture through a fine-mesh sieve into a bowl. Gently fold in the dried coconut.

☙ Place the caramel-lined dishes in a roasting pan. Pour enough hot water into the roasting pan to reach halfway up the sides of the dishes. Ladle the egg mixture into the dishes, dividing evenly.

☙ Bake until the custard is set and a knife inserted into the middle of a custard comes out clean, 30–35 minutes. Remove the custards from the water bath and let cool. Cover and refrigerate to chill well before serving.

☙ To serve, run a knife around the edge of the custards and invert onto individual plates.

serves 8

Vietnamese Coffee

Every morning during our stay in Hanoi, my husband and I took our coffee in a small café near the hotel. Such cafés became part of the urban landscape with the French colonization of Vietnam, and today they offer good people-watching along with croissants, baguettes and butter, and Vietnam's strong, fragrant coffee.

The Vietnamese tend coffee plants in the highlands and treat the harvested beans to a dark French roast. Coffee is brewed at the table in a metal filter that fits over a cup or glass, and it may take up to twenty minutes of agonizingly slow dripping before the last drop falls. An order of *ca phe* will deliver a cup of black coffee, while *ca phe sua* is coffee with sweetened condensed milk, *ca phe da* is iced coffee, and *ca phe da sua* is iced coffee with sweetened milk.

To make *ca phe sua*, unscrew the filter, lift off the top, place 2 tablespoons French-roast coffee into the bottom, then replace the filter top. Pour 3 tablespoons sweetened condensed milk into a cup, top with the filter, and moisten the grounds with a little hot water. Let steep for 30 seconds, then fill the filter to the top with hot water and allow it to drip slowly.

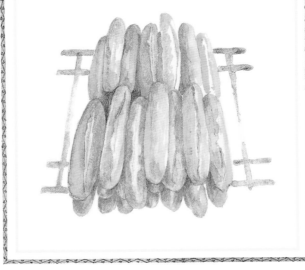

Indonesia

Bubur Ketan Hitam

black sticky rice pudding
with palm sugar

To the ordinary tourist, black sticky rice pudding may not look appealing. Yet once sampled, the dessert wins the votes of even the biggest skeptics. With its subtly nutty flavor, rich texture, and warm coconut sauce, it is the ultimate comfort food. If you can find neither the pandanus leaves nor the extract, add a cinnamon stick for flavor. Palm sugar, in contrast, has a distinctive caramel flavor and is a must for this recipe. In Indonesia, the sugar is extracted from the nectar of the coconut flower. It is cooked down to a thickened syrup, which is then left to solidify in coconut-shell molds.

1½ cups (10½ oz/330 g) black glutinous rice

5–6 cups (40–48 fl oz/1.25–1.5 l) water

2 pandanus leaves or 2 or 3 drops pandanus extract (essence) (page 248)

½ cup (6 oz/185 g) firmly packed palm sugar

1½ cups (12 fl oz/375 ml) thick coconut milk (page 245)

½ teaspoon salt

☙ Wash the rice thoroughly in several changes of cold water until the rinsing water runs clear. Drain well and place in a 1½–2-qt (1.5–2-l) saucepan. Add 5 cups (40 fl oz/1.25 ml) of the water and let stand for at least 2 hours or, preferably, overnight.

☙ Bring the rice and water to a boil over medium-high heat and cook, stirring occasionally, for about 40 minutes. If using the pandanus leaves, scrape the surface with the tines of a fork. Add the pandanus leaves or extract and palm sugar, stir well, and reduce the heat to low. Simmer, stirring frequently to prevent sticking, until the rice is tender and most of the liquid has evaporated, 20–30 minutes longer. Check for doneness and, if needed, simmer a little longer, adding more water if dry, until tender.

☙ Meanwhile, in another saucepan over low heat, combine the coconut milk and salt. Cook, stirring continuously, until it thickens enough to coat the back of a spoon, about 15 minutes.

☙ Spoon into dessert bowls and pour the coconut sauce over the top. Serve at once.

serves 6

Thailand

Med Maenglak Nam Kati

sweet basil seeds in coconut milk

Plump, black lemon basil (maenglak) seeds look like tiny dark eyes staring up at you from this dessert soup. The seeds, with their subtle flavor and slippery texture, are both unusual and intriguing. When you soak them in water, they swell into clear, gelatinous beads with a black dot at the center. They are often thrown into soups and curries at the last minute, and at a favorite restaurant of mine in Bangkok, the wonderfully named My Choice, the kitchen is famous for its basil seed ice cream. The seeds are sold in Thai markets, usually under the label "dried sweet basil seeds," or in Vietnamese markets as hot e.

2 teaspoons sweet basil seeds (see note)

2 cups (16 fl oz/500 ml) water

½ cup (6 oz/185 g) firmly packed palm sugar or light brown sugar

2 cups (16 fl oz/500 ml) coconut milk (page 245)

1½ cups (9 oz/280 g) young, green coconut meat (see sidebar, page 51) or cubed honeydew melon (½-inch/12-mm cubes)

☙ In a bowl, combine the basil seeds with 1 cup (8 fl oz/250 ml) of the water. Let stand until the seeds swell into jellylike beads, about 20 minutes. Drain in a fine sieve.

☙ Meanwhile, in a saucepan over medium heat, combine the remaining 1 cup (8 fl oz/250 ml) water and the palm or brown sugar and heat, stirring, until the sugar is dissolved. Remove the pan from the heat and add the coconut milk. Mix well, cover, and refrigerate until well chilled, about 2 hours.

☙ To serve, distribute equal portions of the coconut meat or honeydew and the basil seeds among individual dessert bowls. Divide the coconut milk evenly among the bowls, pouring it over the fruit and seeds. Serve chilled.

serves 6

Tropical Fruits

Southeast Asians treasure their bountiful variety of fruits, tropical and subtropical specimens that delight the eye and the palate. Every time I am in Asia, I encounter a new member of this large family. On my last trip to Vietnam, I was served what was called a dragon fruit, a stunning sphere with a reddish pink exterior that has the texture of banana skin and a handful of spikes tipped with emerald green. The white flesh had a subtle crispness, much like an Asian pear, and was flecked with tiny black seeds. It was difficult to eat because it was so beautiful.

Although the local favorite throughout the region is the big, spiky durian, I have yet to be able to get beyond its notorious odor and strong flavor and join the crowd. Fortunately, I have many other choices. I can barely control myself in the Southeast Asian sea of crisp, tart, juicy star fruits and red-husked, deliciously sweet mangosteens. Here I can eat all the lichees I want, breaking open their strawberry red skins to extract the shiny white translucent flesh. Stubby finger bananas and large cooking bananas are full flavored, and

the football-sized papayas and golden mangoes are the sweetest in the world. I can also choose from among the blush-colored, faintly sweet rose apple; the teardrop-shaped salak, also called snake fruit for the brown triangular scales that make up its skin; the rambutan, a bright red or yellow-green fruit with hairy spikes and juicy, tart pulp; and the more commonplace watermelon and pineapple.

When I am in the mood for a cooling snack, I head for a fresh-fruit vendor at a hawker center, who makes up a plate from whatever I point out in the usually large display. If I am thirsty, I order a glass of freshly squeezed star-fruit, watermelon, or sugarcane juice. And I can almost never pass a stand with young, green coconuts without stopping. The vendor whacks off the top of the nut and sticks a straw in the hole, and I slowly sip the cool liquid contained inside—guaranteed to hit the spot on even the hottest day.

Fruits are also the everyday dessert for Southeast Asians. They are healthful and satisfying and just the right finish to a meal of highly seasoned dishes.

Indonesia

Pisang Goreng

banana fritters on a stick

Most visitors to Southeast Asia think of banana fritters as dessert. In Indonesia, however, they are also enjoyed for breakfast or as a snack. The fritters are best when made with the small thin-skinned bananas found in Southeast Asia. Thais prefer a small, firm banana called gluay nam wah, *which tends to be particularly sweet, is the perfect size, and stays fairly firm when cooked. Indonesians are partial to the larger sweet king banana, or* raja.

1 cup (5 oz/155 g) all-purpose (plain) flour, or as needed

½ cup (2 oz/60 g) rice flour

2 teaspoons baking powder

½ teaspoon salt

1 cup (8 fl oz/250 ml) water, or as needed

vegetable oil for deep-frying

8 small, firm bananas, peeled

confectioners' (icing) sugar or ground cinnamon

2 limes, cut into wedges

☼ In a bowl, sift together the 1 cup (5 oz/155 g) all-purpose flour, rice flour, baking powder, and salt. Stir in the 1 cup (8 fl oz/250 ml) water to make a smooth, thick pancakelike batter. Adjust the consistency by adding more all-purpose flour or water.

☼ Pour the oil to a depth of 2 inches (5 cm) in a wok or deep frying pan and heat to 350°F (180°C) on a deep-frying thermometer. Spear one end of a banana with a bamboo skewer, running the skewer all the way through to the other end, then dip it into the batter, coating evenly. Carefully lower the battered banana into the hot oil, leaving the skewer in. Repeat with as many more bananas as will fit in the pan without crowding. Deep-fry the bananas until they are crisp and golden, about 3 minutes. Using a slotted utensil, transfer to paper towels to drain.

☼ Serve the bananas hot, still on their skewers. Dust with confectioners' sugar or cinnamon. Each diner squeezes lime juice over his or her serving.

serves 4

Khao Niow Ma-Muang

sticky rice with mangoes

When ripe mangoes are not in season, the kanom *(sweets) vendor offers different toppings for the rice, including a sweet-salty one that uses dried shrimp.*

2 cups (14 oz / 440 g) long-grain glutinous rice

2⅓ cups (19 fl oz / 590 ml) water

1 can (13½ fl oz / 420 ml) coconut milk (page 245)

⅔ cup (5 oz / 155 g) sugar

½ teaspoon salt

2 pandanus leaves or 2 or 3 drops pandanus extract (essence) (optional; page 248)

2 ripe mangoes, peeled, pitted, and sliced

3 tablespoons unsweetened grated dried coconut, toasted

❦ Wash the rice in cold water until the water runs clear. Drain, place in a saucepan, add the water, and let stand for at least 2 hours or, preferably, overnight.

❦ Bring the rice and water to a boil and boil, stirring occasionally, until most of the liquid has reduced, leaving little craters in the rice. Cover tightly, reduce the heat to very low, and cook until tender, about 20 minutes. Remove from the heat and let stand, covered, for at least 10 minutes.

❦ Meanwhile, pour the coconut milk into a saucepan. Add the sugar and salt. Place over medium heat and bring to a simmer. If using the pandanus leaves, scrape the surface with the tines of a fork. Add the leaves or extract, if using, to the coconut milk. Simmer for 10 minutes to blend the flavors. Remove the leaves, if used, and discard. Continue simmering until the coconut milk is thick enough to coat the back of a spoon, 3–5 minutes longer.

❦ Transfer the rice to a large bowl, pour in about half of the coconut sauce, and fold in gently. The rice should be moist but not swimming in coconut sauce. If possible, let the rice stand for 30 minutes before serving, to allow the sauce to be absorbed fully.

❦ Spoon onto individual plates and top with the remaining sauce and mango slices. Garnish with the toasted coconut.

serves 6

Malaysia

Sago Gula Melaka

sago in coconut milk pudding with palm sugar

In Malaysia, gula Melaka *translates literally as Malacca sugar. But when you ask for* gula Melaka *in a restaurant, you will get this popular pudding made from sago, coconut milk, and palm sugar syrup.*

1 cup (6 oz / 185 g) sago pearls or pearl tapioca

8 cups (64 fl oz / 2 l) water

SYRUP

¼-lb (125-g) block dark palm sugar, shaved

2 tablespoons treacle or dark molasses

¾ cup (6 fl oz / 180 ml) water

1 pandanus leaf, scraped with the tines of a fork (page 248)

pinch of salt

1 cup (8 fl oz / 250 ml) thick coconut milk (page 245)

❧ If using sago, pick over for any large impurities, then place in a sieve and shake to release any dust and dirt. If using pearl tapioca, you do not have to clean it. In a saucepan, bring the water to a boil. Add the sago or tapioca in a steady stream, stirring continuously to keep the pearls separated. Continue cooking until the pearls swell and become transparent, about 10 minutes. Pour into a fine sieve and rinse thoroughly with cold water. Divide the sago or tapioca among 6 small custard cups, cover, and refrigerate until set, about 1½ hours.

❧ To make the syrup, in a saucepan, combine the palm sugar, treacle or molasses, water, pandanus leaf, and salt. Bring to a boil over high heat, stirring continuously until the sugar is dissolved. Continue cooking until the mixture reduces to 1 cup (8 fl oz / 250 ml), 5–8 minutes. Remove from the heat and let cool. Remove and discard the pandanus leaf.

❧ To serve, unmold each custard cup into a shallow bowl. Pour an equal amount of the coconut milk and syrup over each portion. Serve immediately.

serves 6

Thailand

Thab Thim Krob

mock pomegranate pearls
in coconut milk

The climate zones in Thailand are often correctly described as hot, very hot, and furnace hot. The heat is humid throughout most of the year, and after strolling through the streets, the most welcome sight is that of a vendor selling cold fresh fruit drinks. The only better sight is Bangkok's Bussaracum restaurant. It serves a first-rate thab thim krob, fresh water chestnuts dyed red and blue with natural colorings, rolled in tapioca flour, and served in chilled sweetened coconut milk in a coconut shell. The red ones are said to resemble pomegranate pearls, hence the name. It is important to serve the dessert well chilled in lots of crushed ice.

1¼ cups (10 oz/315 g) sugar

2 cups (16 fl oz/500 ml) plus 6 tablespoons
(3 fl oz/90 ml) water

1 can (13½ fl oz/420 ml) coconut milk
(page 245)

1 lb (500 g) fresh water chestnuts

½ teaspoon red food coloring

½ teaspoon blue food coloring

1 cup (4 oz/125 g) tapioca flour

crushed or shaved ice

♛ In a small saucepan over high heat, combine the sugar and the 2 cups (16 fl oz/500 ml) water and bring to a boil, stirring until the sugar has dissolved. Continue to cook until a light syrup forms, about 5 minutes. Remove from the heat and let cool. Pour off half of the sugar syrup and set aside. In a bowl or pitcher, combine the remaining sugar syrup and the coconut milk and stir to mix. Cover and refrigerate.

♛ With a paring knife, peel the water chestnuts. Rinse with cold water. Cut into ¼-inch (6-mm) pieces and drop into a bowl of cold water. When all the water chestnuts are cut, drain and divide evenly among 3 bowls. Add 2 tablespoons of the remaining water to each bowl. Tint one bowl with a few drops of red food coloring, tint the second bowl with a few drops of blue food coloring, and leave the third bowl clear. Stir each bowl of water chestnuts until the pieces are evenly colored. Divide the tapioca flour evenly among another 3 bowls. Drain a bowl of the water chestnut beads and toss them into a bowl of tapioca flour, then let stand for 10 minutes. Repeat the coating process with the two remaining batches of water chestnuts and tapioca flour.

♛ Bring a large saucepan three-fourths full of water to a boil. Using your fingers, separate the water chestnut beads in the first bowl. With a slotted spoon, scoop up the beads, shaking off the excess flour, and drop the beads into the boiling water. Cook, stirring frequently, until the beads float to the top, about 3 minutes. Scoop them out with a slotted spoon, drain well, and place in a large bowl. Add cold water to cover. Repeat with the remaining beads, boiling each color separately but combining the cooled beads in the same bowl of cold water. Stir the beads together, cover, and refrigerate until thoroughly chilled.

♛ To serve, drain the beads and divide them evenly among 6 custard cups or, if available, hollowed-out coconut shells. Cover the beads with ice, then top with the prepared coconut milk. Serve at once. Pass the reserved sugar syrup at the table.

serves 6

Myanmar (Burma)

Sarnwin Makin

baked semolina pudding
with sesame seeds

The semolina (called sooji *by the Indians,* shwegi *by the Burmese), cardamom, and ghee in this Burmese sweet reflect the Indian influence on local cooking.*

1 cup (5 oz/160 ml) fine semolina flour

½ teaspoon ground cardamom

¼ teaspoon salt

2 cups (16 fl oz/500 ml) coconut milk
(page 245)

2 cups (16 fl oz/500 ml) water

¾ cup (5 oz/155 g) firmly packed palm sugar

¼ cup (2 oz/60 g) ghee or unsalted butter

2 egg whites, lightly whisked

¼ cup (1½ oz/45 g) blanched almonds

2 tablespoons sesame seeds, toasted

❧ In a dry frying pan over medium-low heat, toast the semolina flour, stirring frequently, until light golden brown, 8–10 minutes. Remove from the heat and let cool. Stir in the cardamom and salt.

❧ Preheat an oven to 325°F (165°C). Lightly butter or oil an 8-by-13-inch (20-by-33-cm) cake pan.

❧ In a saucepan over medium heat, combine the coconut milk, water, and palm sugar. Heat, stirring, until the mixture is smooth and well blended. Gradually pour in the semolina, whisking continuously to prevent lumping. When the mixture is smooth, continue cooking and stirring until you have a thick, dense mixture that pulls away from the sides and bottom of the pan, about 10 minutes. As you stir, you should be able to see the bottom of the pan easily. Beat in the ghee or butter, a small amount at a time, and continue cooking until well incorporated. Remove from the heat and let cool slightly.

❧ Add the egg whites and mix thoroughly. Pour the mixture into the prepared pan. Decorate with the almonds and then sprinkle with the sesame seeds.

❧ Bake until golden brown and firm to the touch, about 1 hour. Transfer to a wire rack and let cool completely. Cut into diamonds and serve.

serves 8

Vietnam

Chuoi Chung

bananas and tapioca in coconut milk

Bananas stewed in coconut milk is a popular afternoon snack in Vietnam. A Vietnamese friend in San Francisco re-created that experience for me when he cooked this sweet soup one day for his three daughters who had just returned home from school.

6 ripe bananas, peeled and cut crosswise into thirds

2 teaspoons salt

6 cups (48 fl oz/1.5 l) water

¾ cup (4 oz/125 g) pearl tapioca

⅔ cup (5 oz/155 g) sugar

1 tablespoon cornstarch (cornflour) mixed with 3 tablespoons water

1 can (13½ fl oz/420 ml) coconut milk
(page 245)

❧ Place the bananas in a large bowl and add water to cover and ½ teaspoon of the salt. Set aside.

❧ In a saucepan over high heat, bring the 6 cups (48 fl oz/1.5 l) water to a boil. Add the pearl tapioca, reduce the heat to low, and simmer until the pearls are clear, about 10 minutes. Add the sugar and the remaining 1½ teaspoons salt and stir to dissolve. Stir in the diluted cornstarch until the liquid is lightly thickened, 2–3 minutes. Drain the bananas and add to the saucepan along with the coconut milk. Cook over medium heat until tender but firm, about 5 minutes.

❧ Remove the pan from the heat and divide the bananas and liquid evenly among individual bowls. Serve hot or warm.

serves 6

The Burmese Buddhist calendar is filled with pagoda festivals, each one a celebration of ritual, music, and foods, both savory and sweet.

Singapore

Kueh Lapis

layered multicolor rice cake

Violet Oon, a Nonya living in Singapore, introduced me to kueh lapis, *sticky multicolored cakes made from rice flour and coconut milk. The flavor is sweet, and the texture, from a Western point of view, is unusual. But with a few bites of one of these steamed sweets, you will undoubtedly become a convert. Although Ms. Oon feels that these cakes are done best by the bakeries that specialize in them, I have developed this home-style version. It is not a match for the best bakery effort, but it is very good. It is important to use a nonstick square metal cake pan and to oil it well. If you have the patience, pour very thin layers of batter to make as many layers as you can. If a layer seems too thin, it probably isn't. Also, be sure that each layer is thoroughly cooked, or firm, before pouring on the next layer. I have included only two colors here, but bakery cakes often include several different colors.*

kueh lapis *is refreshing paired with a cup of tea in the afternoon, a fashionable custom in Asia.*

1 pandanus leaf (page 248)

1⅓ cups (11 oz/345 g) sugar

1⅓ cups (11 fl oz/345 ml) water

2 cups (16 fl oz/500 ml) coconut milk (page 245)

⅛ teaspoon salt

3⅓ cups (13 oz/410 g) rice flour or glutinous rice flour

2½ tablespoons tapioca flour

¼ teaspoon green or red food coloring

vegetable oil for oiling the pan

❀ Split the pandanus leaf in half along the spine. With the tines of a fork, scrape the leaf in several places to release more flavor. Put the leaf into a small saucepan with the sugar and water and place over high heat. Bring to a boil, stirring to dissolve the sugar. Once it boils, remove from the heat and set aside to cool to room temperature. When cool, remove and discard the pandanus leaf and stir in the coconut milk and salt.

❀ In a large bowl, stir together the rice flour and tapioca flour. Slowly add the coconut milk mixture, whisking to blend. Pour 2½ cups (20 fl oz/625 ml) of the batter into a bowl and put the remainder in a separate bowl. Add the food coloring to the larger portion, mixing well. Leave the other uncolored.

❀ Set up a steamer that can accommodate a nonstick 6-inch (15-cm) square metal cake pan. Brush the bottom and sides of the cake pan with oil. Pour water into the bottom of the steamer and bring to a boil. Set the cake pan on the steamer tray above the boiling water and preheat the pan for 5 minutes.

❀ Measure out ⅔ cup (5 fl oz/160 ml) of the colored batter and pour into the cake pan. Cover with a sheet of parchment (baking) paper cut to fit over the edge of the pan, then cover the steamer and steam over rapidly boiling water for 8 minutes. Uncover, remove the parchment paper, and check that the batter is set, opaque, and firm. Measure out ⅓–½ cup (3–4 fl oz/ 80–125 ml) of the white batter and pour it over the first layer. It should just cover it. Cover again with the parchment paper, cover the steamer, and steam for 5 minutes. Repeat the layers, alternating the colors and using the parchment paper each time, until you have 9 layers or more or until the pan is filled to the top, ending with a colored layer. Steam the final layer for 10 minutes.

❀ When the cake is done, remove the pan from the steamer and let the cake cool completely. Using a thin, oiled spatula or knife, run it along the inside edge of the pan to loosen the cake's sides. Place a piece of plastic wrap over the top of the pan and invert onto a work surface. Cut the cake into 12–15 diamonds or rectangles. Transfer to a platter to serve.

makes 12–15 pieces

The Versatile Coconut Palm

The coconut palm, which can soar to a height of one hundred feet (33 m) and flourishes when grown within a stone's throw of the sea, is a fixture in every Southeast Asian culture. Not only are the palm's meat, milk, and juice used in the kitchen, but the trunk, leaves, and shells—indeed, the entire tree—are pressed into service in one way or another.

The leaves are woven into baskets, mats, hats, and roofs, and the fibrous husks, known as coir, are used to make carpets, fishing line, brushes, and cooking fires. The shell makes a perfectly shaped drinking cup or small mixing bowl, and the oil, extracted from the mature meat, not only is an important cooking oil, but also goes into the manufacture of soaps, shampoos, candles, and skin creams. The trunk is used in the building of houses and bridges, and the bud, or palm heart, that crowns the tree is a pricey salad ingredient. In some places, even the roots are put to use by finely grinding them for medicine.

Palm sugar is also made from the coconut palm (as well as other palms). Ranging from a muted yellow to a dark chocolate brown, the sugar is made by boiling the sap until it crystallizes, and then forming the mass into flat cakes or cylinders. Palm sugar, which has a luscious caramel flavor and is not cloyingly sweet, is known as *gula Melaka, gula Jawa,* and *nam tan peep,* in Malaysia, Indonesia, and Thailand, respectively.

The sap is also used for making wine or for distilling into a fiery, tongue-numbing liquor. The blossoms yield a liquid as well, which can be sipped fresh, distilled or fermented into alcoholic beverages, or made into vinegar.

GLOSSARY

The following entries cover basic recipes and key Southeast Asian ingredients called for throughout this book. All of the ingredients can be found in Asian markets or in the Asian section of well-stocked food stores. For information on items not listed below, please refer to the index.

ANNATTO SEEDS

The Spanish introduced these triangular seeds of a Latin American tree to the Philippines. They impart a reddish brown color and fragrant flavor to meat dishes.

BAMBOO SHOOTS

The ivory to white shoots of the bamboo plant are sold sliced, chopped, shredded, or whole in cans. Some Asian markets sell the same processed shoots in bulk, usually displayed immersed in water in large plastic buckets. Fresh shoots, only rarely seen outside of Asia, are toxic if not properly preboiled, a lengthy process. Drain and rinse the canned shoots well before use.

BANANA BLOSSOMS

Also known as banana buds or banana flowers, these are unopened banana flowers, peeled of their purplish petals to leave just the tender hearts. They are sold fresh in some Asian markets but are more commonly available canned in brine. Used sliced or shredded, they tend to discolor on exposure to air and should be rinsed well and sprinkled with lemon juice before use.

BANANA LEAVES

These large, pliable green leaves are used to wrap food for steaming, grilling, or roasting, during which they impart a mildly grassy flavor and, sometimes, a pale touch of color. They may also be pressed into service as plates, placemats, or platters. Look for frozen banana leaves in ethnic markets, and wipe well with a damp towel before using.

CABBAGE, CHINESE PICKLED

Cabbage packed in brine and allowed to ferment. Sold in cans, jars, crocks, and in bulk, the wilted leaves and crisp stems add a sharp tang to soups, stir-fries, noodles, and other dishes. Many brands are sold, all pickled slightly differently, so sample a variety to find the one you like.

CANDLENUTS

Resembling small, waxy hazelnuts (filberts), these oil-rich nuts—known in Malaysia and Indonesia as *buah keras*—are used primarily as a thickening agent in spice pastes. Blanched almonds may be substituted.

CARAMEL SYRUP

This Vietnamese syrup is mixed into savory dishes to add a rich flavor and bronze sheen to sauces.

TO MAKE THE SYRUP: In a saucepan, combine 1 cup (8 oz/250 g) sugar with ¼ cup (2 fl oz/60 ml) water and bring to a boil over high heat; do not stir. Swirl the pan to help dissolve the sugar clinging to the sides. Reduce the heat to medium-low and simmer gently for 10–15 minutes. When the syrup turns a deep brown and the bubbles become sluggish, remove from the heat and slowly pour in ¼ cup (2 fl oz/60 ml) hot water. Return the pan to medium-high heat and cook, stirring continuously, until the caramel is dissolved and is thick and syrupy, 3–5 minutes. Stir in 1 teaspoon lemon juice. Let cool, then store in a capped jar in a cool, dark place indefinitely. *Makes about ¾ cup (6 fl oz/180 ml).*

CARDAMOM

The dried pods of this highly aromatic spice may be used whole, or their papery husks may be split open to free the small, spherical seeds. Ground cardamom is also available.

TO TOAST CARDAMOM: Heat whole pods or seeds in a dry frying pan over medium heat for a few minutes until their aroma develops.

CHICKPEA FLOUR

Also known as *besan,* this flour is ground from dried chickpeas (garbanzo beans) or sometimes from dried yellow peas or lentils. A popular ingredient in the Indian vegetarian kitchen, it is used to make doughs and batters and also is sometimes toasted like toasted rice powder (page 251) for use as a condiment. Store in an airtight container in a cool place to retard spoilage.

CHINESE BROCCOLI

This member of the cabbage family vaguely resembles broccoli, thus its English name. When Chinese broccoli

CHICKEN STOCK

Southeast Asian cooks use chicken stock rich in natural chicken flavor and with little or no seasoning. Once the stock is made, strip the meat from the chicken pieces and use it in other dishes. If you are short of time, purchase chicken broth in cans or cartons, or use a dehydrated concentrate. Do not buy products that contain European-style seasoning.

1 chicken, cut up

2 green (spring) onions

♨ In a large pot, combine the chicken with water to cover. Bring to a boil, skimming any impurities off the surface until the liquid is clear. Add the green onions, reduce the heat to low, cover, and simmer for 2 hours. Lift out the chicken pieces and set aside. Strain the stock, skim the fat from the surface with a large spoon, and use immediately, or cool, cover, and refrigerate, then lift off the congealed fat. Refrigerate the stock for up to 3 days or freeze for up to 2 months. *Makes about 6 cups (48 fl oz/1.5 l)*

flowers, it produces small white blossoms that are also edible. The crisp stems and rich green leaves have a slightly bitter taste that is delicious in stir-fries and noodle dishes. Also known as Chinese kale and as *gai lan* in Cantonese.

CHINESE CELERY

This relative of the familiar broad-stemmed celery of Western kitchens has slim stalks and leaves that look like those of flat-leaf (Italian) parsley. Its pleasant celery taste is a good addition to soups and braises.

CHINESE CRULLERS

Resembling the long, twisted Western doughnuts of the same name, these deep-fried treats are served as a snack in China and in Chinese communities in Southeast Asia. Called *yu tiao* in Mandarin, they are most easily found in Asian markets that also carry fresh noodles.

CHINESE SAUSAGE

Known most commonly by the Cantonese *lap cheong*, this variety of air-dried pork sausage has a sweet, slightly pungent flavor and a coarse texture. The slender links are usually steamed first and then cut up for adding to fried rice or dumplings. Many Chinese delis hang the sausages in the window, ready for sale. They also are available in vacuum-packed pouches. Some shops carry similar sausages made from duck liver.

COCONUT CREAM AND COCONUT MILK

To make coconut cream and milk at home, see the sidebar on page 51. Good-quality unsweetened canned coconut milk, with an excellent ratio of cream to milk, is a welcome shortcut when time is at a premium. Do not shake the can before opening. Once open, first scrape off the thick mass on top, which is the cream. The next layer is an opaque white liquid, which is coconut milk, and finally there is a clear liquid, which is thin coconut milk.

CORIANDER

Fresh green coriander leaves, also called cilantro and Chinese parsley, add an aromatic taste when used as a garnish or seasoning. The seeds of the plant, used whole or ground as a spice, have a bright, almost citruslike flavor. In Thailand, the flavorful roots of the fresh plant are also used. Although not common, sometimes they can be found still attached to fresh coriander stems.

CRAB

Fresh crabs abound in the coastal waters, rivers, lakes, and swamps of Southeast Asia. Fresh nonnative crabs work equally well in authentically styled dishes of the region, and freshly cooked crabmeat is always preferable.

TO CLEAN A FRESHLY COOKED CRAB: Hold the top shell of the crab in one hand while grasping the legs and claws with the other hand. Gently twist and pull away the shell. Turn the crab's body over and twist off and discard the triangular apron. Pull off and discard the feathery gills, then cut out the mandibles at the face end.

CHILE PASTE

Cooks in Southeast Asia make use of pastes that combine roasted fresh or dried chiles with a variety of other seasonings. Various commercial chile pastes are sold, but a good chile paste is also easy to make at home. See also *sambal ulek* (page 250).

THAI ROASTED CHILE PASTE

6 large dried red chiles

6 cloves garlic, unpeeled

2 shallots, unpeeled, halved

2 teaspoons dried shrimp paste

2 tablespoons dried shrimp

3 tablespoons tamarind water (see sidebar, page 114)

2 tablespoons palm sugar or brown sugar

1 teaspoon salt

⅓ cup (3 fl oz/80 ml) vegetable oil

❧ In a dry wok or frying pan over medium heat, fry the chiles, garlic, and shallots, stirring often, until they darken and become dry and brittle. When the chiles are charred on both sides, after 3–5 minutes, transfer them to a plate. Leave the garlic and shallots in the pan until they darken and feel tender when pressed, 5–8 minutes longer, then transfer to the plate. Split open the chiles and shake out the seeds. Peel the garlic and shallots. Wrap the dried shrimp paste in a piece of aluminum foil, and place the packet directly on a stove-top burner turned on to medium-high heat. Toast, turning once or twice, until fragrant, 1–2 minutes. Open the packet; if the shrimp paste crumbles, it is ready. Let cool.

❧ In a blender, process the dried shrimp to a fine powder. Add the chiles, garlic, shallots, dried shrimp paste, tamarind water, palm sugar or brown sugar, salt, and about 1 tablespoon of the vegetable oil. Blend until a smooth paste forms. In a small saucepan over medium-high heat, warm the remaining vegetable oil and add the paste. Reduce the heat to a gentle sizzle and fry the paste, stirring frequently, until it darkens to a deep reddish dark brown and has a sticky, oily consistency, 10–15 minutes. Let cool, transfer to a jar, cover tightly, and refrigerate for up to 1 year.

Makes about 1 cup (8 fl oz/250 ml)

Gently bend each leg and claw backward and twist them free from the body. Spoon out the creamy yellow tomalley and reserve it for another use, if desired. Rinse the body and pat dry with paper towels. Using a cleaver, chop the body into quarters. Crack each leg and claw at the joint with a mallet. At this point, the crab is ready to stir-fry or braise. To extract the crabmeat, pick it out from the body and legs.

CRAB PASTE

Similar to fish paste and sold in small jars, this powerful-tasting seasoning is made by salting and fermenting crabmeat. Shrimp paste (page 250) may be substituted.

CURRY LEAVES

These small leaves of a tropical shrub are used whole, fresh or dried, to add aromatic flavor to simmered dishes. They are also sometimes pounded to a powder to season egg dishes and marinades. Bay leaves may be substituted, although their perfume differs.

DEEP-FRIED BEAN CURD

When deep-fried in hot oil, soybean curd (also called tofu) takes on a golden brown color, rich flavor, and satisfyingly chewy texture. Deep-fried bean curd is sold in Asian markets usually packaged in plastic and sometimes refrigerated. It is available in cubes generally about 1½ inches (4 cm) square. Use within 3 days of purchase.

FISH CAKES

Made from mild-tasting fish, eggs, and rice flour or other binders, ready-cooked fish cakes are available fried, steamed, or baked in a variety of shapes, the most common of which are slabs and balls. They also come in different ethnic styles—Vietnamese, Chinese, Japanese, Korean—with different seasonings and textures. Look for them in the refrigerated section of Asian markets.

FISH SAUCE

In many Southeast Asian kitchens, fish sauce assumes the same seasoning role played by soy sauce in China and Japan. Made by layering anchovies or other tiny fish with salt in barrels or jars and leaving them to ferment, the dark amber liquid adds pungent, salty flavor to many dishes. The two most common types are Thai *nam pla* and Vietnamese *nuoc mam*, with the latter having a milder flavor. Fish sauce is known as *patis* in the Philippines, *tuk trey* in Cambodia, and *ngan-pya-ye* in Myanmar (Burma).

FIVE-SPICE POWDER

The components of this popular southern Chinese spice blend vary, but star anise, fennel seeds or aniseeds, cinnamon, cloves, Sichuan peppercorns, and sometimes ginger are usually part of the mix.

GALANGAL

Similar in appearance to ginger, to which it is related, this gnarled rhizome adds a mustardlike, slightly medicinal flavor to simmered dishes. Known in Thailand as *kha,*

CURRY PASTES

In many Southeast Asian nations, and especially in Thailand, cooks use curry pastes to prepare curries and other dishes. Although commercial curry pastes are sold in markets, freshly made pastes deliver the best flavor.

THAI RED CURRY PASTE

1 tablespoon coriander seeds

2 teaspoons cumin seeds

½ teaspoon peppercorns

½ teaspoon coarse salt

12 dried long red chiles, cracked, seeded, soaked in warm water for 20 minutes, and drained

8 red Fresno or jalapeño chiles, seeded and chopped

4 slices fresh galangal, peeled and chopped, or 2 slices dried galangal, soaked in warm water for 30 minutes, drained, and chopped

2 fresh kaffir lime rind strips, chopped; 2 dried kaffir lime rind strips, soaked in warm water for 30 minutes, drained, and chopped; or rind of 1 regular lime, chopped

3 lemongrass stalks, tender midsection only, chopped

6 cloves garlic, quartered

2 large shallots, quartered

2 tablespoons fresh coriander (cilantro) roots or stems

1 teaspoon dried shrimp paste

vegetable oil or water, if needed

In a small, dry frying pan over medium heat, toast the coriander seeds, cumin seeds, peppercorns, and salt until fragrant, about 5 minutes. Transfer to a mortar or spice grinder and pound or grind to a fine powder.

Transfer the ground spices to a blender and add the drained chiles, fresh chiles, galangal, lime rind, lemongrass, garlic, shallots, fresh coriander roots or stems, and shrimp paste. Blend until a smooth paste forms. If necessary, add a few tablespoons of vegetable oil or water to facilitate the blending. Transfer the curry paste to a jar, cover tightly, and store in the refrigerator for up to 3 weeks. For longer storage, transfer the curry paste to a lock-top plastic freezer bag, seal closed, and freeze for up to several months.

Makes ¾–1 cup (6–8 oz/185–250 g)

THAI GREEN CURRY PASTE

1½ tablespoons coriander seeds

1 tablespoon cumin seeds

1 teaspoon salt

½ teaspoon peppercorns

4 green Fresno chiles

1½ oz (45 g) green serrano or Thai chiles

4 slices fresh galangal, peeled and chopped, or 2 slices dried galangal, soaked in warm water for 30 minutes, drained, and chopped

2 fresh kaffir lime rind strips, chopped; 2 dried kaffir lime rind strips, soaked in warm water for 30 minutes, drained, and chopped; or rind of 1 regular lime, chopped

2 lemongrass stalks, tender midsection only, chopped

in Indonesia and Malaysia as *laos,* and sometimes also referred to in English as Siamese ginger, galangal is available fresh and frozen whole and as dried slices. If only the dried form can be found, use half the quantity you would for fresh. If dried galangal will be pounded or blended, reconstitute it first by soaking in warm water for 30 minutes until pliable. For some soups and curries, the unsoaked pieces can be added directly to the simmering liquid.

GARAM MASALA

This keynote spice mixture of northern India turns up in Southeast Asian kitchens. The blend—sold commercially or made at home—features coriander seeds, cumin, black pepper, cardamom, cloves, cinnamon, nutmeg, and mace. It is typically used to season dishes at the beginning of cooking and is sometimes sprinkled over finished dishes.

GARLIC, PICKLED

These popular Thai and Chinese pickles are made by preserving whole peeled heads of garlic in vinegar. Both tart and sweet varieties of pickled garlic may be found in jars or cans, ready to eat as a relish or to add a spike of aromatic flavor to meat or noodle dishes or to sauces.

GARLIC CHIVES

Although they resemble common chives, these slender grasslike stalks have a noticeable edge of garlicky flavor. Also known as Chinese chives.

GARLIC OIL

Garlic is favored throughout Southeast Asia, and one of its most appealing forms is as a combination of garlic-scented oil and crisp fried garlic bits.

TO MAKE GARLIC OIL: Preheat a small frying pan or wok over medium heat. Add ⅓ cup (3 fl oz/80 ml) vegetable oil and heat to 325°F (165°C) on a deep-frying thermometer. Meanwhile, chop 8 garlic cloves. Drop a bit of the chopped garlic into the oil. If it sizzles right away without burning, add the rest of the garlic and fry, stirring with a spoon to break up any clumps. When the garlic begins to turn golden, after about 3 minutes, remove the pan from the heat and let the garlic continue frying until golden brown, about 2 minutes longer. Let cool to room temperature and pour through a fine-mesh sieve placed over a glass jar. Store, tightly sealed, in the refrigerator for up to 1 month. *Makes about ⅓ cup (3 fl oz/80 ml) oil and 2 tablespoons garlic bits.*

4 cloves garlic, quartered

2 large shallots, quartered

2 tablespoons fresh coriander (cilantro) roots or stems

1 teaspoon dried shrimp paste

vegetable oil or water, if needed

In a small, dry frying pan over medium heat, toast the coriander seeds, cumin seeds, salt, and peppercorns until fragrant, about 5 minutes. Transfer to a mortar or spice grinder and pound or grind to a fine powder. Transfer the ground spices to a blender and add all the chiles, the galangal, lime rind, lemongrass, garlic, shallots, fresh coriander roots or stems, and shrimp paste. Blend until a smooth paste forms, adding a few tablespoons of oil or water to facilitate the blending if needed. Store as for red curry paste. *Makes ¾–1 cup (6–8 oz/185–250 g)*

THAI MUSSAMAN CURRY PASTE

10 large dried red chiles

4 slices fresh galangal, peeled and chopped, or 2 slices dried galangal, soaked in warm water for 30 minutes, drained, and chopped

2 lemongrass stalks, tender midsection only, chopped

3 large shallots, quartered

4 cloves garlic, quartered

2 fresh kaffir lime rind strips, chopped; 2 dried kaffir lime rind strips, soaked in warm water for 30 minutes, drained, and chopped; or rind of 1 regular lime, chopped

1 tablespoon coriander seeds

2 teaspoons cumin seeds

seeds from 4 cardamom pods

4 whole cloves

1 teaspoon peppercorns

1 teaspoon salt

¼ teaspoon freshly grated nutmeg

1 tablespoon fresh coriander (cilantro) roots or stems

1 teaspoon dried shrimp paste

vegetable oil or water, if needed

In a dry frying pan over medium heat, toast the chiles until they begin to blacken, 1–2 minutes. Remove the chiles from the pan, crack them, and shake out and discard the seeds. Set the chiles aside. In the same pan, combine the galangal, lemongrass, shallots, and garlic and toast, turning occasionally, until lightly charred, about 5 minutes. Transfer the contents of the pan to a blender, add the lime rind, and blend until a smooth paste forms. In a small, dry frying pan over medium heat, toast the coriander seeds, cumin seeds, cardamom seeds, cloves, peppercorns, and salt until they are fragrant, about 5 minutes. Transfer the toasted spices to a mortar or spice grinder and pound or grind to a fine powder. Add the ground spices to the mixture in the blender along with the nutmeg, fresh coriander roots or stems, and shrimp paste. Blend until a smooth paste forms, adding a few tablespoons of oil or water to facilitate the blending if needed. Store as for red curry paste. *Makes ¾–1 cup (6–8 oz/185–250 g)*

GHEE

Sometimes simply described as clarified butter from which all milk solids have been removed, this popular Indian cooking fat is actually simmered beyond the clarification step to eliminate all moisture, giving it a richer flavor. Ghee is sold in jars and cans.

GINGER, SWEET PICKLED

Also known as pickled red ginger, this garnish, popular in Chinese and Japanese cooking, is made by preserving thinly sliced fresh ginger (preferably young ginger) in salt, sugar, and vinegar. A natural chemical reaction turns the slices a pale pink, which is often enhanced by the addition of food coloring. Look for the ginger in the refrigerated section in small plastic tubs or on the shelf in vacuum-sealed bags.

GINGER, YOUNG

Most fresh ginger available in markets is mature ginger, which has thin brown skin and a gnarled surface and is used as a seasoning. Young, or baby, ginger has cream-colored skin and pink shoots. Available in spring, it can be very thinly sliced and eaten like a vegetable and is used for making pickled ginger (see above).

HOISIN SAUCE

Fermented soybeans, vinegar, garlic, chile, and other ingredients are combined in this thick Chinese savory-sweet sauce used as an ingredient and a condiment.

KAFFIR LIME LEAVES

The kaffir lime contributes its rich, citrusy flavor to curry pastes and other savory and sweet dishes through its dried, fresh, or frozen leaves and its gnarled rind. Its juice, however, is not used. Pesticide-free lemon or lime leaves may be substituted.

LEMONGRASS

This stiff, reedlike grass has an intensely aromatic, citrusy flavor that is one of the signatures of Southeast Asian cooking. Use only fresh lemongrass, as it lacks good flavor when dried. Lemon zest, often mentioned as a substitute, can play its role but in no way equals its impact.

TO PREPARE LEMONGRASS: If a recipe calls for the tender midsection of a stalk, use only its bottom 4–6 inches (10–15 cm). Peel off the tough outer layers of the stalk to reveal the inner purple ring. To release the aromatic oils, smash or chop the stalk before use.

LILY BUDS, DRIED

Sometimes descriptively labeled "golden needles," these dried buds of the tiger lily add a delicately chewy texture and mildly astringent taste to Chinese dishes. Soak in water for 10 minutes before using.

LUMPIA WRAPPERS

Resembling thin crepes and sold fresh or frozen in plastic-wrapped stacks of 20 or more, these wrappers, also known as *lumpia* skins, are used for making Philippine spring rolls and other Southeast Asian appetizer rolls.

Lumpia wrappers are made from a thin batter of egg, cornstarch, flour, and water.

MUSHROOM SOY SAUCE

This form of dark Chinese soy sauce (see page 250) gains extra rich flavor and deep color by adding an extract of straw mushrooms. Some brands also include a little sugar.

MUSHROOMS

Southeast Asian cooks have a wide variety of preserved mushrooms at their disposal. Among the most commonly used types are the meaty-tasting dried Chinese black mushroom, also known as the Japanese shiitake, which is usually reconstituted in warm water before cooking; the dried cloud ear, a crinkly two-toned mushroom similar to the smaller and darker-colored tree ear; and canned straw mushrooms, plump, bite-sized brown specimens with a mild taste and smooth texture.

MUSTARD SEED

Asian cooks use black mustard seeds to add a pungent note to Indian-style curries and vegetable dishes.

PALM SUGAR

Derived from the sap of the coconut or other palms, and sometimes called coconut sugar, palm sugar is prized for its fragrant caramel-like flavor and dark brown color in Indonesia, Malaysia, and Thailand. Vietnamese cooks use a lighter, milder version. The sugar is often sold formed into dark, hard disks or cylinders, which may be grated or shaved for use. Very hard palm sugar can be softened by heating it briefly in a microwave oven. Light or dark brown sugar, depending upon the color desired, can be substituted, although the flavor will not be the same.

PANDANUS LEAVES / EXTRACT

With a taste reminiscent of butterscotch or vanilla, the pandanus leaf, which resembles a small green whisk-broom, is plucked from the screw pine tree. It adds flavor and green color to sweet dishes in Malaysian and Indonesian kitchens. Dried or frozen leaves, as well as a powerful extract (essence), are more readily found in markets. If fresh leaves are not available, use frozen.

PLUM SAUCE

A specialty of Chinese cuisine, this thick commercial sauce made of plums, apricots, sugar, chiles, and vinegar is appreciated for its tart-sweet flavor.

POLYGONUM LEAVES

Known also as Vietnamese mint and in Malaysia as *laksa* leaves or *daun kesom,* these slender green-and-purple leaves have an exotic, herbaceous flavor. They are added fresh to noodle dishes in Malaysia and to salads in Laos, Thailand, and Vietnam, where they are called *rau ram.*

PRAHOK

A popular Cambodian seasoning sold in jars, this fish paste is more easily used as a seasoning if an extract is made from it.

LONTONG

Lontong is compressed cooked rice that originated in Indonesia and then traveled to Singapore and Malaysia. The rice is cut into small chunks and picked up with the fingers to eat or added to soups and curries.

1 ½ cups (10 ½ oz/330 g) medium-grain white rice

2 ¼ cups (18 fl oz/560 ml) cold water

4 pieces banana leaf, each about 12 inches (30 cm) square, plus extra banana leaf scraps for making ties

boiling water, as needed

❀ Wash the rice in several changes of cold water until the rinsing water runs clear. Place in a saucepan, add the cold water, and bring to a boil over high heat, stirring to separate the grains. Boil until the water on the surface has been absorbed, about 5 minutes. Reduce the heat to low, cover, and cook until the rice is plump and tender, about 20 minutes longer. Remove from the heat and set aside.

❀ Place all the banana-leaf pieces in a baking pan and add boiling water to cover. Let stand until softened, about 30 seconds for frozen leaves or 5 minutes for fresh. Remove a square of banana leaf and place it shiny side down on a flat surface with the veins of the leaf running horizontal to you. Wipe dry with paper towels. Spoon one-fourth of the rice onto the leaf about one-third of the way up from the bottom edge, and spread the rice across the middle to form a log 7 inches (18 cm) long and about 1 ½ inches (4 cm) in diameter, leaving 2 inches (5 cm) on both ends free of rice. Starting from the edge nearest to you, roll the leaf around the rice to form a taut log (like rolling sushi). Flatten each end and fold them back toward the middle. Use a scrap piece of banana leaf to make ties: Working with the grain, tear off strips about ½ inch (12 mm) wide by 10 inches (25 cm) long. Using 3 strips, securely tie the logs at each end and once in the middle.

❀ Bring a large pot three-fourths full of water to a boil over high heat. Add the rice logs, reduce the heat to medium, and cook at a gentle boil for 1 hour. Remove the logs, let cool, then refrigerate for at least 4 hours or, preferably, overnight.

❀ To serve, remove the banana leaves and cut the logs into slices or cubes ½ inch (12 mm) thick. Serve at room temperature.

Serves 8

NUOC CHAM

Every Vietnamese cook has his or her recipe for *nuoc cham*, a sauce eaten with nearly every meal and snack. Adjust the ingredient amounts to suit your taste.

1 large clove garlic

1 fresh red chile, seeded

¼ cup (2 fl oz/60 ml) fresh lime juice

5 tablespoons (2 ½ fl oz/75 ml) fish sauce

3 tablespoons sugar

6 tablespoons (3 fl oz/90 ml) water

2 tablespoons grated carrot

❀ In a mortar, pound together the garlic and red chile until puréed (or pass the garlic clove through a garlic press). Mix in the lime juice, fish sauce, sugar, and water. Pour into a dipping saucer and add the carrot.

Makes about 1 cup (8 fl oz/250 ml)

TO PREPARE PRAHOK JUICE: Put ¼ cup (2 fl oz/ 60 ml) of the fermented fish (including the fish meat) into a saucepan with 1 cup (8 fl oz/250 ml) water and bring to a boil over high heat. Reduce the heat to a simmer and simmer uncovered, stirring once or twice, for 10 minutes. Pour through a sieve placed over a bowl, pressing against the solids to extract as much liquid as possible. Discard the solids. Store the strained liquid in a covered jar in the refrigerator for up to 2 weeks. *Makes a scant 1 cup (8 fl oz/250 ml).*

RADISH, PRESERVED

A preserved form of the large white radish commonly known by its Japanese name, daikon, this Chinese ingredient is sold in plastic packages labeled "preserved white radish" or "preserved turnips." The brown-tinged strips add pungent flavor to braises, stews, and other dishes.

RICE

Most Southeast Asians prefer long-grain white rice, which they usually cook by the water-absorption method, producing so-called steamed rice. Washing the kernels beforehand is essential to remove the surface starch that would otherwise make the rice sticky. Plan on 2 cups (14 oz/440 g) of long-grain white rice to serve four healthy Asian appetites. Long-grain rice is also ground into flour that is used largely for making noodles. Do not confuse it with glutinous rice flour (page 250).

TO MAKE STEAMED RICE: Rinse 2 cups (14 oz/440 g) long-grain white rice thoroughly in several changes of cold water until the rinsing water runs clear. Drain. Choose a saucepan in which the raw rice takes up at least one-third but no more than one-half of the pan. Add the rice and 2 ¼ cups (18 fl oz/560 ml) water. Asian cooks use the knuckle method to determine if the water level is correct: the water should cover the rice by the depth of one knuckle of the index finger (a generous 1 inch/2.5 cm). Bring to a rapid boil, stir to separate the grains, and boil until all of the surface water is absorbed, about 5 minutes. There should be craters on the surface. Cover the saucepan, reduce the heat to low, and cook until the kernels are plump and tender, about 20 minutes. Remove from the heat and let stand, covered, for at least 10 minutes or for up to 45 minutes, then serve. *Makes about 5 ½ cups (1 ½ lb/750 g).*

RICE, GLUTINOUS

Also known as sticky rice or sweet rice, this starch-rich white rice is the daily grain of people living in the Golden Triangle and throughout Laos. It cooks up into a sticky mass, and traditional diners, eating with their hands, roll the rice into small balls, which they dip into sauces and curries and then move swiftly to their mouths. Elsewhere the rice is used primarily to make sweets. Both short-grain and long-grain varieties are available, as is black glutinous rice. Glutinous rice flour, sometimes labeled "sweet rice flour," is used for making cakes and other sweets.

RICE PAPER

Made from rice flour and water, tissue-thin rice paper, indispensable to the Vietnamese pantry, is commonly purchased rather than made at home (see sidebar, page 62). It comes dried in rounds and triangles of different sizes, with 8-inch (20-cm) rounds the most common. Before use, it must be made soft and pliable by dampening it with water (or another liquid), either by dipping it briefly in a bowl of water or by brushing it with water.

SAGO PEARLS

Sago is a starch extracted from the sago palm. The pearls, extruded tiny pellets made by pressing the wet starch through a sieve, are sold dried. When cooked, usually in a pudding, they become translucent, much like tapioca pearls. In general, sago and tapioca pearls can be used interchangeably in recipes.

SALAM LEAVES

Malaysian term for aromatic laurel leaves similar to bay, used dried or fresh to flavor simmered and stir-fried dishes. Although bay leaves are the usual substitute, some cooks prefer curry leaves (page 246).

SAMBAL ULEK

The term *sambal* is used in Indonesia and Malaysia to refer to often-spicy condiments and side dishes used to add flavor to other dishes. *Sambal ulek* is one such embellishment, a commercial or homemade Indonesian product combining chile, vinegar, and salt.

SAW-LEAF HERB

Known as saw-leaf herb because of its slender serrated leaves, this fragrant herb recalls coriander (cilantro). Called *ngo gai* by the Vietnamese, the fresh leaves are typically added to soups at the table.

SHALLOTS AND PICKLED SHALLOTS

Members of the onion family, shallots are added to dishes throughout Southeast Asia, usually as part of the seasoning base for curries and stir-fries. Asian markets also carry jarred pickled shallots, which have been packed in a vinegar brine.

SHISO LEAVES

Related to mint but with an aromatic flavor faintly recalling ginger or cinnamon, these serrated, heart-shaped leaves tinged with purple on their undersides, also known as perilla or beefsteak leaves, are used in noodles, salads, and other dishes.

SHRIMP, DRIED, AND SHRIMP POWDER

Usually sold in cellophane packages, dried shrimp (prawns) range in size from very tiny to nearly 1 inch (2.5 cm) long and are used as a seasoning in many Southeast Asian countries. They add a salty, briny flavor to everything from soups to stir-fries. Shrimp powder can be purchased in jars, but, if possible, grind it yourself to ensure quality. Store the whole shrimp in the refrigerator for up to 6 months and the powder in a cool, dark place indefinitely.

SHRIMP CHIPS

These featherlight chips are made from ground dried shrimp (prawns) and are sold in the form of translucent, hard disks of various sizes and shapes that puff up when deep-fried (see sidebar, page 38).

TO DEEP-FRY SHRIMP CHIPS: Preheat a wok or deep frying pan over medium-high heat. Pour in vegetable oil to a depth of 2 inches (5 cm) and heat to 375°F (190°C). Drop a few small chips into the hot oil. Using a wire skimmer, submerge the chips in the oil. They should expand within seconds. Stir for a few seconds to make certain that the entire chip has puffed. They are ready when they float and have turned just slightly darker than their original color. Using the skimmer, transfer to paper towels to drain. Let cool. If you are frying large chips, use a wok, fry them one at a time (you'll need the full width of the wok), and turn them over once they puff, so that they cook evenly.

SHRIMP PASTE, DRIED

Intensely flavored, this Southeast Asian seasoning paste is made by salting, fermenting, and then drying shrimp (prawns). Depending on its source, the dried paste may range in color from pinkish tan to deep purple-black. Called *blacan* in Malaysia, *trasi* in Indonesia, *kapi* in Thailand, and *ngapi* in Myanmar, it is most often sold in hard blocks from which slices can be easily cut with a sharp knife. Do not confuse the dried paste with shrimp sauce, called *bagoong* in the Philippines and sometimes shrimp paste in English, a highly pungent, thick grayish sauce sold in jars. It is easily found in Chinese grocery stores.

SOY SAUCE

Typically made by fermenting and aging soybeans along with wheat, salt, and water, soy sauce is an indispensable seasoning in kitchens in China and, to a far lesser degree, in Southeast Asia. It is used in local dishes with Chinese roots, and it is popular with strict Buddhists who eschew fish sauce. Dark soy sauce, a Chinese product also known as medium soy sauce, gains its dark color, thicker consistency, and edge of sweetness from the addition of caramel. Chinese light soy sauce, also called thin or regular soy sauce, has a thinner consistency and a lighter flavor. Japanese soy sauces tend to be milder tasting, slightly sweeter, and less salty than Chinese varieties. Other types of soy sauce include the sweetened Indonesian variety known as *kecap manis* (see note, page 46) and mushroom soy sauce (page 248).

SOYBEANS, FERMENTED BLACK

Also commonly labeled "salted black beans," this Chinese seasoning is made by fermenting cooked black soybeans and then aging them for 6 months in a salty brine that may also be seasoned with ginger, five-spice powder, or orange peel. Sold in plastic bags, the beans should feel soft. After opening, store in an airtight container in a cool, dark place; they keep well for months.

SPICE PASTES

Pastes built from a pantry of spices and other ingredients are central to the cuisines of Malaysia, Indonesia, Singapore, and Thailand. Once the pastes have been assembled, they must be properly cooked so that they will release their flavors fully into the dishes they are seasoning.

TO COOK A SPICE PASTE: Place a generous amount of oil for a Malaysian, Indonesian, or Singaporean *rempah* or coconut cream for a Thai curry paste in a wok or saucepan, usually ⅓ – ½ cup (3–4 fl oz/80–125 ml) for most recipes. (Although at least twice as much would typically be used, this amount works fine.) Place the pan with the oil over medium heat and allow it to warm, so that the spice mixture will sizzle slightly when you add it. Or boil the coconut cream over medium-high heat, stirring often, until oil beads appear on the surface, about 5 minutes. Add the spice mixture and stir until the coconut cream and curry paste, or the oil and the *rempah,* are combined and emulsified, 3–5 minutes. Continue cooking at a gentle boil (soft bubbles should break on the surface), stirring occasionally, for 10–15 minutes longer. When the oil separates from the spice mixture, the mixture is ready. If the paste turns dry during frying, add more oil or coconut cream to keep it moist.

SQUID

Many seafood merchants sell squid already cleaned, in which case you will need to buy only about two-thirds the amount indicated in the recipes, as there is considerable waste. To clean the squid yourself, work with 1 squid at a time. Pull the head and tentacles away from the body. Cut off the tentacles just above the eyes and discard the lower portion. Squeeze the base of the tentacles to force out the hard beak. Rinse the tentacles and set aside. Pull out the quill-like cartilage and entrails from the body and discard. Peel away the thin mottled skin that covers the outside of the body, rinse well, then cut as directed in individual recipes.

SRIRACHA SAUCE

Named for the seaside Thai town in which it originated, this bottled, hot or mild, sweet-tart all-purpose sauce is made from red chiles and resembles a light-colored ketchup. Keep in mind that even the so-called mild Sriracha sauce is quite hot.

STAR ANISE

Named for their resemblance to eight-pointed stars, these small, brown, hard seedpods have a sweet licorice flavor and are used frequently in Vietnamese and Chinese dishes. The whole pods or individual points broken from them may be added to long-simmering dishes. Pulverized star anise is one of the key elements in five-spice powder (page 246).

SUGARCANE

Peeled of their green skin, fresh sticks cut from the bamboolike sugarcane plant are used in Vietnamese cooking as skewers on which a minced shrimp mixture is molded for grilling. Canned sugarcane is readily available.

TAPIOCA PEARLS / FLOUR

Made from the tubers of the cassava plant, pearl-shaped particles of tapioca contribute a mild, soothing flavor and thick, slightly gelatinous consistency to a wide variety of Southeast Asian sweets and some savory dishes. Finely ground tapioca flour, also called tapioca starch, is used to thicken sauces, to coat steamed dumplings, and as an ingredient in batters for fried foods.

THAI BASIL

Three types of basil are used in Thailand: *kraprow, maenglak,* and *horapa. Kraprow* has serrated green leaves with a tint of purple and a hint of anise flavor overlaying the familiar basil scent. *Maenglak,* also known as lemon basil, has smaller leaves and a lemony scent. *Horapa* has purple stems, shiny leaves, and an anise aroma. All three can be used interchangeably in the recipes in this book, or European sweet basil can be substituted.

TOASTED RICE POWDER

Sold commercially in Asian markets and sometimes labeled as "roasted rice powder," this seasoning and binding agent is known in Vietnam as *thinh* and in Thailand as *khao kua pon.* Pale brown and with a hint of nutlike richness, it is sprinkled on soups; tossed together with finely chopped meat, poultry, or seafood for salads; or added to minced shrimp or meat for kabobs.

TO MAKE TOASTED RICE POWDER: Put raw white rice in a dry frying pan over medium-high heat and toast, stirring occasionally, until golden brown, 3–5 minutes. Transfer to a spice mill and grind to a powder.

URAD DAL

A type of small black-skinned dal, or lentil, used in the making of *thosai* and other Indian dishes. Sometimes labeled in English as white split gram bean, *urad dal* is usually available already skinned. If the skins are still intact, before using, soak the dal in water to loosen the skins and then rub them off.

YARD-LONG BEANS

Also called long beans or snake beans, these thin green beans sometimes grow to nearly 3 feet (1 m) in length. Crisp, crunchy, and mildly flavored, they are used in stir-fries, soups, salads, and other savory preparations.

INDEX

ACKNOWLEDGMENTS

Joyce Jue wishes to thank the following individuals and organizations for their recipe contributions and assistance: I am greatly indebted to Mr. Yap Lim Sen for introducing me to the world of Southeast Asian cooking. I also wish to extend my gratitude to Chris and Shaymie Liew; Mrs. Lee Kum Choon; Christine Hooi; Chris Yeo of Straits Café, San Francisco; Dennis Wong of Le Soleil Restaurant, San Francisco; Lac E. Minh; film producers Paul Kwan and Arnold Iger; Executive Chef Didier Corlou and Sous Chef Nguyen Thi Kim Hai of Hotel Sofitel, Hanoi; Executive Chef Serge Rigodin of Hotel Sofitel, Saigon; Chef Wan; Mai Pham of Lemongrass Restaurant, Sacramento; Charmaine Solomon; Sharifah Danial and Raja Normala Raja Shamsudin of the Malaysian Tourism Promotion Board; Teresa Pereira Capol; Seet Tiang Chye of Restoran Ole Sayang, Melaka; Shangri-la's Rasa Sayang Resort, Penang; Chef Azhar Alias of Hotel Nikko, Kuala Lumpur; Restoran Seri Angkasa, Kuala Lumpur; Juliet David and John and Eve Read of The Oriental Hotel, Bangkok; Jennifer Martin; Randy Kay; Wendely Harvey; Hannah Rahill; and Sharon Silva.

Noel Barnhurst wishes to thank his assistant, Noriko Akiyama, and Jefferson Finney for help with props. George Dolese thanks food stylist Leslie Busch, and her assistant, Elizabet Der Nederlanden, for their excellence in the kitchen. The photo team also thanks Tom Panoa and J. D. Staub for granting access to their collection of Asian treasures.

Weldon Owen would like to thank Wendely Harvey, Gaye Allen, Desne Border, Linda Bouchard, Ken DellaPenta, Lisa Lee, and Jamie Leighton. We also thank the following photographers and organizations for permission to reproduce their copyrighted photographs (b=below, c=center, t=top): From **Aurora & Quanta Productions**: ©Dominik Obertreis 172–173t; ©Thomas Ernsting 225b; ©Jose Azel 88b, 227t. From **Black Star**: ©David Portnoy 88t; ©Erica Lansner 27. From **Contact Press Images**: ©Dilip Mehta 129t, 167b. From **Corbis**: ©Michael Freeman 169b; ©John R. Jones 172b; ©Catherine Karnow 171b, 226; ©Kevin R. Morris 28; ©Steven Raymer 1; ©Nevada Weir 126; ©Nik Wheeler 93t; ©Michael Yamashita 84–85, 129b. From **Indopix**: ©Tantyo Bangun 92, 132, 171t; ©Tara Sosrowardoyo 30b, 227b. From **Liaison Agency Inc**: ©Wolfgang Kaehler 26b, 90b; ©Christophe Lovigny 131b; ©John Penisten 14b. From **Woodfin Camp & Associates**: ©Geoffrey Clifford endpapers, 24b, 30t, 173b; ©Lindsay Hebberd 6–7; ©Catherine Karnow 90t, 124–125; ©Adam Woolfitt 127b; ©Michael Yamashita 15, 19t, 164–165, 166, 222–223. From **Individual Photographers**: ©Lou Dematteis 4–5, 12–13, 169t, 224; ©Michael Freeman cover, 8–9, 17t, 17b, 18, 20, 22–23, 24t, 25, 86, 91, 93b, 127t, 127c, 128, 131t, 170, 228b; ©R. Ian Lloyd back cover, 14t, 16, 19b, 26t, 29t, 29b, 31, 87, 89, 133, 167t, 168, 225t, 229; ©Stuart Isett 130, 228t; ©Michael Yamashita 21.

OXMOOR HOUSE INC.

Oxmoor
House.

Oxmoor House books are distributed by Sunset Books
80 Willow Road, Menlo Park, CA 94025
Telephone: 650-321-3600 Fax: 650-324-1532

Vice President/General Manager: Rich Smeby
Director of Special Sales: Gary Wright

Oxmoor House and Sunset Books are divisions of
Southern Progress Corporation

WILLIAMS-SONOMA INC.
Founder and Vice-Chairman: Chuck Williams
Book Buyer: Cecilia Michaelis

WELDON OWEN INC.
Chief Executive Officer: John Owen
President: Terry Newell
Chief Operating Officer: Larry Partington
Vice President International Sales: Stuart Laurence
Associate Publisher: Hannah Rahill
Consulting Editors: Sharon Silva, Norman Kolpas
Design: Kari Ontko, India Ink
Photo Editor: Sandra Eisert
Production Director: Stephanie Sherman
Production Manager: Chris Hemesath
Editorial Assistant: Dana Goldberg
Prop and Style Director: George Dolese
Calligraphy: Jane Dill

THE SAVORING SERIES
conceived and produced by Weldon Owen Inc.
814 Montgomery Street, San Francisco, CA 94133
Telephone: 415-291-0100, Fax: 415-291-8841

In collaboration with Williams-Sonoma Inc.
3250 Van Ness Avenue, San Francisco, CA 94109

Savoring® is a registered trademark of Weldon Owen Inc.

pp 4–5: Dawn welcomes the local fishing boats to Vietnam's Vung Tau, a major port and well-known seaside resort. The fishermen distribute their catch among the enterprising vendors, who then sell the impeccably fresh specimens farther along the beach. **pp 6–7:** Climbing every available patch of land, Bali's terraced rice fields rely on a system of canals, dams, tunnels, and dikes developed over centuries to produce three high-yielding crops every fourteen months. **pp 8–9:** Housed in Wat Phra Kaeo, the royal temple adjoining the Grand Palace in Bangkok, this bronze Buddha, encased in gold and precious stones, is one of two that flank the Emerald Buddha, the most venerated Buddha image in Thailand. **pp 12–13:** Every morning, boats loaded with locally grown fruits and vegetables make their way along Vietnam's Can Tho River, a tributary of the Mekong.

A WELDON OWEN PRODUCTION
Copyright © 2000 Weldon Owen Inc.

First printed 2000
10 9 8 7 6 5 4 3 2

Library of Congress
Cataloging-in-Publication Data

Jue, Joyce.
    Savoring Southeast Asia : recipes and reflections on Southeast Asian cooking / Joyce Jue, recipes and text ; Chuck Williams, general editor ; Noel Barnhurst, recipe photography ; Marlene McLoughlin, illustrations.
    p. cm.—(The savoring series)
    ISBN 0-7370-2043-1 (hc.)
    1. Cookery, Southeast Asia. I. Williams, Chuck. II. Title.
III. Series.
TX724.5.S68.J84 2000
641.5959—dc21   99-057164
                                                                CIP

Separations by Colourscan Overseas Co. Pte. Ltd.
Printed in Singapore by Tien Wah Press (Pte.) Ltd.